Partners

Everyday working dogs being heroes every day

Service dogs
for Military
Veterans receives
a percentage
of author
royalties

Nan Walton

The Hubble & Hattie imprint was launched in 2009 and is named in memory of two very special Westies owned by Veloce's proprietors.
Since the first book, many more have been added to the list, all with the same underlying objective: to be of real benefit to the species they cover, at the same time promoting compassion, understanding and respect between all animals (including human ones!)
Hubble & Hattie is the home of a range of books that cover all-things animal, produced to the same high quality of content and presentation as our motoring books, and offering the same great value for money.

More great books from Hubble & Hattie

A Dog's Dinner (Paton-Ayre)
Animal Grief: How animals mourn (Alderton)
Because this is our home: the story of a cat's progress (eBook) (Dowson)
Camper vans, ex-pats and Spanish hounds (Coates)
Cat Speak: recognising & understanding behaviour (Rauth-Widmann)
Clever dog! Life lessons from the world's most successful animal (O'Meara)
Complete Dog Massage Manual, The – Gentle Dog Care (Robertson)
Dieting with my dog: one busy life, two full figures … and unconditional love (Frezon)
Dinner with Rover: delicious, nutritious meals for you and your dog to share (Paton-Ayre)
Dog Cookies: healthy, allergen-free treat recipes for your dog (Schöps)
Dog-friendly Gardening: creating a safe haven for you and your dog (Bush)
Dog Games – stimulating play to entertain your dog and you (Blenski)
Dog Speak: recognising & understanding behaviour (Blenski)
Dogs on Wheels: travelling with your canine companion (Mort)
Emergency First Aid for dogs: at home and away (Bucksch)
Exercising your puppy: a gentle & natural approach – Gentle Dog Care (Robertson & Pope)

Fun and Games for Cats (Seidl)
Know Your Dog – The guide to a beautiful relationship (Birmelin)
Life Skills for Puppies: laying the foundation for a loving, lasting relationship (Zulch & Mills)
Miaow! Cats really are nicer than people! (Moore)
My dog has arthritis – but lives life to the full! (Carrick)
My dog is blind – but lives life to the full! (Horsky)
My dog has cruciate ligament injury – but lives life to the full! (Haüsler)
My dog is deaf – but lives life to the full! (Willms)
My dog has hip dysplasia – but lives life to the full! (Haüsler)
Older Dog, Living with an – Gentle Dog Care (Alderton & Hall)
Partners – Everyday working dogs being heroes every day (Walton)
Smellorama – nose games for dogs (Theby)
Swim to recovery: canine hydrotherapy healing – Gentle Dog Care (Wong)
The Truth about Wolves and Dogs: dispelling the myths of dog training (Shelbourne)
Waggy Tails & Wheelchairs (Epp)
Walking the dog: motorway walks for drivers & dogs (Rees)
Walking the dog in France: motorway walks for drivers & dogs (Rees)
Winston … the dog who changed my life (Klute)
You and Your Border Terrier – The Essential Guide (Alderton)
You and Your Cockapoo – The Essential Guide (Alderton)

www.hubbleandhattie.com

First published in April 2013 by Veloce Publishing Limited, Veloce House, Parkway Farm Business Park, Middle Farm Way, Poundbury, Dorchester, Dorset, DT1 3AR, England. Fax 01305 250479/e-mail info@hubbleandhattie.com/web www.hubbleandhattie.com.
ISBN: 978-1-845844-20-2 UPC: 6-36847-04420-6.
Readers with ideas for books about animals, or animal-related topics, are invited to write to the editorial director of Veloce Publishing at the above address. British Library Cataloguing in Publication Data – A catalogue record for this book is available from the British Library. Typesetting, design and page make-up all by Veloce Publishing Ltd on Apple Mac. Printed in India by Replika Press, India.

Contents

Dedication &
   acknowledgments 4

Prologue 5
   Understanding the 'Whys'
      of your dog's behavior 5
   Marshall and Prince 6
   Nan and Teak 6
   Nan and Madge 8

Communication through
   trust 10
   Why and how dogs do
      what needs to be done . . . 12
   The stories 17

Scent-detection
   specialists 18
   Anything, anywhere: partners
      who find and deliver 18
   Mike and JJ 19
   Scent work basics 26
   Illegal drugs are
      everywhere 30
   Narcotics specialists Blake
      and Enzo 31
   Steve and Louis, Henry and
      Riley 37
   Forensic remains
      specialists 41
   Laura and Nike 41
   Nan and Katie 43

K9 law enforcement
   partners 48
   Loving a living 'tool' 48
   Kevin and Django 50
   Jon and Bo and Drago 57
   Reed and Olk 63
   Chris and Joker 71

Stan and Abby, Mike and
   Arrest 74
Bob and Nanto 77

Search and Rescue 80
   That others might live 80
   Erica and Bart 82
   Margaret and Ashley 89
   Judy and Frita 93
   Jodi and Winnie 96
   Jim and Rusty 99

Guide Dog partners . . . 103
   Brad and Tommy 103
   Suzanne and Coral and
      Martina 110
   John and Traveler and
      Mick 114
   LaDoris and Remca 118
   Rebecca Carines 122
   Rachel Carines Walton
      DVM 122
   Melissa Carines Ellis 123
   Clint and Libo and Sachmo . .124

Therapy partners 132
   A gift to those in pain 132
   Nan and Lex 133
   Lisa and Hoop and Dunk . . .133
   Kathy and Jerry Lee 138
   Judy and Barrett, Jim and
      Truman 141
   Lyn and Holly 145

Epilogue 152

Bibliography and Notes   155

Index 159

Dedication & acknowledgments

Dedication

This book is dedicated to the entire canine species – highlighting 26 working dog teams whose stories typify their everyday contribution to society and humanity. The pain at their loss touches not only the heart of their human partner but all they have bravely saved, served or walked beside.

"They have not gone—they have simply 'gone ahead,' as any devoted shepherd would for her beloved human." – Quote inspired by Maria Dales, German Shepherd Rescue Orange County, California.

Knowing in my heart that they have just 'gone ahead' makes their loss somewhat bearable ...

Teak 1967-1978

Katie 1993-2004

Lex 2003-2012

Acknowledgments

To the 30 individual story contributors who gave me a part of your heart, I hope *Partners* will cause you to smile as you remember the hours of love and dedication you spent at *your* partner's side. I have treasured your stories and know that, without each and every one of you, *Partners* would not be.

To the two remarkable ladies that made *Partners* readable – seriously. Red pencil in hand Joan Reed and Rachael Hardy gave me encouragement when the task seemed impossible, and grammatical correction after correction when it seemed I couldn't even write a complete sentence. – there is no way to thank you enough.

And finally, Jude – and Hubble and Hattie – who personally polished and refined our project: your help was truly remarkable. What an experience to see the energies of so many come together: thank you all so very much.

Nan Walton
Bountiful, Utah,
United States of America

Enjoy! Nan

Understanding the 'Whys' of your dog's behavior

In *Partners* – a collection of true dog stories – you will explore the unparalleled dedication, diversity and loyalty inherent in the only species that has ever chosen to walk with man. These stories were collected with the express purpose of introducing you to today's canine heroes, and the innate senses driving their actions.

For anyone sharing their life with a dog, understanding the senses that motivate him or her is the first step in shaping their dog's behaviors into good-mannered, predictable actions.

Written as tributes to their departed canine partners, this collection tells of a unique interaction between man and his canine partner: a partnership that allows basic daily tasks, feats of bravery, phenomenal detection work, and therapy that comforts strangers in pain.

While reading about teams that locate lost children, solve crimes, find illegal narcotics and criminals, you will learn how a Guide Dog named Traveler pulled his blind partner from the path of a moving car, and how Therapy Dog Holly touched the soul of an abused child. Look for the stories between the lines about the courage of the people who partner these amazing animals as they make life and death decisions based on canine senses. Consider the challenges that these special pairings deal with every day, which give rise to the trust and communication and resultant bond that makes the team so successful. Appreciate how these teams become partners – not man owning dog; not dog working for man – but true equals.

Previously considered the reason for problematic behavior, words like 'inherent' and 'instinct' became directly associated with negative dog behavior. For years, attempts to stamp out these instinct-based behaviors only caused greater frustration and deeper psychological problems, eventually leading to neurotic, unmanageable dogs. Fortunately, current attitudes redress that error in philosophy, and, today, mainstream behaviorists and trainers are working hard to introduce new and inventive ways to cope with undesirable behavior that is the direct result of instinct.

I feel strongly that the instinct-driven behaviors of our canine partners are the exact qualities that make dogs man's best friend, both at home and in the workplace.

Direct descendants of wolves, domestic dogs exhibit inherent behaviors that make possible a highly valued and unequaled variety of tasks, tasks performed by one unique species: Canis lupus familiaris of the family Canidae. In working dogs these instincts provide essential qualities and skills, and in the family pet they allow the nurturing that enables undying devotion, love and protection.

Throughout history the diversity of our partners seems to defy categorization. Our dogs' uncanny ability to be there and do what is needed can seem beyond explanation. From the tiny Poodle's tender diligence as cancer claimed my Dad's body, to the 'bomb sniffers' saving countless lives in Iraq and Afghanistan, their phenomenal range is unquestionable, and their dedication to man without equal.

In the words of Maurice Materlinck, in his charming book *My Dog*, written in 1904 "[He came to us] ... to serve us better, to adapt himself better to our different needs, he has adopted every shape and been able infinitely to vary the faculties, the aptitudes which he places at our disposal. Is he to aid us in the pursuit of game in the plains? His legs lengthen inordinately, his muzzle tapers, his lungs widen, he becomes swifter than the deer. Does our prey hide under wood? The docile genius of the species, forestalling our desires, presents us with the basset, a sort of serpent, almost without feet, which steals into the closest thickets.

"Do we ask that he should drive our flocks? The same compliant genius grants him the requisite size, intelligence, energy and vigilance. Do we intend him to watch and defend our house? His head becomes round and monstrous, in order that his jaws may be more powerful, more formidable and more tenacious. Are we taking him to the South? His hair grows shorter and lighter, so that he may faithfully accompany us under the rays of a hotter sun. Are we going up to the North? His feet grow larger, the better to tread the

A perfect example of trust and communication: Jim and Rusty train at rappelling down a steep cliff in preparation for a possibly dangerous recovery in search and rescue.

by my father's old hunting partner, Prince. Re-told over and over as I grew up, the story explains the beginning of my connection with this species ...

Marshall and Prince
In the words of my father ...

"Prince, my very large German Shorthair Pointer, had been pushing hard, holding the body of my frightened three-year-old daughter against the concrete wall, and preventing the water from pulling her under.

"As I lifted Nan to safety, Prince tumbled backward and was pulled under, unable to regain his footing. Knowing our daughter was safe in her mother's arms, I raced to the metal grate: if Prince went through that grate, he would be lost forever. Luckily, though exhausted and bloodied, Prince did land on that grate just long enough for me to pull my old hunting partner to safety.

"That same summer Prince jumped through a 5x5 foot plate glass window, prompted by that spoiled three-year-old's cries of anguish, not realizing she had simply heard the 'no' word, and was throwing another tantrum.

"Prince spent his thirteen years protecting our daughter from all manner of mishaps: Gila Monsters in the dessert; concrete irrigation ditches; whatever, whenever, Prince was there.

"But when the autumn leaves turned color and it was time to hunt pheasants, Prince took time out from protecting Nan to join me in the hunting field. He was first and foremost her protector but, second, Prince was my hunting partner. He loved hunting, a job he was born to do, and those Fall days were times treasured by two deeply connected old friends."
Marshall, my Dad

Nan and Teak
An unexpected bond

I believe my connection with dogs began that day as Prince held me against the concrete wall, and was reinforced some seventeen years later when hiking a deserted mountain trail where a would-be attacker started explaining in detail his evil plan for me.

Fortunately, about a year before, while

snow; his fur thickens, in order that the cold may not compel him to abandon us."

I started collecting working dog stories six years ago, but my life with dogs really began many years before, and I hope that my book will give you a glimpse of the evolution of a perspective based on a lifetime of experience. Until her recent passing I was the partner of a German Shepherd who touched the souls of the abused and the abusers, but for the past 19 years I have followed working dogs searching for the lost on mountains, in avalanches or in the desert; scouring crime scenes for human remains with a forensic canine partner, and most recently searching for illegal narcotics in schools, businesses and homes.

But my first experience with a dog was as a very young child when my life was literally saved

Public displays demonstrate the powerful instinctual drives used by law enforcement to protect and defend the public.

volunteering at a local humane society, I had taken home a retired police K9. Teak was a beautiful, strong, 110lb (50kg) German Shepherd, who seemingly didn't care about developing a relationship with me. I knew nothing about canine bonds, so we just existed in the same apartment – or so I thought. That day she was just off running, hunting, doing whatever dogs do on a mountain. Now, frozen in fear, I knew my life was over, or at least it would never be the same, as I listened to this person while staring into eyes I will never forget, wondering what I could do, where I could run?

Then Teak came, but where did she come from; how did she know? Was it his threats she sensed, or my fear? I remember thinking how dumb I had been, coming up here to such an isolated spot, alone. But I wasn't really alone, I just didn't know it!

Teak appeared at my side with her fangs bared and a deep primal rumble coming from her throat. As my would-be-attacker tumbled down that mountainside, Teak repeatedly explained to him, over and over, whose plan would be implemented, and it was not his. I still remember my fear in those moments; her strength and ferocity. Had there been any prior question

Trusting his very life to his Guide Dog, Brad is safely escorted across a busy intersection.

about the depth of my involvement with this species, it was erased that day as my allegiance became permanently planted, always, completely and occasionally irrationally, on the side of all canines.

My life was saved twice by dogs, which created an immediate connection, although understanding that connection came much later. I had no idea at the time that both Prince and Teak were using pack survival instinct to do what they were born to do: protect, at all costs, their pack; fortunately for me, I was part of their pack.

The following, subtle experience did not make much of an impression at the time, but epitomises how an extraordinary relationship can develop with a dog. If you want that special bond, if you hope to experience the moments that all of these stories are full of, the next short story highlights the first essential step in the development of that partnership.

Nan and Madge
My awareness begins

The responsibility and compassion I learned for animals came directly from my Uncle Tom, who I knew was simply the best veterinarian in the world. Before it was the in-thing, in a very

rural farming community, Uncle Tom provided sanctuary and health care for unwanted animals; any that needed him found warmth, food, shelter, and a loving home. He had always been there and his unspoken connection was something I just took for granted.

So it was natural that I found myself anxious when it became necessary to introduce our beloved family pet to a new vet. Fortunately, my fears were quickly alleviated the moment Dr Martin stepped into the room and touched my dog, Madge. Just as Uncle Tom had done for years, he simply walked in and touched.

Immediately the level of trust was absolute, seemingly achieved by some mystical means. I now understand that this trust was based on communication, not mysticism, and is the first step. The silent communication offered by Dr Martin and Uncle Tom was immediately perceived through olfactory senses and confirmed by touch. That unique connection, that depth of trust and communication developed between working partners united in purpose, is the basis of *Partners: everyday working dogs being heroes every day*.

Forty-five years later I am finally beginning to understand the canine species, and I remain

Instincts that protect and defend also protect and nurture – as this small child experiences with a therapy partner.

fascinated by the depth of its commitment to us. I know our partners are absolutely necessary, their involvement with mankind is complete, their service to mankind boundless and totally inherent to their very nature, and we are the fortunate recipients of this devotion and service.

The nature of this collection of stories – which covers five unique disciplines – is especially intriguing as an awareness of the similar instincts that determine the behaviors of each dog evolves. From the tough police K9, the search and rescue and scent detector specialists, the tireless devotion of Guide Dogs, to the tender therapy partners, the same inborn senses are responsible for this instinct-driven behavior, which itself stems from survival instincts that enable tracking and hunting, the need to herd and protect the pack, and their social interdependency that nurtures and loves man as one of their own.

And what about the contrast and similarities of the human partners, from the tough street cop facing potentially deadly situations, to the blind, High School wrestling coach, and the myriad of volunteers working search and rescue and therapy partners?

To illustrate the adaptability and versatility of the canine species, I have included quotes by noted canine specialists to provide information relating to the behaviors, bonds and drives within each story. By demystifying instinctual behavior, every dog owner will be able to expand and improve their relationship with their family pet. Better understanding of the drive behind behavior is the key to responsible, quality relationships

between man and dog. The dogs in these stories were working dogs which had a specific job, but everyone can develop a deeper relationship with his or her dog by understanding the 'whys' of their behavior, and giving him something to do to provide a purpose to his day.

Most importantly, though, you can do this by giving your dog your time; by giving him *you*. Your dog is always available to you, waiting to become the partner to you that you have always been to him ...

Realistic training scenarios shape and develop communication that illicits necessary action when dangerous situations require law enforcement intervention.

Visit Hubble and Hattie on the web: www.hubbleandhattie.com and www.hubbleandhattie.blogspot.com

f **twitter**

Details of all books • Special offers • Newsletter • New book news

... being heroes every day

Communicating through trust

Today's world revolves around technological advancement, relying heavily on man's newest inventions to secure and maintain that warm, safe spot in an unknown future. Yet we cling tightly to one connection with our past, a past that started at least 26,000 years ago[1] as a small child walked side-by-side with his dog in a deep cave in Chauvet France. The sets of fossilized footprints are quite possibly the first dated proof of a unique relationship that man has enjoyed from the beginning of time.

"Did he come spontaneously to us? We cannot tell. So far as our human annals stretch, he is at our side, as at present; but what are human annals in comparison with the times of which we have no witness? The fact remains that he is there in our houses, as ancient, as rightly placed, as perfectly adapted to our habits as though he had appeared on this earth, such as he now is, at the same time as ourselves." Written in 1906 by Maurice Materlinck, *My Dog* simply states our fascination with this species and a partnership with mankind that seems to have been in existence forever.

Almost a hundred years later, Jon Katz in *Tending To Life, Love and Family,* wrote: "Every dog is descended from creatures who aided primitive, frightened humans when they most needed it. Today, when we are less primitive but still frightened, they are working harder than ever."

The give and take that our two species have shared from the start varies from partnership to partnership, dependent on our needs. And while we passionately preserve a relationship based first on our survival, protection, tracking and dispatching of prey, today's need for the canine species continues to expand as we find new and innovative ways to keep him walking at our side. Fortunately, his ever-present senses have adjusted as he has moved from that ancient fireplace into each and every imaginable branch of our existence.

From those 26,000BC ancient and intriguing footprints in that far away cave to Abb'e Henri Breuil's early 1900s tracing of a 17,000BC polychrome wall painting of a wolf, canines have been at our side. Men of the *Old Stone Age*, written by Henry Fairfield Osborn in 1915, discusses the lives of the ancients, accompanied by numerous pictures of the environment, tools, art and theorized ways of living. The 230-plus drawings catalogued in the Grotte de Font-de-Gaume in France mostly show bison and mammoth, but this wolf painting is among only a handful representing their species found throughout the entire world. The theories behind cave art – who and what was painstakingly depicted – will always remain a mystery, and although depictions of wolf and man are extremely rare, I believe that they were walking and working with man even then.

Painstakenly created by ancient artisans, this 17,000BC wall painting of a wolf is extremely rare, providing proof of the presence of canines in the life of early man.

No other interspecies relationship has been more totally dissected or analyzed, and, for many, their relationship with a dog enables their daily existence, whilst others develop a truly unique partnership as they work together to find solutions to an astounding variety of difficult tasks. Watching canine teams in action inspire feelings of wonder and envy: wanting that same togetherness, that same level of connection, and, yes, that same apparent degree of obedient compliance. How did they do that? Why is that dog so obedient? If only my dog behaved that way. If only!

The five specialty disciplines that this book covers – scent detection, law enforcement, search and rescue, guide, and therapy – demonstrate the emotional bonds that make possible tasks which even technology can't begin to replicate or explain. And yet, a commonality of purpose runs deep between all of these specialized partnerships: canine heroes who work tirelessly to help us function; prevent bad guys from winning; rescue the lost from a mountainside or provide the depressed with a reason to smile. The union forged via an incredible amount of time, patience, consistency, and a common goal creates a team that develops a working interdependency and creates a bond like no other.

How and why are these relationships formed? What enables this peerless species to master such a vast array of unique specialties? And why are dogs still walking at our sides, working tirelessly at such difficult tasks every day, always available and ready to try new and inventive ways of using their skills to help man?

Is the answer simply that we own them?

Perhaps, although these stories are not just about dogs that are owned: these stories are about working partnerships that begin through mutual need – maybe born of necessity – but ultimately bound by love and purpose.

These true stories, as told firsthand by the everyday, real-life partners, highlight those RinTinTin and Lassie attributes – trust, communication, and devotion to man – which are made possible by a dog's innate senses and survival instincts, and overflow with heart-stopping, feel-good moments.

Likewise, the stories spotlight the courage of the people walking beside their canine partner as they first learn to trust their dog – and ultimately have to say 'goodbye.'

How a dog uses his unique set of skills and senses is demonstrated in the stories within this book. Some will claim that man has bred and tweaked the genetic make-up of dogs to enable them to be what they are today, but bear in mind

The gaze of this small child, and the obvious meeting of minds expresses the meaning behind this therapy canine's 'heart.'

that without the adaptability and inborn senses that all dogs possess, man's genetic tweaking would prove pointless.

Even so, there is legitimacy in this claim. The Labrador Retriever pulling a wheelchair or guiding a sightless person is not the same Lab found in the duck-hunting blind: genetics have played a part in emphasising certain traits. Guide dogs – with their strong, gentle, nurturing temperament – have been selected for trainability, intelligence, patience, and a desire to please.

Selective breeding increases the presence of specific attributes, but doesn't change the inborn senses that drive the behaviors – they remain constant. Working dogs used for military and police work – where fearless determination along with explosive strength and agility are required – are selectively bred for these characteristics. The same protective behavior, driven by survival instincts to nurture and protect the pack, can be equally employed to gently care for a child or a flock of sheep.

Job-specific training refocuses instinctual canine skill sets, and the biggest challenge is for the human team member to learn to follow his canine partner without hesitation, allowing the dog's senses to decide their every move.

It is only through constant training and communication that the partners in this alliance can maintain their trust, and nurture the growth of the bond that they have: an ongoing process that is enhanced by time and field experience. These canine partners didn't just guide the blind down a crowded street or find drugs in a school locker, or a child lost on a mountain. Their fundamental working relationship goes a stage further and develops into an almost symbiotic partnership.

Clint, in one of the stories, describes it best when he says: "That's what I mean when I say he is I, I am he, our purpose is so totally the same, the meeting of minds, the uniting of souls, a synergy like no other." A unique characteristic of this affinity is what is simply known as 'canine heart,' that rare quality which motivates dogs to run into burning buildings, showing bravery beyond reason and uncompromising loyalty to man, saving the lives of complete strangers.

Recent, genetic manipulations have resulted in dogs who are bigger, smaller or hairless, and, with careful breeding, does allow for some fairly predictable, breed-specific personality traits and characteristics. But the dog's inborn instincts remain constant, and it is these that have strengthened the bond with man and intensified that mystical element: the canine heart.

Inborn senses drive the survival instincts which, ultimately, are behind most dog behaviors, and the stories here will provide an insight into what these senses are, and why the behaviors are so crucial in working dogs, whilst drawing a parallel between breed temperament that explains why the little Cocker Spaniel is as determined and unwavering a working partner as the avid, drug-finding Malinois.

Developing the necessary working relationship between man and dog begins by understanding the fundamentals of the four main canine senses: smell, touch, sight and hearing. Our partners and companions are part of the animal kingdom, of course, just as we are: predators whose survival is dependent on the senses they were born with, simple, basic survival essentials. In order to gain understanding of our companion, some knowledge of how the environment communicates information to him is essential.

Why and how dogs do what needs to be done

The brilliant architecture of the dog's nose allows scent – with all of its complex undertones and emotions – to be transmitted directly to his brain.

"It is in the brain that odors are recognized, interpreted, and filed for memory," writes William G Syrotuck in *Scent and the Scenting Dog*. The canine 'sniff' carries scent-permeated air to the brain where a powerful scent-discrimination process determines and causes action based on categorization of the odor (an ability that can be compared to our sight: we see, and, based on prior experience, we understand immediately what we are seeing). This ability to instantly categorize the potential of a scent (is it my dinner or am I its dinner?) – constantly learning and categorizing new scents – is obviously of major importance for survival.

Comparing a dog's scenting ability to our own is humbling. Dr Ian Dunbar, in *Dog Behavior*, writes: "It has been suggested that olfaction in the dog is up to one million times superior to man." Determining whether this ability varies from breed to breed is not an easy task, but the one fact that cannot be disputed is that canine noses are superior to ours.

Today's canine pee-mail – the who, what, and why, in addition to the emotional and physical state of the messenger – is determined by a single sniff, and, even if only with a single drop or two of urine, an answer – I was here, too – must be left for all other passers-by. It's as important to canine communication to leave that drop as it is to take that sniff, because the latter reveals messages fresh and old in the environment they are passing through. Obviously, it's vital to know if the messenger was prey or predator, but the actual success of the species depends on knowing more intimate details, such as sex, friend or foe, dominant or submissive, pack member or enemy, via a finely-tuned ability to discriminate and analyze scent that is an obvious throwback to a dog's wolf ancestry.

An odor's unique composition is what allows olfactory senses to distinguish one scent from another. For example, individual people have a unique odor based primarily on their DNA, although this is affected by numerous factors, such as detergent, diet, or change in mood or health. Studies indicate that genetic factors regulating metabolic processes lead to a discharge of distinctive body odors for each individual, which is exuded onto the body's surface where it combines with any number of environmentally unique factors to create a specific aroma. When trained to locate a particular scent, olfactory senses impel our canine searcher to locate that precise scent.

Flooding his nose with air as he sniffs, a canine fills a complex cavity lined with olfactory receptors with some of those DNA flakes of skin. Unlike normal breathing, sniffing consists of a series of rapid short breaths, which provide air for

"Every day we shed forty million flakes of skin, each one supporting a rich flora of bacteria with characteristic odors. All this invisible and odorous dandruff drifts along behind us in a vapor trail, leaving a track that leaps out at a hound like neon lights. Even on a quiet day, we produce several pints of sweat, the smell of which is so distinctive that most dogs can retrieve a pebble from a riverbed and return it to the hand of the man who threw it.

"The truth is that there may be more than half a million odors loose in the world, any one of which could waft our way. Most of these smells are of biological origin, and many carry vital information about things beyond the reach of our eyes and ears.

"Even the cleanest air, at the centre of the South Pacific or somewhere over Antarctica, has two hundred thousand assorted bits and pieces in every lungful. And this count rises to two million or more in the thick of the Serengeti migration, or over a six-lane highway during rush hour in downtown Los Angeles." – Lyall Watson, *Jacobson's Organ*

respiration while also funneling air to the brain, where the odor is analyzed, and a response made based on instinct or training. At that same time the slightest variance in the strength of that odor is detected individually by the nostrils, and the process of locating the source begins.

Robert Burton, in *The Language of Smell*, writes: "In Man, the [olfactory] membranes add up to about the size of two postage stamps, if laid out, compared with the pocket-handkerchief size of the membranes in a fair-sized dog. The difference in size of the smell membranes in dog and Man give an idea of the difference in their ability to smell odours."

Tens of millions of biological cells full of DNA messages about health, sex, mood, fear, perfume, which are affected by wind, moisture, temperature, altitude, and tracked by German

Shepherd vs Bloodhound vs Border Collie, searching the desert, a mountain, an avalanche, a river or a backyard full of family pets and curious neighbors, are all variables interwoven to present countless combinations providing ongoing, continual challenges. And these are only a minute sampling of the variables affecting all canine searches and interactions with their partners, explaining the need for a consistent level of communication and trust between them. It also explains the necessity of solid training and the need to expose a working canine to as many combinations of the foregoing variables as possible, building on his confidence and focus for whatever job might be just around the corner.

In *The Dog's Mind*, Bruce Fogle DVM MRCVS writes: "Anatomically speaking, sensory stimulation causes nerve cells in the brain to actually grow and make new synaptic connections with other nerve cells. The network expands to accommodate and assimilate new information."

The introduction of new scents experienced during training makes use of that fact. Ultimately, these new networks incorporate new scents and imprint them onto the brain – where they will be categorized – and produce an appropriate response. Now, through training, we can shape that response or behavior.

A major contribution to survival is how a dog uses his nose to find food. Connecting the new scents that we want him to 'hunt' to his survival/hunting instincts means that he will pursue these with the same focus and urgency he uses when hunting for his dinner. He instinctively goes into hunting mode in order to find food to survive, and now our new scent will initiate that same behavior. But the hunter will not completely forget about hunting live prey: the inherent scents and connected instincts will never be totally extinguished, and, genetically-speaking, they cannot be eliminated. These crucial, natural drives should not be considered negative, however, as they can simply be rechanneled into an activity that is acceptable to the current circumstance. The hunting instinct is a deep-rooted survival essential that provides the wherewithal to sustain life. By its very nature

Opposite: "A person's scent changes according to mood." Milo D Pearsall and Hugo Verbruggen, MD, Scent

survival is essential, and the powerful behaviors it supports must be positively channeled. Maintaining that same intensity for a refocused new scent (not a survival necessity) requires continuous training.

Entire books have been written about how the feelings of a handler can be transmitted via the leash, and the negative effect that can result if those feelings are of frustration or anger. The message we transmit through body language, verbal praise and internal calmness directly affects the relationship with our canine partners, and, as a result, their work. Our bond is based on (1) the emotional messages our partners receive through their olfactory senses, (2) the tactile messages we send every time we touch our partners in work or play, (3) the spoken word reflecting positive or negative emotion, and (4) the visible messages we project through body language.

When reading the stories here, it will become apparent that the dogs knew the emotions behind every thought, movement and touch of their human partner, based on their senses receiving the messages telegraphed to them; they just knew. Simply put, their olfactory senses smell the facts and start the action.

A dog's entire body has tactile nerves at the base of each hair follicle, which make the sensation of touch a very relevant method of communication. This sense and the type of touch can ultimately determine the strength of the bond between dog and person. Because physical touch can actually cause canine heart and respiratory rates to slow, how we touch our dogs can be crucial in the formation of that all-important emotional bond.

The connection between man and dog begins through smell, and is reinforced when we touch him. In the photos opposite and overleaf notice first the touch of a stranger, and second the touch of a trusted partner: both of these working dogs are receiving and benefiting from the connection. Facilitating the trust and communication poignantly visible in both of these images are olfactory senses that first told the therapy partner the child needed her, and

"Touch remains forever the most potent reward that a dog can receive ..."
Bruce Fogle,
The Dog's Mind.
What message does your touch send?

secondly went to work locating drugs in the knowledge that success would elicit a touch – the ultimate reward.

Born without the ability to see for the first 8-12 days (and, it is believed, unable to hear for three weeks), the senses of touch and smell are immediately crucial to the comfort (touch) and survival (food smells) of puppies, and remain influential throughout their entire lives. Being so helpless in terms of senses creates a strong dependency on dam and siblings for survival, and is a major element in the development of that all-important bond when the same feelings are transferred to their human family. Development of

vision and hearing skills are key to their success as a predatory species, but it is that early family connection with dam and pack that makes our bond possible.

Hunting success is boosted by a large pupil that collects more light and enhances vision during low light at dawn or at dusk (crepuscular vision). In addition, a wider field of vision and movement sensitivity allows canines to recognise and understand what they see moving in the distance.

"Although their ability to see detail is limited, they are quite exquisitely sensitive to movement, and are able to pick up even very slight movement of hiding prey. A stationary object may not be noticed from a distance, but the dog will see it as soon as it makes a move." says Virginia Wells in *Making Sense of your Dog's World*.

Hearing is one of the dog's best-developed senses, and, as our stories reveal, is highly important in his understanding of the environment. Bruce Fogle writes in *The Dog's Mind*: "The dog's ability to hear high-pitched sounds is an aspect of the wolf in him."

Identifying the location of imminent danger is vital for a Guide Dog, who has been trained to react to vehicles in much the same way that a wolf would react to his prey. Being able to locate a sound in one six-hundredth of a second, our canine partners also hear sounds in a higher, wider range of frequency than does man, and locating his dinner underground is made possible by this acuity. Anatomical features that support this survival adaptation are the finely-tuned antenna ears which provide directionality simply because of the distance between them, and their ability to swivel in opposite directions at the same time.

Acute hearing and unique visual adaptations allow perception of dangerous situations. When these two senses work in tandem with olfactory expertise and a strong bond that has developed through touch, dogs have the ability and desire to help the blind move safely across busy intersections, capture a fleeing felon, find a lost child in the wilderness or locate a vast array of newly-introduced scents that have simply been categorized as something, anything, that man wants found.

The stories

Now read the firsthand accounts of exceptional behavior, that extra – the canine heart – taking over, and getting done what needs doing regardless of training or previous experience.

"All dogs have magnificent cognitive powers. Cognition is defined as the brain processes through which a dog acquires information about his environment. The dog's mind is eminently good at cognition. They are amazingly perceptive to nuance and observe the most imperceptible changes in us," writes Bruce Fogle in *The Dog's Mind*.

Because the senses that drive and support canine behavior are different to ours, understanding said behavior can sometimes seem difficult. Demystifying and properly understanding instinctual behavior will expand and improve relationships with your canine partner or companion. Better appreciation of the senses that drive the behavior is the key to responsible, quality relationships. While reading the stories, look out for unique moments, not just the obvious finds and rescues, but those special moments between partners, which will never be forgotten.

Visit Hubble and Hattie on the web: www.hubbleandhattie.com and www.hubbleandhattie.blogspot.com
twitter
Details of all books • Special offers • Newsletter • New book news

... being heroes every day

Scent-detection specialists

Anything, anywhere: partners who find and deliver

Canine scent-detection specialists work on a phenomenal variety of assignments today. "The major restriction to the use of trained scent-detection dogs appears to be human imagination," reported a research team in New Zealand after studying 'The use of scent-detection dogs,' Clare Browne, Kevin Stafford and Robin Fordham, *Irish Veterinary Journal.*

From today's explosive, fire-accelerant and forensic crime scene specialists, finding illegal contraband and gas leaks in Ontario, to early alert warnings of melanoma cells or oncoming epileptic and hypoglycemic attacks, and conservation specialists scenting for tiger and grizzly bear scat, enabling the safe study of endangered species, this unique species aids man in so many intriguing and varied searches. His legendary scenting abilities are a direct result of a need to eat and provide for the pack, and, as part of that pack, we are privileged to make use of this highly-prized skill set. Whether solving crimes or benefiting our planet, canines have adapted their inborn skills to meet man's ever-expanding requirements.

University research reveals that a dog's nose can determine scent at one part per trillion (1,000,000,000,000,000,000) – that's eighteen zeroes! – simply amazing. Highlighting olfactory prowess, the stories in this section demonstrate tracking, illegal narcotics, an atypical example of human imagination, and forensic crime scene recovery. While most of the canines in this section had two jobs – referred to as dual-purpose – these stories focus on one specialized skill set – canine olfactory senses – the most widely used in the most diverse range of jobs, with no apparent limitation, and driven by the most basic instinct: eat to survive.

Initiating a search for anything requires scent-specific molecules to enter a dog's nose, and the two ways this happens are through tracking (scent on the ground), and air-scenting (scent in the air). The canine tracking specialist is used primarily for hunting any manner of moving object, and our tracking specialist, JJ, successfully hunted the bad guys. For years the pre-eminent canine expert has been the Bloodhound, a name given to this floppy-eared tracking marvel years ago when it was believed that tracking dogs actually followed a trail of tiny droplets of blood left by the lost or a fleeing convict. Today, we know the dog is actually following flakes of skin which carry the unique, odor-specific DNA markers that slough off us as we move.

JJ, the first tracking Bloodhound in Salt Lake City, blazed the way for other tracking

"The task is to locate this person. The traditional method, of course, the tracking or trailing dog ..."
William G Syrotuck,
Scent and the
Scenting Dog

Bloodhounds and hard surface trackers by facilitating exceptional arrests based on his tracking skills. With raw and very new emotions, Mike Serio, JJ's partner, explains how his life was forever changed, from the day this little puppy first came into his family until his last breath. JJ's tracking abilities reprogrammed the lives of Mike and his family, and his influence eventually spread into the community.

Bloodhounds have distinct character traits: they're stubborn, not so good at taking direction or actually apprehending the bad guy, but are excellent trackers. Retired police K9 handler Julia Priest puts it clearly when she states "... understand your dog's motivation for tracking, understand that he can track and you can't, and try to learn how to use what he has to your best advantage by convincing him that he wants to find what you have laid down. Be a partner in the marvelous skill that he has, rather than a dictator, and let him teach YOU what you need to know about scenting. Once you have that, the rest is just details, and if you learn how to read your dog's indications, the two of you will be a team that's hard to beat!" 'Canine Scenting Ability Makes Teaching Tracking a Treat.'

Mike and JJ
That 'bay' became JJ's signature
"JJ came into our home to be our best friend, not a police dog. Named after a particularly special dog in our college life, he quickly became part of our family. From day one, when I arrived home from work, this eight-week-old puppy would dart past me, without a greeting, nose down, tracking straight to my police car, then backtrack me into the house. It was the strangest, coolest thing watching this little guy track. Tracking was something I knew close to nothing about, but I would learn. I think, even then, JJ had a different idea about what his future would hold.

"My wife and I took JJ everywhere: after all, he was family. Intrigued by his desire to keep his nose on the ground, we watched as everywhere we went JJ's nose would go down. In a funny lumbering position, he checked out and explored his world, making decisions on which direction to

" It looks as though those doleful dogs, the Bloodhounds, who would as soon lick a quarry to death as bite him, have put together the perfect odour detection system.
"It has to focus on that single stimulus beyond all the usual limits of sensory attention span." – Lyall Watson, *Jacobson's Organ*

go based on what he smelled. He seemed to know the right way, even as a puppy, and was most interested in ground scents: watching him come across a track, you could see him hit the scent, and then start following whatever scent it was that day. I thought it was just the coolest thing to watch – exciting, and, we thought, unusual.

"My wife and I knew we had a very special pup from day one. On one particular trip to Lake Tahoe we stayed in a cabin, and enjoyed long walks on the beach – with JJ, of course. One time, it was obvious that JJ was getting tired, and finally he simply turned around and backtracked to our cabin. He was only four months old at the

JJ and Mike – Salt Lake City's first Bloodhound team – introduced a new method of finding the 'bad guy.'

time, and it was at least a mile, but he simply wanted a nap.

"Those early months with JJ were fun, and watching one incredible feat after another had us exclaiming in wonder, although neither my wife nor I had any idea just how important and special JJ and his talents would prove to be for us.

"Bloodhounds need a lot of exercise or they will chew your house apart, so we hiked a lot, and between hikes JJ chewed – a lot. Even after 11 hours of hiking, JJ still wanted more: he just didn't want to quit. Between chewing on our cable wires or the barbeque grill, JJ slept: sleep – chew – sleep – chew – he never quit. Bloodhounds don't know the word 'quit' either while tracking, chewing or playing, and JJ was all Bloodhound. He definitely loved to sleep, especially as he got older, but once he was on a track, his drive was phenomenal. JJ and I did a lot of hiking, otherwise he would have destroyed our home. JJ used his own devices to entertain himself, and it usually involved chewing; he wasn't especially fussy about what he chewed, either.

"I had just finished at the police academy and was on the streets of Salt Lake City, though not a K9 officer, when JJ joined our family. Some time went by, and even though the small tracking scenarios my wife and I would set up for JJ became more complicated and longer, he was still always successful. Intrigued, I finally asked a K9 handler to watch JJ: to set up a track, any track, and JJ would work it.

"Well, did he set up a track! It was short, over grass, onto cement and black top, into bushes and flowerbeds, and ultimately in the top of a tree, in an area full of tracks and distractions. I should have been concerned, but I wasn't. JJ tracked beautifully, finding my friend easily, and together JJ and I began a very long journey. Ultimately, a career change would give rise to years of success as the first Bloodhound K9 team in the State of Utah.

"Before any of that could happen, however, it was my turn to play catch-up.

JJ already knew his job, but the handler part of the team needs to carry his load, too, and I knew virtually nothing. I had watched JJ work all the tracks we had set for fun, but things had changed; I needed to understand just what JJ could and couldn't do, and how to enhance his training and maintain his interest at all times. What was JJ's motivation? It was no longer simply a matter of keeping him from eating the furniture. I needed to learn how to turn JJ into a tracking Bloodhound, on command, regardless of his desire to nap or play. I had a lot to learn.

"We began with basic runaways: an apparently simple concept that is actually quite complex as the handler learns to read his dog's body language. The K9 handler who had set the track for JJ inspired me by saying how he wished that their dogs would track that naturally. I read books from the National Police Bloodhound Association, and started training using the methods described there. Quite soon training was filling my every thought, and neighbors, my wife (more times that I can count) and Boy Scouts became the 'runaways' for whom JJ searched. It's good to use different scents, but sometimes you have to use a familiar scent simply because that's the only person available. It was important that JJ learn his reward would come from the scent he was tracking, not just my wife, but the logistics and practicality of that didn't always come together. And I figured any track was better than no track. Yes, I know that a lot of authorities say it is wrong to use family members more than a couple of times, and you should never use yourself, but I did what I needed to do, which was to get in more and more tracks.

"I especially remember a track around Alta View Hospital, when JJ started to 'bay.' As soon as I left the car, he knew I was setting a new track for him; he was going to track, something he truly loved to do. He got so excited he started to bay, and that became JJ's signature, his announcement to everyone that he was 'on the job.'

"In most any situation this species is such a wonderful presence, such a great tool, but that does not mean it is foolproof; nothing is 100%. Tracking is one of the most difficult things for any dog to do; your search area is the world. Never, in reality, are you deployed into an area where you know the subject's location: obviously, that's the point.

"Locating a source of scent at a crime scene, such as a footprint or scent article, becomes your first challenge. It is particularly important in this instance to be extra careful and know exactly where the 'bad guy's' footprints are, or acquire a clean scent article from his car. Next, you present this scent to your K9; remember, your partner will follow the scent you present him with, right or wrong, so now is the time to be very careful because this is the scent he will follow, and the focus of your and your agency's energies.

"Once a particular track is begun, its odor is set in a time frame, combining human scent with ground disturbances. Identifying that particular odor, the K9 focuses exclusively on it. In the training process we observe and follow, needing to understand the dog's reactions to the track and its variables. He makes it all look so easy, but confusion and inconsistency can occur if an inexperienced tracker finds himself following more than one track, and it is here that an uncontaminated scent article can mean the difference between right and wrong. Still, training, to simulate likely situations, will eventually teach the tracking K9 to focus on just one scent: developing his track loyalty formula, he will ultimately utilize all available information.

"When I started training JJ, he was much better initially as the training tracks had not been contaminated. But now, JJ was facing contaminated, parallel, or crisscross tracks, and he became confused. I encouraged him to follow any scent that had bailed out of the suspect's car. I would put JJ in the suspect's car full of scents: the owner's scent, the person who stole the car's scent, the three guys' in the back seat scents, and now JJ's nose. I could actually see his confusion when trying to choose a scent, but I couldn't help him, he was on his own. In reality, even if it is not the actual guy who stole the car that JJ chooses to follow but someone else who got out of that car, we will eventually find that bad guy, which is exactly what happened.

That's why JJ was so successful: he learned to follow someone from that crime scene. But initially his confusion was palpable: I kept pushing: 'choose, JJ, just choose.' I could hear his nose sniffing, sniffing more, his head moving methodically yet frantically back and forth over the area, that quizzical expression, until he finally made his decision. The tension in those moments actually seemed to increase his intensity and drive him forward with yet more determination, if that's possible for a Bloodhound. But, JJ was actually selecting and presenting himself with a scent; he was remarkable.

"How does it happen? No one really knows. But we do know that JJ utilized instinctual hunt drives, drives that come before anything else, drives that assure success. Remember, JJ had been displaying those exact skills from the day I took him home.

"Bloodhounds are extremely stubborn: they can stay on task, and their focus is so intense they will almost track until they drop. In a rural setting, in his prime with a fresh track, JJ would drag me into the ground. He could go ten or 15 miles, but tracking through one block in the city is equivalent to tracking through one mile in a rural setting, because of the different distractions and hard surfaces such as concrete and black top that don't hold raft scent [DNA] well, or provide crushed organic scent. So, in just one example, going through a dark alley, I could see six or seven different prowling cats, a Pit Bull bashing into a fence, garbage cans and dirty diapers, an old dead pig, not to mention trash! But JJ was the master in simply getting through the distractions, unless of course I took him into an area with no track; then maybe food would distract him, depending on the food.

"Our trial period, full of starts and stops, ultimately ended with JJ earning the respect of the patrol officers, and we earned respect not just from finding people, but by involving the officers in JJ's everyday training. I would have the officers set tracks, and then watch the resulting track and find, observing firsthand how it worked. They began to understand how JJ could help, and how his efforts would ultimately benefit them by solving problems on the street. This interaction allowed me to become confident in what JJ could do: one more way I learned and developed a deeper respect and love for the partner I was following.

"Finally, we're on the street, working as partners, and the following stories should give you a small window onto our lives for the next nine years. Most of our searches were within Salt Lake City and Salt Lake County over variable surfaces, with blacktop and pavement being the predominate ones. As a patrol officer, when you answer a call and you find out that someone has had their house broken into, or their purse stolen, you feel pretty helpless. Where do you start when you don't have anything to go on, no direction to pursue? You just say: 'I'm sorry, here's a case number and we'll try.' But now, with JJ's skills, we could pick up the track leaving the crime scene, and our chances of success went up enormously. All those previous demonstrations showing the officers how JJ worked, well, that got others to call, because when we got to a scene JJ's skills would help. That's just what happened, everyone called.

"I was initially on the patrol squad, I wasn't assigned to K9, and it was really beneficial to be assigned to the patrol because they would see me every day, and we trained together every single night. It got to the point that even in my trial period they were calling just for JJ specifically, and this did cause some angst. I was really trying to introduce a new skill that Utah POST did not train for, tracking on concrete and blacktop for long distances. I was showing how beneficial a city tracker could be in apprehending criminals, and the patrol officers I worked with were as excited about using this new tool as I was. I saw the potential, but I really didn't know how good JJ would get.

"Because of the success I had in that short trial period, I got another six-month trial period, and was eventually assigned to K9. New programs are always difficult, and it was very stressful for a long time, but fortunately the department – and the patrol in particular – were behind us 100%. JJ's success was the bottom line, and –

particularly in law enforcement – if they don't see it work quickly, they're going to get rid of it even quicker. This was new and different: it wasn't your typical police K9, he didn't bite, but he did find the bad guys; he found a lot of bad guys.

"By the time one particular early morning search was over, everybody had developed complete trust in JJ. It was a quiet morning, and a lot of officers were available who had arrived to help (coincidentally, many of them were really close to where our suspect was reportedly headed). A parked vehicle had been broken into, and a suspect was seen calmly strolling away, apparently confident he could get out of sight before anyone arrived and began looking for him. When JJ and I arrived about 25 minutes later, JJ located the track and started baying immediately (obviously, our suspect did not know that JJ would be there). From our training, I knew he was going in the right direction, and now everyone would be able to see firsthand what he could do.

"What a pivotal search this turned out to be for the two of us. I was very confident, watching JJ's intensity, sorting out intersections, figuring out the right direction: he was on a good solid track. The officers behind me didn't understand how I could just keep following, just following JJ for such a long distance when they couldn't see anyone. They must have been wondering why they should keep following, block after block after block. I'm telling the officers: 'Go northbound and then west, the suspect is only about 20 minutes ahead of us.' We eventually tracked all the way through that neighborhood, and then the track went into a golf course.

"Based on JJ's directionality, I could see exactly where this guy was going to cross the fence. I directed the officers to the exact spot on the other side of the fence, and told them to wait. They were probably thinking I was crazy: we're about a quarter of a mile behind him; how could I possibly know where he was going to cross that fence? But, sure enough, all of a sudden, this guy Spidermans over the fence, and drops down, surrounded by cops. During this process, about six or seven officers were giving me a play-by-play over the radio, and from then on everyone knew that when JJ was on a track – especially if he started baying – they had a really good chance of apprehending the bad guy.

"Prior to JJ's bays, his body language changed: he would slow down, inhale intensely, over and over, working feverishly, methodically, until finally the baying would start, usually when he was close, about 50 feet (15m) away from the bad guy, but in this case he started almost immediately. I can only speculate why, but it was an exciting 45 minutes following him, baying all the way, and exciting for everyone to understand and see just what JJ could do in the field. I knew the answer was in his nose and now every one knew.

"Our longest track was about two hours. We were tracking a robbery suspect responsible for a drive-by shooting, and we took up pursuit right after the suspect bailed from his car. I was especially proud of JJ that day. It was in the spring and he was suffering a lot of sinus discharge because of bad allergies, but still he tracked this guy about two miles, through junkyards, and finally located him hiding, pretending to sleep in a transient camp. He probably sensed the heightened angst associated with that track due to the shooting and possibility of more gunfire.

"Another very pivotal case was a deployment for Salt Lake County in pursuit of homicide suspects. Emotions run especially high in a homicide, and this was also a neighboring agency deployment, so more pressure. The initial responding K9 units were just starting to search; containment had been set, but was likely to be insufficient. 'Wait for Serio and his Bloodhound, JJ, he's the best chance we've got of bringing these guys in.' was the directive from Sergeant John Ritchie, a former German Shepherd handler. John was well respected, and chanced alienating all of the other handlers with this remark, but they reluctantly put up their dogs.

"John had called for me and I was really, really sweating. My own agency would simply have called JJ, but this was the city, and it was a homicide. A different agency was already in pursuit, and it was obviously very difficult to be

called down. JJ did have a good reputation by then, but I certainly felt the pressure. The track had been contaminated because the other dogs and officers had been canvassing the area, and I had found that if you don't get a good start, you don't usually get a good finish.

"For what was the longest ten minutes of my life we couldn't pick up the track. Sergeant Ritchie was following at my back, wondering out loud: 'Mike, what's going on, what's going on, where is the track?' I probably burned 10,000 calories in that short time, or at least lost 10lb (5kg), but JJ finally hooked into the track, which immediately went over a fence. I've got a German Shepherd and a couple of officers behind me, and we've all got to get over that fence. That achieved, the track is pristine, and conditions for tracking now excellent.

"We tracked about two-and-a-half blocks, well out of the containment area and, ultimately, the suspect was found hiding in a backyard: he's now serving his sentence in prison. Respect for our previous work for the county was good, but this was the city, and this was a homicide, and this particular success was sweet!

"Working with Officer Limburg and Elvis, a really big German Shepherd, JJ and I found ourselves part of a crime-fighting team comprised of two great K9 partners: tracking par excellence, and great big jaws, working side-by-side just waiting to bring down the bad guys. Having trained together we had developed a great plan of attack, so when a particular kidnapping suspect ran from LDS hospital, JJ was on the track, baying through the Avenues. JJ and Elvis, in pursuit, tracked several blocks and located the suspect in a tree. The suspect immediately Peter Panned out of the tree and started rooftop jumping.

"JJ had worked his butt off to find this guy and now it was my turn, so I handed the leash to Officer Limburg and jumped up on the roof, running, jumping; jumping from rooftop to rooftop after this guy. Jumping into one yard he met Elvis and those jaws, waiting not so patiently. Back up he went and started coming over the fence. Gun drawn, I tried to give him commands, but I knew I couldn't really shoot: there was no good reason to shoot. Sensing my hesitancy, he got back on the roof and began running again. At this point, I tackled him on the roof, doing everything in my power to take him into custody. We were in a big fight, my gun had been pointed directly at him, and he just kept saying: 'What is that noise, what is that noise, what kind of dog is that, just don't let that dog get me!' He was deathly afraid of what might be behind that 'bay,' which sounded like a huge foghorn, echoing throughout the Avenues. He couldn't imagine what could be making that sound – something worse than Elvis?

"I shouted and threatened with my fists, trying to get his arms behind his back, but he was so fearful of that dog, not the German Shepherd that nearly tore his arm off, but the Bloodhound that he heard following him, block after block after block, and JJ was still baying while we were on the roof, fighting. He was really proud of himself that day; he knew we had all done well.

"When JJ was nine, he was diagnosed with melanoma in his mouth. He lived a little over a year after that diagnosis, and during that year he caught over fifty bad guys. When he was initially diagnosed, I was devastated. He was at the top of his game, incredibly smart, catching one bad guy after another. I had noticed he was having trouble eating; something was different. Hoping he simply had a bad tooth, but secretly fighting fears of cancer, I took JJ to the ER, where they confirmed my greatest fears: JJ had cancer in his mouth.

"With the diagnosis came the estimate of one month to live, so I immediately started looking for different options. A vaccine created for human melanoma sent JJ and I to New York. It was extremely important to know that I had exhausted every option before making the decision to let JJ go. We were there eight days, and JJ underwent CAT scans, X-rays, and surgery. The tumor was removed but the surgery was not totally successful: however, with the vaccine and following radiation (which does not affect dogs the way it does humans – my decision might have been different if it did), we were all hopeful. And there was reason to hope for one, two, or even three more years, not just a single

month: that seemed like a good trade-off for the treatment he had to have.

"Between treatments we'd come home and JJ would catch the bad guys. Looking at those statistics his success rate never dropped, which was absolutely incredible to me. He lost that 'bay' of his for a while, because he seemed to have a hard time lifting his neck, but he did get it back before the cancer returned one last, awful time. JJ made it through the first six months and then another six months went by and he had made it a year, not a month, but a year.

"While in California on vacation, he really seemed to enjoy everything: maybe a little tired, maybe a little lethargic with some breathing difficulties, but he still had a good time. On the way home his panting was heavier, and I thought he was having kidney failure. I honestly thought we had licked the cancer but something was wrong. A chest X-ray showed the cancer was back: carcinoma and melanoma in his lungs, which was sucking all of the oxygen from him. Seeing the X-rays I broke down; I broke down even harder when the doctor told me I would need to put him down by the end of the month. This time, there were no other options.

"I took him to work thinking the best painkiller in his world would be distractions. A photo shoot at the park, some pictures, some old friends, and he perked up a little. But he just kept panting, and I knew he was running out of time. Only two days after taking him to the photo shoot and to see the other dogs he had been working with, it was obvious he was breathing even heavier. We rented an oxygenator and wrapped his kennel trying to get him more oxygen and some comfort. The kennel was too hot so we bought 300 dry cool packs to cool the air, but they didn't help, it was too hot, and he kept moving, trying to get comfortable. At the park he would sniff around for just a second, and then just sit and pant, looking, taking everything in.

"Because this damn oxygenator thing wasn't working, I took him downstairs where it was cold, and we opened the window. I wrapped myself in a comforter and tried to sleep. I wanted so badly to hold him and to comfort him, but JJ had never wanted to be held, he was really finicky that way. Wanting to be around you, keeping you in sight, knowing you were with him, he would allow an occasional pat on the head, but JJ was born to work and being held did not fit into his job description. When I knew he was dying, it didn't matter where I went, he kept watching me. I know JJ knew how really hard this was for me; I just wanted to lay there with him, but he simply couldn't let me, not because it would make him too hot, not because he wasn't comfortable with that kind of hugging stuff, but JJ knew it was time for us to let go.

"I had made arrangements with JJ's doctors to come day or night. The night I found JJ lying in the snow, uncomfortable, trying to get air, and then he'd move, trying to breathe, searching for an answer, a way to get comfortable. He could walk only a few steps and then stumble once or twice, probably from the lack of oxygen. That was the night, JJ didn't even sniff the ground once, he just kept moving, trying to get comfortable, trying to breathe. We went to the corner just a few steps and I knew. I came back in and called JJ's doctors.

" It was the hardest thing, it was the hardest thing looking back at it, but at the time I couldn't get them there soon enough. At that moment, I could not cry or even shed a tear until after, because I knew exactly what I had to do. Looking back, I made the decision at such a late hour, I've wondered if I was thinking clearly, but I know I was. I just didn't want it to be time. But then, there was never going to be a good time.

"My mother was in town for a trip to California, so she provided JJ's last meal, one of her meatballs, his favorite. I hand-fed him while he laid in our bed, his favorite comfort spot. This part was supposed to be easy for him, but it wasn't. Everyone always says 'it's easy,' but not for JJ it wasn't. He didn't go quietly into that good night: he cried, trying to jerk away, the line caused pain, not what I wanted. Pain was so not what I wanted to happen, not more discomfort. The last thing I wanted to do was cause him pain before he left this world, but when they finally got the line in his back, he did relax and calm down. But he had this scared look in his eyes, and again, I just

wanted to hold him, but I knew that wouldn't help.

"So, instead, I simply said, as positively as I could: 'JJ, do you want to go to work?' He tilted his head like he always did, when I said, this, and, with that look of anticipation, that's when JJ went, within seconds his heart had stopped. I felt – hoped – that I put him in a good state of mind, and now I could hold him. That day was very stormy, and I lay on the bed with him for three hours before I could move. After a biopsy at our veterinarian for research, I took JJ to the crematorium and said goodbye again.

"JJ started out as our family pet, a great part of our family, which would have been more than enough, but he also became instrumental in my career, in finding my life's vocation. Creating with me a new appreciation for Bloodhounds in Utah, enabling a new tracking potential to be used in the arsenal of weapons against the bad guys. JJ helped define who I am today.

"But dealing with the grief and finality associated with his death seemed impossible. Always previously content to live life as it happened, saying goodbye and not knowing how or where JJ was this very minute, intensified my grief beyond my level of understanding. For JJ to simply not *be* any more was incomprehensible; a pain I had never before experienced. I just wanted to know he was okay, and I hurt for him not being able to live life. Philosophically I know it's not possible, but I needed somebody, anybody, or JJ to just knock on the door and say: 'hey I'm okay.'

"At that particular point in my life, I didn't know anything about *The Rainbow Bridge*[2] poem. If someone had simply handed it to me, I would have thought, well, that's great, someone just wrote a lovely little poem to make people feel better, isn't that cute? But the following incidents still make me wonder and watch for rainbows.

"The next afternoon, Lisa, my wife, had gone to the neighborhood market to distract our four-year-old daughter and our five-month-old son from the sadness in our home. As she returned home, turning up our street, there, stretched across our road, was a glorious rainbow. Lisa stopped the car in awe. She desperately tried to call me, but I was in bed, all curled up, not answering the phone. Lisa kept calling and finally came running into the house to tell me about the rainbow: 'JJ's okay! He's okay!' Somehow a strong sense of peace accompanied that rainbow and its beauty. Lisa knew we had made the right decision to help him go peacefully: she didn't know anything about a rainbow bridge poem at that moment, she just knew the rainbow was beautiful, and somehow, with its beauty came peace and some hope.

"The next day – and here's the part that's tough – when JJ's ashes were returned, I was handed a poem entitled *The Rainbow Bridge*.

"This summer, looking at the tribute stone with JJ's picture on it, I said: 'Okay, give me something else, give me something else, so I can know you're okay,' and an hour or so later a raincloud brought a rainbow right over our home.

"I wonder how many rainbows I'll need to see, sitting on my front door, before my grief subsides, and the assurance of JJ's comfort finally

> "He is your friend, your partner, your defender, your dog. You are his life, his love, his leader. He will be yours, faithful and true to the last beat of his heart. You owe it to him to be worthy of such devotion." – Unknown

gives me peace. Unfortunately I'm more into absolutes, but it does give me some hope." Police K9 officer Mike Serio and K9 partner JJ, Salt Lake City, Utah, America. Current K9 partner Bloodhound Junior

Scent work basics

JJ was a tracking fanatic: a Bloodhound who tracked methodically and obsessively using

This picture was taken the day before JJ became a memory.³

ancient instincts – driven by inborn senses that are present in all dogs – that absolutely would not allow him to fail. JJ did not need training to become a great tracker: JJ was born to track. Good scent work starts with the natural inborn instincts of the canine species, which is born with a uniquely qualified tool that its members know how to use to find what they are looking for simply by following a scent. Training only becomes necessary when we want the dog to track a particular scent, which we repeatedly and positively introduce to him in order that he can focus on what we want found.

Obviously, intense hunt drives are highly-prized qualities in all search work. Canine partners with bold, dynamic energy, all-consuming determination, unbelievable tenacity, and olfactory prowess are essential to the quality and efficiency of any search. And because we are constantly turning this tenacity on and off at will, these sometimes hard-to-live-with characteristics need to be continually maintained and nurtured to maximize search efficiency. Defining terminology, and describing the processes of training dogs to track/trail/air-scent or detect specific odors, can fill volumes, and our goal here is not to create another training manual. All of the various methods allow us to access the hunting skills and olfactory prowess of our canine partners, and whilst each search method has advantages in specific situations, the outcome is ultimately to make a 'find' using a dog's nose.

These hunting skills, naturally present in all dogs, need to be channeled constructively, and this holds true for all of the partners in the stories you are about to read, and for your canine companion – the one sleeping at the foot of your bed or lying under the kitchen table: he needs those same challenges to fulfill his life and preclude the development of destructive, unacceptable behavior.

Our partners were born knowing how to search, but initially, even for them, a search begins blind, so survival skills are brought into play. Needing to locate a single specific scent molecule – on air-currents, on the ground, on rocks, or on bushes – entails smelling virtually everything in the environment, to ultimately identify that one molecule which will lead to its source: the find. As the search progresses, the dogs use a technique known as 'quartering' [turning the muzzle side-to-side (left and right) in order to take in all of the immediate environment via the olfactory system, either on air currents or the ground, ultimately working toward the source of the scent].

Any proficient hunter will use all methods available to make his find, and will systematically pattern-search all of the physical features of the environment. Search and rescue dogs are taught to 'find' human odor on command from an article of clothing from the lost person, or tracks. If neither of these is available, a basic 'find' command precipitates a search for any human scent – track/air-scent/trail – any method that makes the find.

Tracking dogs begin by following the scent of crushed vegetation on the ground, footprint to footprint, until it combines with the human scent and creates a unique odor. Detection dogs given the 'find' command respond in the same manner, and search their immediate environment, again, using the very same skills they would to hunt dinner. When these innate skills are refocused to track the bad guy, explosives or narcotics, or to search for a lost child, our partner's nose will get the job done in the most efficient manner his instincts direct him to use, and it is our responsibility to have trained with him enough to accept that we can trust him, understand his body language, and know he is following the scent he has been given or trained to locate. And we need to trust that the method he has chosen to search with is the best for that situation, because our canine partners absolutely know where the scent is – and we absolutely don't.

I think Mike said it best: "I needed to learn how to turn JJ into a tracking Bloodhound on command, regardless of his desire to nap or play. I had a lot to learn." JJ obviously came equipped with all the mechanics, and Mike and JJ developed the necessary bond, establishing communication and trust. Now Mike needed to determine when and how JJ's senses could be

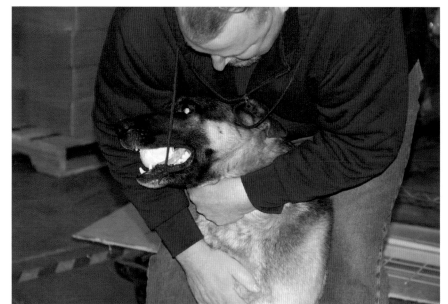

Totally content after a difficult training search, this German Shepherd's reward is a tennis ball and a hug from his trusted trainer. Who could ask for more?

No! Mine is the best.

And yet this Retriever obviously thinks his reward is the best ... and that's the point: each must have a reward that he regards as the absolute best!

turned on and off, and exactly how they could be applied successfully to find the bad guys – not his wife or a neighborhood scout.

Shaping a specific search technique that will best suit future working situations starts early – tracking/air-scenting/trailing/detection/point source – it's all the same to the dog: hunt, search, find. A simple game of hide-and-seek: finding a favorite person around the corner or hidden in a tree, or chasing and catching a tennis ball that has been scented with narcotics or explosives – creating a stimulating game that replicates the hunt and then presenting him with a reward he simply can't live without.

Coaching natural instincts to follow a specific search technique in initial training is facilitated by using an excited tone of voice and animated actions. At first, the search must always result in a 'win,' followed by the dog's choice of reward – a tennis ball, a stick or favorite toy –

whichever lets him know he's won. As training progresses, the challenges will become harder and longer, but success always results in a really big, animated "What a good job you did!" reward – always.

Always staying positive when introducing a new scent while working with 80lb (36kg) of unrestrained energy can be challenging for the other half of the team, and giving the reward at the exact location of the scent source is crucial in order to keep the dog on track. He needs to recognise that the reward is for finding the new scent: precisely the same emotion he would feel when successfully catching prey.

Because absolutely no environment leaves scent unaffected, odor molecules are in constant motion; this critical part of training is extremely difficult. Milo D Pearsall and Hugo Verbruggen, MD in *Scent: training to track, search and rescue* wrote: "Corrections serve no purpose and must be avoided: no handler can possibly tell what the dog does or does not smell."

Illegal drugs are everywhere

The illegal drug trade around the world is terrifying. Growing at an alarming pace, drugs endanger our children every day by enticing their participation, and making them vulnerable to violence and crime. Over several years working for a federal agency, my narcotic canine partner and I located illegal drugs in dorms, lockers and workstations at occupational training facilities, and I was amazed at the amount of drugs and associated paraphernalia she found. Participating in drug sniffs at our local High Schools and Junior Highs, I became painfully aware that the presence of illegal drugs is not restricted by financial means, ethnicity or social class: they are everywhere. If you always thought, as I did: "Not in my back yard," you're probably wrong.

One of the major assignments for law

All searches require realistic training in every imaginable location. These two pictures show drug sniffers locating drugs in a bus gas tank and in a school locker. Keeping our schools drug-free is one of law enforcement's everyday challenges.

"A dog and his handler can process 400 to 500 packages in 30 minutes. It would take a person several days to inspect this many packages. At border ports a dog can inspect a vehicle in four to five minutes. Even a cursory search by a customs inspector would require at least twenty minutes." – Milo D Pearsall and Hugo Verbruggen MD, *Scent: Training to track, search & rescue*

enforcement K9s is the drug 'sniff.' Illegal drugs are just that, illegal: dangerous to one's health they also contribute to the presence of really bad guys in our community associating with our children. They rob our children of their youth, their future, and frequently their lives. The futility

of this work became depressing for me. I have a great deal of admiration and respect for the K9 officers who work at this seemingly impossible endeavor every single day. It's a task that will never end, and maintaining a positive attitude with that knowledge requires strength of conviction of the hope of keeping crime and violence away from our children and off the streets. And, of course, a positive attitude must be transmitted through the leash to K9 partners to encourage enthusiastic productivity in the field.

Narcotics specialists Blake and Enzo
"... not ounces but pounds: pound after pound after pound"
The next story is about Enzo, who was responsible for removing over ten million dollars' worth of drugs from the streets of Utah in the 1990s.

An energetic, high-powered Malinois who loved his job, Enzo was also a dual-purpose K9 who protected Blake on the backroads of Southern Utah. I chose to include his story because of the sheer volume of drugs he located in really unusual places. Enzo introduced the bad guys to a new kind of drug 'sniff.' The bad guys thought it was easy to fool law enforcement and started to become inventive, but Enzo kept finding the drugs; not ounces but pounds: pound after pound after pound.

"My wife and I had traveled to Kentucky to pick up a dog that had been selected for our department, and flown from Holland. Enzo was scheduled to become part of the first drug interdiction program in the State of Utah.

"My partner and I had been working interdiction, more specifically the I-70 corridor, for about one-and-a-half years. During that time we had learned what to look for, how and when to find it, or at least we thought we knew where to find it. We had recovered about 38lb (17kg) of drugs during that time, and felt certain that if we had a dog we could find more. It was with this objective that our department okayed our first K9.

"Enzo was acquired – or should I say

Enzo acquired us? He was a strong, long-legged Belgian Malinois with one floppy ear, not especially pretty to the eye, and hell on wheels because of a higher-than-normal energy level and strength of purpose. We'd never had a honeymoon, so, for my wife and I, the trip to collect Enzo was intended to double as a honeymoon. Excited about both, it became obvious on the way home that the honeymoon was over. Within 48 hours of our meeting, Enzo claimed me as his future. The bonding process between man and dog has never been completely understood; sometimes it takes weeks or months, but in our case it was hours.

"Enzo's bond was instantaneous and complete, and although many times throughout the following years the question of who was boss arose, there was never any doubt about our loyalty to each other, even in the middle of the night on the freeways of Southern Utah. Knowing he was at my back let my family and I sleep soundly. Enzo would do anything to ensure my safe arrival home each night.

"I had had Enzo for only six days when we conducted our first narcotics search. I hadn't been through POST (Police Officers Standard Training), and neither had Enzo, although he had been introduced to narcotic scent memorization in Kentucky, so had a head start.

"So, there we were, six days into our relationship, and my fellow officer had pulled over a van. Questions we asked gave rise to suspicion, but neither of us could see anything that alerted us to the obvious presence of drugs in the van. I asked if we could use Enzo to search the van and was given the okay. Remember, I had had Enzo for just six days when we conducted this, our first search, and hadn't deployed him yet, so was anxious, not really knowing what to expect.

"Within seconds of entering the van I was wondering what I had gotten myself into. Literally bouncing from one side panel to the next, tearing at windows, curtains, carpet, and side panels, I was certain we had acquired a mad dog; at the very least an erratic and totally uncontrollable canine. Making no attempt at the civilized, methodical searching I had hoped for, this

animal went literally nuts in the van, giving the impression that there were drugs in every corner.

"And that's precisely where the drugs were: in every corner, behind every panel. As the panels of the van were removed one by one, packages of drugs were found lining the spaces between the interior panels and the outside frame. If I had had any doubt about whether or not I had a drug dog, that doubt was dispelled that day, as we recovered 38lb (17kg) of marijuana on our first search. That was the beginning of Enzo's career, and I never questioned him again as he went on to locate over 10.1 million dollars worth of illegal drugs.

"Fortunately, I had a dog who was at the top of his game, so a combination of my time and effort, and Enzo's natural ability allowed us to develop into one of Utah's most valuable drug-finding teams ever. Enzo ended up being a phenomenal 'dope' and patrol dog, realizing his full potential.

"Bandits became inventive at hiding their drugs. Knowing that a K9 search was likely during transit, they became more resourceful and hid the stash wherever they felt the dogs couldn't

physically reach, or disguised their scent by surrounding them with all sorts of noxious odors. But Enzo would still find them: that's what he did, he found drugs. He also supported me when the use of force or tracking into the night desert became necessary, and the following stories are just a few examples of the interesting locations in which we found drugs, and what Enzo's reactions were when I needed help.

"The drug interdiction program started in 1969, and was aimed at slowing the travel of drugs known to be happening on the I-70 Corridor in Utah. During the first year-and-a-half that we ran our program we kept our department busy prosecuting bandits, and destroying large finds of illegal narcotics. We thought we knew what we were looking for prior to getting Enzo as we had been quite successful already, and felt confident that getting a dog for our program would just make it easier. Little did we know. After working with Enzo for only a short time it occurred to us that, previously, a huge amount of stuff would have been missed.

"I was constantly on the freeway and now

(Left) 113lb (51kg) of drugs that almost got away but for Enzo. In the door (below), just one of the many cut access panels used to hide drugs throughout the van's walls.

I had Enzo. If Enzo told me drugs were present, that's exactly where the dope was. If Enzo gave me an indication, seats were coming out, walls were opened up, he didn't lie, and consequently we did a very thorough search when he told us drugs were present. His finish remained crazed, like the first day: he would scratch, bite, scratch, and keep scratching. That initial high drive search where he looked like a crazed fool was a sign to all of us that drugs were present.

"Based on Enzo's record, and the support my department gave our drug program, aggressive searches of gas tanks and interior walls in vehicles become commonplace. Previously, illegal drugs were transported in hidden compartments in vehicles, and we had no legal way of confirming their presence, which meant that illegal drugs were being successfully trafficked without any way of locating them. It was not possible for law enforcement departments – regardless of suspicion – to start ripping open truck beds, gas tanks, or van walls without violating an individual's civil rights, and besides,

where would you start? But now, with Enzo and the other narcotic K9 teams, suspicion (the

officer's training), accompanied by probable cause (K9 indication) was sufficient to allow full and thorough searches, resulting in find after find in gas tanks, air filters, tires, mufflers, and other previously undetectable places.

"Another time Enzo indicated on a gas tank, and we ended up taking over 100lb (50kg) of narcotics out of that gas tank, which held about 8 gallons of gas with the rest of the space full of drugs. It's claimed that K9s can't detect through gas, but oh yes they can!

"A search that really stands out was at a roadblock. The highway patrol requested our presence based on Enzo's success, and was hoping he would make a difference here. The patrol had stopped a car, and we were asked to search.

"As usual, I started at the front to go around anti-clockwise, but Enzo went around me and under the door of the truck. He went directly to the gas tank of that Ford truck and started scratching, so into town that Ford Ranger went. In Green River we dropped the gas tank, but didn't see any extra compartments cut into the tank as we'd expected: nothing. As we let the gas tank down, however, a rattling noise could be heard inside the tank. We set the tank on the floor and discovered seven pieces of glued, capped pvc pipe, each filled with a kilo of meth!

"The gas tank of a Ram Charger was found to be the hiding place when Enzo kept indicating in the back of the Charger. After removing a piece of the carpet we could see an access door, under which was the gas tank with an access cut into the top: 75lb of packaged marijuana was floating around in *that* gas tank.

"Another unusual find was made in a unique creation of two stacked truck beds blocked with spacers, which looked like one truck bed, allowing the transportation of pounds of illegal drugs. Enzo kept hitting on the taillights; I mean really hitting on the taillights. A blowtorch allowed us to cut a hole behind the taillight, and we could see the packages stacked solid between the two truck beds. We simply cut off the top bed and shook out the packages of drugs: a find we never would have made without Enzo.

The red van that almost got away

"The 63-year-old driver of the van and his two grandchildren, visiting from Los Angeles, were traveling to Chicago. The grandkids were 22- and 23-years-old, a brother and sister. Talking to them for a minute or so after we stopped them for a motoring infraction, none of their stories seemed right, but I couldn't see anything obvious by just glancing inside; nothing seemed out of the ordinary.

"So, I simply asked the grandfather if he had any illegal drugs, and if I could search the van with my dog? He hesitated, saying he was in a hurry and wanted to get going. I told him it would take 30 seconds for the dog to search, and then he could be on his way.

"This had been my pullover, and my back-up had just arrived, so we could get started. I reiterated a search would take only 30 seconds because I had the dog right in my patrol car: you could see the color literally drain out of his face, a sign that confirmed my suspicions.

"Starting Enzo at the front of the van, I passed the front doors, to which Enzo said 'no' and veered off to the back doors, practically tearing the paint off them. I asked the occupants to get out of the van and put Enzo inside, where he just went crazy. There was 113lb (51kg) of dope in the panels of that van and Enzo hit every single one of them. They almost got away with it: even though my suspicions had been aroused by stories that didn't quite gel, without Enzo there was nothing visually that would have enabled us to search for drugs, and I probably would have let that one go, along with all those drugs.

"The dog program was in its infancy in Utah when we got Enzo, and I was in a position to learn and understand the amount of training and upkeep that was and still is necessary to have a good partner that is dedicated to you and your work. Personally, I enjoy the hunt, I don't care how much there is, I'm the biggest drug addict of all. It's just a game of Cat and Mouse and finding and destroying the drugs is second only to the sheer pleasure of working at the side of a phenomenal partner like Enzo. I don't know how many finds of 30 or 40 kilos we made, one right after another; quantities like that add up quickly. He was hard to work but he was fun to follow because trusting him always led me to drugs. He didn't miss the dope, he wasn't fooled by anything and he didn't lie, but I wasn't afraid to deploy him, either.

"On one particular occasion we pulled over a rental car, and could actually smell burnt marijuana, so out came Enzo. The car's occupants were asked to step out and in he went, immediately removing a chunk of dashboard about the size of a 50 cent piece. As he continued his search along the roof and the headliner in the rental car, his mouth opened again and he proceeded to remove part of the ceiling liner, whereupon three bags of heroin, each about the size of a cookie, fell out. Continuing with the search we eventually located enough lab equipment to send the suspects to jail for both distribution and possession of a traveling lab. I clearly remember making a call to the rental company, telling it about the location of the car and why and where the damage was. The agent wasn't too worried since he had an open credit card on the guy who had hired it, and indicated he would get everything fixed.

"That degree of damage to a rental car is not unusual when a narcotics search is carried out by an aggressive finisher. I'd deploy Enzo in a BMW with leather seats, say, which, of course, I didn't want him to destroy for a two-inch 'joint' – but he would. He didn't differentiate between a half-filled pipe and 113lb (51kg) when showing me its location. I've seen him literally remove air conditioning vents from cars, and that stuff can get expensive. Luckily, he was not wrong in the case of the BMW, so I never had to buy a leather seat, but I've seen him take chunks out of dashboards, and he did remove parts of the headliner from that rental car.

"There are obvious occasions where more passive dogs are essential: explosives, for sure, and a lot of departments want passivity for criminal forensic searches to protect the scene and any evidence located. Having an aggressive-finish canine means that when he locates drugs, he will use whatever method is necessary to show

Enzo didn't miss the dope; he wasn't fooled by anything ...

you where those drugs are. With most aggressive finishers, this usually means scratching or biting, but really scratching or biting. Damage to property can obviously occur since there are just seconds, literally seconds, between his olfactory confirmation and the need to show his partner where the stash is located. This aggressive indication leaves no doubt in a courtroom situation as the jury is shown what occurred via a simple video taken at the time, and can actually see the dog try to take off a fender or rip open a suitcase.

"Personally, I prefer the aggressive finish because it's part of the image I need while traveling the highways of Utah at night. My back-up is at least 30 minutes away, and a little black, passive, indicating Lab – regardless of how good a drug-sniffer she is – does not intimidate a bandit. Bring out a 92lb Mal and the situation is very different, preventing matters from getting out of hand. Just one of the obvious benefits of traveling the night roads with Enzo.

"Enzo wasn't just a dope dog. Driving the dark highways in the desert of Utah made nights long and sometimes dangerous. Having him there gave me companionship, and comfort to me, and my family.

"His very first patrol deployment concerned a bandit who had stolen a car, and wanted to have a gunfight with us and go out in a blaze of glory. Suicide-by-officer is a tactic used by desperate people, and we work hard to prevent it from happening, but in this case it was obvious that the bandit wanted us to facilitate his death.

"Attempting to avoid gunfire and injury to

anyone, we sent Enzo under the bridge where the bandit was hiding. For any of us to have done that would have been suicide, but that was exactly what Enzo was trained for. Even so, making the decision to send Enzo into obvious danger was always a tough call, but necessary to assure everyone's safety, and I knew Enzo's speed, agility and training gave him a great chance of avoiding harm. Enzo finally dragged out the guy to where we could see him, and we realized that he had already taken his own life. We all went home to our families that night, and Enzo went home with me.

"On another occasion a trooper asked us to search a suspicious car, and Enzo positively indicated a headlight. The initial search by the trooper and I was negative until the trooper popped off the air cleaner, and that's where the drugs were: 12 kilos of meth, down in the ductwork. Enzo had located the drugs right away, and we just needed to look further, which is often the case.

"At this point the bandits decided that as there were just two of us against three of them, they weren't going down on this particular deal. One guy ran into the desert a few feet, but, looking into that dark desert night, probably decided he didn't want to die out here on this freeway so came back and gave it up. The other two, however, decided they could take us: they weren't in handcuffs yet, and it looked like there was going to be a fight. Apparently they had forgotten about Enzo, or maybe they hadn't noticed those teeth, or thought he only did drugs, but I simply brought Enzo back out and sat him down, whereupon he immediately switched to patrol mode. Enzo did enjoy drug work, but he really, really enjoyed patrol work, and the possibility of a chase and a bite made him come to life. With all his energy focused directly on them, it didn't take the two bandits long to offer up their hands for the cuffs, whilst anxiously requesting that Enzo be put back in the car.

"Department policy dictates you never search alone. So, because of our remote location, and the time it would take for assistance to arrive, when pulling over someone for a potential

search, a call for back-up is made. The initial conversation and questions which eventually lead to 'Are drugs present?' and 'Can I search your automobile?' determine what action ensues. If a search is warranted and back-up is present the occupants are asked to step out, and are searched and placed about 30ft (9m) in front of the vehicle. I put them where I can see them at an observable distance in case a large amount of drugs is located, as it's safer that way. A joint or two in the ashtray or their pocket usually does not warrant fighting, but distribution amounts – the hidden stashes the K9 will find – create another problem.

"After finding the narcotics, I'll go over to the bandit with the dog on the lead, put him in a guard position and tell the bandits to 'stand still:' the patrol command for the K9, who immediately focuses on the bad guys. I drop the leash and again tell them very firmly: 'Stand still, he will bite you, do not make quick movements, do not, do not, whatever you do, get aggressive with me, because he will engage you.' I let them know what he will do, and by now he's quivering and has drool down the sides of his mouth, and they are so focused on the dog at that point that they don't care what I'm doing, they just know he's going to bite and they don't want it to be them that he bites. After that getting them handcuffed is easy ... Hopefully, this type of posturing sets the stage for a quiet finish to a potentially dangerous situation. Deterrence in this type of volatile situation is of immense value.

"One of our most exciting deployments was to assist a trooper in Salina Canyon, who had gone out on an accident call, and figured that the guy was driving whilst under the influence. The driver was arrested and put in the back of the patrol car. The City of Price called for back-up when it realized the car also contained illegal narcotics. While the officer was talking with dispatch, explaining what to do with the automobile to be confiscated, a female passenger slid into the driving seat and took off in the trooper's patrol car. The bandits drove about 60 miles in our direction (where we had been working a roadblock), finally coming over the top of the canyon by Salina.

"During the time they were driving directly towards us, the patrol car radio made a call for help with their apprehension, which, of course, they heard, and knew that 15 police cars were coming from all directions right at them. They abandoned the vehicle and took off on foot. It was dark by the time we got there, and I immediately deployed Enzo, on-lead, and tracked them for about three-quarters of a mile.

"The dark desert night is a frightening thing, and they never went far enough into the desert that they couldn't see the freeway. Knowing that we had officers everywhere. and there was a 6ft (1.85m) wash to the other side of the freeway, I decided that I wasn't going to track down into it. We had a good perimeter so I announced my decision and unleashed Enzo, who jumped down into the wash with us following. As soon as we hit the wash and put our lights up, we could see them at the end of the wash, huddled together. Enzo went right to them and stood about 12ft (4m) away. There was a lot of commotion and shouting and, confused and frightened more by the gun than Enzo, the woman got up in response to the trooper and his gun. When she moved it triggered Enzo, and immediately he went in, landing on the man, breaking the wrist that was still handcuffed and pulled behind him. I kept telling the people not to move while the highway patrolman was yelling 'Get up here, get over here,' with his gun pointing at them, not knowing whether they were in possession of firearms or were even still handcuffed. Emotions ran high until Enzo made contact, whereupon the situation immediately calmed, as he took control.

"Enzo never quit being hell on wheels: he always found the drugs, regardless of their location, and I was always safe at his side."
Deputy Blake Gardner and K9 partner Enzo, Emery County Sheriff's office. K9 adjunct detector instructor and judge; Utah Police officers' Standards and Training. current K9 partner Malinoise Nieko

The first two stories are examples of the canine olfactory system at its best – tracking the bad guy and locating illegal drugs. – not necessarily unusual endeavors – but unique by their very nature. The following story, however, is a very unique example of human imagination.

All high-energy working breeds need to use their innate instincts: they need a job, a purpose to their day. Couches, shoes, gardens, neighbors, an inexhaustible list of destruction just waiting to happen would undoubtedly decline if purpose – a job – replaced boredom. The obvious efficiency with which dogs adapt to the various jobs in this collection of stories is evidence of a high level of versatility, and the desire to 'do' so inherent in their very being. Tracking the bad guy or finding drugs obviously fills that need with working canines, but our partners at home, our companions on the couch, also need and deserve jobs: maintaining their sanity and enabling them to be a good family member can actually depend on it.

The following story illustrates the depth of bond and communication that can occur while using a dog's inborn instincts, and working side-by-side, united in purpose. The depth of your relationship with your dog is directly proportional to the quality time you spend 'working' with him to develop that connection: that bond.

Steve and Louis, Henry and Riley
Not your usual 'find'
"I have thought long and hard about how to tell this story, and many otherwise silent moments have been busied with contemplation of how to do this best. The common theme or thread that stitches all my thoughts together is how one born in the shadow of greatness would eventually shine through. He would do this via a very unexpected route and will always be held dearly in his lofty position.

"Louis was my first Labrador, and he was acquired for a very specific purpose. Deer and elk lose their antlers annually; I like to find them but am limited to a visual sense when searching. Canines have both visual and an incomprehensible olfactory sense that I hoped to tap into with Louis.

Henry and small son, Riley, carry the morning newspaper the quarter mile from the box to the house (in the evening it's the mail), proudly maintaining a tradition that Henry learned from his father, Louis.

"He proved to be a quick study and, by the time he was eight months old, it would have been difficult to find more antlers than he did in our frequent forays into the surrounding mountains. Louis was potent: he was driven, muscular, ambitious and connected.

"Bill Tarrant writes of the imprinted dog that knows his master's thoughts sometimes before the master does. Louis was such a dog and the best example I can give of this occurred on a day when he was roughly one year old. I was shooting my bow, and the arrow found its way past the target and hit an old building in the background. The arrow tip snapped off and I was on hands and knees searching for it in six-inch-deep, dead, dry fall grass. Soon, it became evident that my ever-present companion had something in his mouth. Given the simple command to 'drop,' Louis deposited the one-inch metal field tip in my hand. No command to seek, search, find or otherwise assist had been given. No exposure to archery equipment or other random searches had

ever been attempted. How could any other dog ever compare?

"Henry was one of two butterscotch-colored pups amongst ten born from Louis' first breeding. My wife was sure our family would not be complete without him, and so home he came.

"From his first days with us and throughout his life Henry would prove the antithesis of his father. Louis was boisterous, hard-charging, playful, and not above a full measure of puppy mischief. Henry was calm, relaxed, content and loving. He truly did stand in his father's shadow, and – with virtually no formal training – learned all that his father knew: down, sit, stay, come, heel, get behind, were all commands given to Louis that Henry mirrored flawlessly, and this also included hand signals in the field given from several hundred yards away. His focus on his father even led him to become a better antler hunter than his dad, and Louis was excellent.

"Henry also missed out on puppy misbehaviours as his father had none of these left to emulate. At six months of age Henry and Louis were left in our home for several hours while we attended holiday festivities in town. I won the five dollar bet that not a single cookie of the forty-four dozen that were left on our tables and countertops would be touched! At an early age, I began to ask him if he was the perfect dog living the perfect life.

"Henry was such a contrast to his dad. Around the house, I would frequently hit a softball for them to retrieve, and have them take turns doing so. Louis would charge out, charge back and shake nervously until his turn came again. Henry would trot out to the ball, walk back with it, then lay down until his turn came again. In the woods, Louis was darting and dashing hither and yon while Henry strolled along at my side. Henry's only competitive streak manifested as Louis would return with an antler. He always intercepted his father and made sure he delivered the prize.

"His approach to the antler game was soft as well. As we walked along he would stop and shoot me a glance, then look up or downhill. Given the command to 'find a bone,' Henry would casually stroll off in the direction of the desired aroma and soon return with his find. Driving down the road Louis would have his nose out of the pick-up truck window feasting on the smells in the passing air, while Henry had found a comfortable napping place to replenish his exhausted energy stores.

"The ever-present images in photographs of Labs launching off either dock or shore and exploding into the water were also contrary to Henry's approach. He would ease into the water as if it were a family swim; he was most content swimming out to my arms to be held. He was also quick to tire of the pointless redundancy of the 'retrieve a stick from the river' game: a shady tree at water's edge held far greater appeal for him.

"My wife contends that Henry's soft nature was a direct result of the many hours she sat with him in her lap as a puppy, and rocked him in her chair. I counter this with the fact that all our other Labs have been far too feisty for extended rocking chair therapy, with which she agrees.

"At roughly 80lb (36kg), Henry could easily dominate or terrorize our cat, Chew Toy. He was only slightly tolerant of the cat's stalking attacks. As I passed through the kitchen one day, Chew Toy bounded out from under an antique cabinet, and pounced on Henry much like a cougar would an elk. Henry slumped onto his side under the onslaught of the multiple bites to his head and neck as if in defeat, but, within the hour, Henry was slowly backing across the room dragging what appeared to be a totally lifeless cat. The cat's entire head was in Henry's mouth, her lower teeth firmly grasping the tender flesh of Henry's lip. All Henry had to do was bite down, but he never did: it was not in him. The only aggressive behavior I ever witnessed were in defense of us, our home, and our vehicles in response to people he perceived as a threat. In these instances he was both serious and – weighing what he did – convincing.

"In spite of his laidback nature, Henry was absolutely committed to his chores: each morning began with him carrying the newspaper a quarter of a mile from the box to our house; in the evening it was the mail. In between, he carried socks or shirts to the dirty laundry or fresh ones

to the shower at the start of each day. During projects around the home he was ever-vigilant of my workgloves. If left out of reach, without prompting he would deliver them to my hand. During breaks, my wife might call him to the house and send him back with a cold beverage. One of my hands was for the drink, the other was to be rested on his head or neck, and a soft nuzzle was all I needed to be reminded. He lived to serve and was visibly disappointed if not allowed to.

"As dedicated as he was to work, he was also the consummate companion at the fishing hole. If Henry ever exhibited nervousness it was at river's edge with poles propped in holders waiting for a bite. His Newfoundland ancestors – who had retrieved cod from nets – had communicated through their genes the relationship between rod, line, bait and prized catfish fillets. As Louis had shaken in anticipation of his next softball retrieve, Henry would sit and stare and shake until one of the several rod tips twitched, at which sign he

Henry's gentle nature was innate, and extended to all of Steve's friends and the smallest member of his family.

would whimper and stand or pace. If I was able to successfully set the hook, Henry just had to jump in and swim to where the line disappeared to provide what assistance he could. We only lost a few as a result of this, and it usually came down to the added challenge of netting the fish and not the dog. It was consistently the most excited I saw him, and he eliminated the need for bells on rod tips that usually indicated a bite during these long night vigils. I have no better explanation for his enthusiasm for this sport than genetics. I'm not sure how I could convey these relationships to him, or even how he made the connection and why they were so important to him. Only one thing was certain: after a night of cat fishing, Henry was exhausted.

Holding tight to his most recent find, the locating talents of Riley – Steve's third generation canine partner, and Henry's son – are obvious.

"Frequently, in discussions about age you will hear that one 'mellows with age,' but in Henry's case that was just not possible. He had been suppressed by the boldness of his father who battled me at times for the alpha position in our pack. His calm and gentle manner was the perfect sponge to the profuse affections my wife showered him with. With the coming of the dreaded day that Louis' shadow would be forever lifted from Henry, his amazing, gentle spirit again shone through.

"After liberating my incredible first Lab, Louis, from the body those years had made infirm, he was wrapped in a blanket and placed under a pine while I created his final place of rest. While I dug in soil softened by the tears of his mother and I, Henry lay with his head on his father's shrouded body. On placing Louis in his grave, I began to cover him when Henry rose and got in the grave with his dad. He gently pulled back two paws of dirt, and when told 'no,' simply lay down on top of his dad. At that point, two people who had cried hard learned how hard they *could* cry. After allowing Henry some time and fearing dehydration, we coaxed him out and finished this arduous task.

"It had not been uncommon, through all his years, for Louis to engage me in wrestling matches that would occasionally escalate to near-war. Twice after Louis' passing, Henry approached me for his own version of a mock battle, which he never had before. Was he trying to fulfill a role, or was he yet again trying to satisfy my needs and fill a void created by his father's death?

"It had been a long-standing joke between my wife and I that Henry's relaxed approach to life was his way of 'saving himself' for us so we would have many more years to enjoy him, and it would be nearly two full years before our family once again congregated under the pine, softening the soil with our tears on Henry's behalf.

"As our wonderful vet traveled to our rural home to administer his freedom, you know I made sure that the last words Henry heard were:

'You are the perfect dog who lived the perfect life.'"

Steve

Almost without exception, working breeds need a job: wonderful, tender moments on the couch do not facilitate the communication or trust necessary to develop the depth of bond needed to become partners. Only long, goal-specific hours of fieldwork, training, practice and simulated working scenarios will elicit the trust and communication necessary to create an accomplished partnership.

The team that was Steve and Louis and Henry was not searching for a lost child, nor tracking a felon or looking for drugs, but were partners, nonetheless. The time and energy spent together in the field working toward a common goal cemented the relationship, and created that unique bond. Utilizing the high energies of this hunting breed in an unconventional pursuit created this team, this partnership, and kept safe the couches and shoes at Steve's home.

Forensic remains specialists
Sniffing out the truth behind the crime

Forensic remains specialists locate trace evidence and the residual scent of humans at natural or man-made disasters. The expertise of the dogs in this specialty have earned the respect of law enforcement, as they locate evidence that finds its way into courtrooms around the world.

Considered forensic tools, the dogs have olfactory prowess that permits tenacious, methodical sniffing, and have been responsible for making remarkable finds at crime scenes: blood-drops, buried remains, remains underwater or embedded in cement, remains scattered by scavengers or blown apart by man – anywhere the bad guys try to hide bodies, forensic remains specialists are trained to search and recover. They have the ability to recognize a corpse or parts of a corpse across a wide range of environmental conditions.

Maintaining the integrity of the crime scene is a priority, so the majority of these forensic 'tools' are taught to be passive in their finish: simply sitting at the location of their find. However, their nature is anything but passive, and their hunting instincts – coupled with a drive

seemingly without limit – leaves absolutely no doubt that they will continue until they find what they are looking for. Methodical, intensely driven by a need to get the job done, regardless of the exhaustion extensive sniffing can cause, their objective consumes every movement and thought.

Laura and Nike

"Another Halloween. This day wouldn't be like any other Halloween, though, this day would be terrifying!

"My pager went off before 6am. Nike, my eight-year-old German Shepherd, raced to my bedside and then ran downstairs to wait for me to open the door to the garage and the truck. I picked up the phone to answer the page ... cadaver dogs were needed in Duchesne County, Utah, to search for people, people who had been blown-up! Did I mention it was Halloween?

"I grabbed my gear and my dog and jumped into the truck. The drive to Duchesne, over several mountain passes, was breathtaking. Despite the beauty, my mind was contemplating the up-coming search, and this made the two-hour drive painfully slow. We arrived at the Lake Canyon Ranch exit at 8:30am. Nike was pacing in her small space, and whining to let me know she was ready to work. I joined my fellow team-mates and walked over to brief with the Sheriff. Details were given: it was thought that a man and a woman had been strapped with explosives and blown to pieces. The pieces were then bulldozed

Nike's work was important, but for Laura her greatest value was the companionship she provided.

here and there in an attempt to cover up the crime scene. Our job? To find the pieces.

"After our lengthy briefing (how's that for an oxymoron?), we followed the Sheriff up a long, dry, dirt road to the crime scene and eventual search site. I parked my vehicle, opened the door, and stepped outside for a quick stretch before grabbing my gear and my dog. My eyes caught something on the hillside ... my jaw dropped. I quickly grabbed my lead, hooked-up Nike and headed for the command post. At the command post we were assigned an area to be searched and given specific details of what to do if we found anything. I pulled the lead officer aside and asked him about what was on the hillside. I was right about what I thought I'd seen: a leg, severed at the ball and socket, the explosives still strapped to the thigh!

"The search began. Nothing easily identifiable was found at first, just bits and pieces of flesh. Whoever the criminal was, he or she had tried very hard (though not very thoroughly, as witnessed by the leg on the hill) to cover up the crime scene by bulldozing the entire mountainside to bury any remains. A few hours into the search, half a torso and a head were found: parts of a man. It was a horrifying sight. His eyes were wide open and his hair stood on end as if he had been electrocuted. His arms, legs and hips had been blown off, and all of his organs were exposed. He was staring face-up at us and, fortunately, he was very dead.

"The search continued for many days. Nike worked hard, pulling against her harness to unearth more and more pieces ... a kneecap here, a fingertip there. The search crew was frantic because the female victim had not been identified. As yet there had been no recovered parts that would distinguish a male from a female victim. We searched on, and I would frequently play with Nike to break up the work and re-energize her. I would even make her sniff coffee beans to help clear out her cadaver-saturated nose. Would it help? I didn't know.

"The search teams were worn from exhaustion and the gruesome nature of the work. Evidence of the female victim was desperately needed, but hadn't been found. I refreshed Nike again and headed back out to the crime scene, this time deciding to head up the canyon a little and out of the assigned search area. Something drew us up and out, and Nike was hot, hot on a scent, pulling fiercely on her harness, with me following as quickly as possible.

"Suddenly, she stopped, motionless, and I almost fell over her. Her nose pointed to a small bush, less than a foot away. There lay a piece of human remains the size of a large hand. I knew it was something important; Nike knew it was something interesting, too. I strained to control her while I radioed for the medical investigator, Felix, who rushed up the hill. He gloved-up and picked up the remains, 'molding' it in his hands for a minute. He turned it upside down and sideways, then looked into my eyes: 'A UTERUS!' he exclaimed.

"For the dog teams on the case, the search work ended that day, and it was months before jurors sentenced the suspect to two life terms in prison without parole for the two murders of a man and a woman.

"Nike was a very headstrong, determined, full-blooded female German Shepherd. I chose six-week-old Nike from a litter of pups because she was the one who would run after and seek me out when I would run and hide from her. Nike – certified in wilderness, water, and avalanche search and rescue – matured into a 75lb (34kg) dark beauty, who searched in five states, and was called on approximately 100 searches in her lifetime.

"After much time working in the mountains, Nike seemed to develop an interest in cadaver work. On one search she alerted on an area in a river where a boy's body had been removed two years prior; on another, and after being scented from a single drop of blood, Nike led police to several areas where the bad guy had broken into buildings and vehicles.

"The result of her love for methodical detail work was a specialized cadaver-training program where she spent the last two years of her life. She truly loved her work and demonstrated this during one of her tests by carrying the 'correct answer to the test' (a tube with cadaver scent, which was not supposed to be disturbed) over to the State Medical Investigator and dropping it at his feet. Nice work, Nike!

"Nike's work was important, but to me her greatest value was in the companionship she provided my family. Tough and resilient in the search field, Nike was gentle, loving and fun at home; she loved her family. She helped me raise my two children, Alley and Riley, since I was raising them on my own, always keeping a watchful eye on them. She always had a 'wag' waiting for us when we came home, and she was a constant companion to me.

"Nike died at the age of ten from leukemia, with her head in a large container full of dried liver treats (her favorite). She went with the same enthusiasm with which she had lived her whole life, and we all still miss her presence."

Laura

Nan and Katie

An obsessive workaholic who drove me nuts

The next story is about my partner, Katie, who is the reason I began collecting stories of our working partners.

Katie was my friend and mentor always, and my partner in the search field. She had a strong, bold attitude: belligerent, determined and methodical. She was an obsessive workaholic, and frequently drove me crazy with this, although her problem-solving abilities never ceased to amaze me. Walking behind her, watching her check her surroundings for scent, was fascinating. If she became bored on a hike Katie would drop her stick (she always carried a stick), and later would find it again, delighted when she rediscovered it. She always found the right stick, and appeared to consider every job the most important thing she could be doing at that moment.

Katie loved using her nose, and could frequently be spotted sitting on a high spot overlooking her environment, nose held high, methodically savoring each scent as it came her way. Acknowledgement and recognition seemed to twinkle in her eyes as she sniffed one scent after another. As she aged, I observed this activity in our backyard in Montana, as Katie seemed to digest and savor the odors in her favorite domain. She appeared to experience pure pleasure as familiar scents allowed memories in her data bank to invade her senses and retell their story. Watching those eyes, her careful, soft sniffing and her nose twitch during those moments, I was envious, imagining myself sharing those same stories, but unable to access her memories.

I always wondered how old those stories were. How aged, how deep-rooted were the odors that carry those emotions and their associated memories? I know it's my imagination and wonderment of the canine species that paints this image in my mind, as there really is no way to know her thoughts, but I saw those eyes filled with recognition, wisdom and sheer pleasure as scents and their accompanying emotions flooded her very essence, retelling stories of her yesterdays.

Katie spent five years actively searching for the lost on mountains and in the desert. A knee injury slowed her down and made her perfect for the methodical requirements of forensic crime scene recovery, while she refocused and refined a drive that enabled long hours of methodical work. She was tenacity at its best with attitude to spare.

It's unusual for bodies to be buried over two feet (0.6m) deep: fear of detection, along with lack

Nike searched in five states and was called on around a hundred searches in her lifetime.

of equipment, usually lead to the hasty disposal of a body in a shallow grave. However, in this case, an available backhoe (earth mover), knowledge of several open ground holes, and access to a remote location gave this really bad guy the perfect conditions to dispose of a child he had murdered. Fortunately, determined detective work and a uniquely aware supervisor led authorities to the same location.

The day Katie and I arrived, we were to work with a backhoe operator in that location. Katie and five other forensic K9s had previously selected one spot as a human burial, and her first search produced another finish at the exact same spot.

The backhoe operator began working. He was incredibly skilled as he removed 1-2 feet (0.3-0.6m) of earth in an area 20 to 25 feet (6-7m) square. After the first couple of feet of earth were removed, Katie was asked to work the area again, and again she went to the same location and sat.

During the morning, after the removal of more earth, Katie would work the area again. At first we were using a ladder to climb down, but a ramp was created that enabled us to descend more easily. As the hole became bigger and wider, we kept checking the entire excavated area, and I directed Katie to check the rest of the hole, but she would always return to that one spot. And sit. She became increasingly adamant, almost belligerent, finishing with loud body thumps and obvious, verbal angst as she sat.

We were down about five to six feet (1.5-2m) by this time, and the tension and frustration were palpable. Eventually, Sergeant Bennett asked if Katie knew what she was doing. Everyone was beginning to question her. 'Yes,' I replied, looking at around fifty men working the site, and a backhoe that was now almost at maximum depth. Would I mind having Katie work an animal burial, just to double-check, make everyone feel better? he asked.

We were taken to a site a few blocks away where I asked Katie to search. By this time it was around two in the afternoon; hot and dry, and everyone was tired – except Katie. She worked the area thoroughly, apparently wondering why we had left the other area where she knew the child

was buried. But she did her job, covering the area and coming back to my side. Katie turned and looked out at the area, then simply stood quietly, looking up at me, wondering, I think, what we were doing there. She did nothing in that area: exactly the right thing.

So back to the larger pit, and Katie worked the area again, this time with a level of intensity I had never previously observed, going back to the same spot in an area 7 feet deep (2m) and 25 (8m) x 20ft (6m) wide. At a depth of nine feet (3m), once again there was extremely intense sniffing, sniffing, meticulous and fixated, checking the same area over and over, sniffing loudly. Katie finally licked the soil and sat.

Katie always licked the faces of the victims she located, so immediately I knew we were within inches of the body. The medical examiner now proceeded gently, brushing and digging with small hand tools for about an hour. Tension continued to build, but nothing. Katie kept indicating at the same place; still nothing. One more backhoe shovel and as the soil dropped to the earth, a tiny white bone fell.

Quickly from the falling earth the medical examiner retrieved the jawbone of a small child (retrieved from 9.5 feet (2.9m). Within 24 hours, a positive ID was made and a family was able to find some closure, and begin the grieving process, their search over.

As we continued to excavate, Katie stood on the ramp and pointed like a bird dog to the area across from the ramp where the small bone had been found. This was new and extremely unusual behavior for a German Shepherd. With what seemed to be irritation Katie also indicated at the top of the hill, directly above the find, giving us the idea that we should dig wider, but nothing. At ten feet (3m), she looked up not down as she had previously indicated, trying to tell us, I believe, that further digging was pointless, but it took us another day and a further ten feet to realize that the rest of the body was not at this location.

Katie had continued to work the same location for more than eight hours, adamantly confirming her initial find, reworking the area over and over. After all her sits, each one indicating

Katie helped me look outward beyond the narrow framework of my life. At that time my experiences centered on my family and a business I had owned for twenty years. A good life, but with the inevitable moving out of our children, my life needed more. Sheltered from many of life's realities, Katie helped me take gigantic steps in becoming more balanced within myself. She introduced me to a completely new and purposeful endeavor, while enabling me to work at the side of a species I had been connected to for years.

When Katie was given a tedious assignment, she became obsessively focused: asked to search a mountain without the aid of a scent article, she methodically showed me everyone on the mountain. Shown footprints of the lost, she air-scented over the ridge; asked to wait in the car during training or at the beginning of a search, she either escaped or howled with irritating enthusiasm. Her heart opened my soul to

Left: Pulling me across this large open valley, Katie was determined to unite me with my lost family member – also her pack: search and rescue work she took very seriously.

Katie was tenacity at its best – with attitude to spare!

that she had done her job, and finally licking the soil, Katie's attitude alerted me to the fact that we were there. On that day, in that place, for that family's child, Katie's attitude kept us digging.

The tears flowed freely that day: Katie had done her job. I believe she was born for that day. She was filled with attitude, determination, and a bold work ethic that would not allow her or me to quit. She methodically led a group of 50 people, hour after frustrating hour; shovel after shovel, to that last shovel, and the one small bone that brought closure to this tragedy.

Katie was a hero that day, but in my life she produced miracles daily. Coming into my life at just the right time, she worked at my side for 11 years. I will always wish I had held her in my arms longer on the day she left this earth, but there was no question that it was her time, and as the veterinarian drove away with her body, my empty arms ached for their loss. Katie's ashes were scattered over the spot she had done her most memorable work while the mother of the child Katie found held me as I cried. And while the tears have dried, the lump in my throat and ache in my heart will never completely go away.

"**Dogs mirror us back to ourselves in unmistakable ways that, if we are open, foster true understanding and change. Dogs are guileless and filled with spontaneity: unlike people, they don't deceive.**

"**When we take seriously the words they speak to us about ourselves, we stand face-to-face with the truth of the matter. We must learn to reflect on these words – they are inscribed on their bodies, in their expressions, in the way they approach and interact with us." – The Monks of New Skete,** *I & Dog*

possibilities and never let me give up. Like all the other canine partners in this book, Katie will never be forgotten.

Nan

There is absolutely no question that the experience of our partners fortifies their intelligence and influences the direction of their focus. If they are encouraged to function, based on their instincts, not on our perceptions, their bold, assertive personality gains strength: insight sharpens, and self-confidence encourages a new level of communication as they perceive with excited anticipation the job ahead.

After experiencing various situations in real life, they can differentiate between training and reality, sensing the environment with its associated dangers and emotions while reading all the signs surrounding a new assignment, knowing when boldness and courage or gentle compassion is needed; whether forceful guidance or intelligent disobedience is called for, they know which to use, when and how. Based in part on their training, they step forward, meeting their task with energy and enthusiasm. And when that extra is called for, it is always provided by their senses, intelligence and heart.

Intelligent disobedience is one of the many phrases used to describe a reaction based on changes in the environment that requires our partners to not follow our directives. Instinct-driven behavior that pulls people from the path of cars or finds a lost child down – not up – the hill is behavior that requires the human part of

the team to trust implicitly in canine instinct. Working in such a wide variety of places we frequently place our partners in situations that require actions not previously trained for, but the responses need to be based on trained facts and procedures. Canine senses can identify subtle differences in their environment and change course accordingly: remember, no two searches are the same, so all successful search teams need to learn to adapt. While training provides a plan of action based on the type of work that is being done, unique environmental situations require complete trust as canine senses take control, and potentially shift the direction of the entire search.

Intelligent disobedience increases as trust and communication develop between team members, with the human part of the team learning to understand that his partner's responses and actions are based on his inborn senses which dictate he follow his nose; in many cases in direct opposition to his human partner's directives.

Encouraging development of intelligent disobedience enables these canines to proceed with the confidence that their partners will follow, even if they want to go in a different direction. Remember, they absolutely know where the scent is, and we absolutely do not!

Developing a deeper relationship with your companion simply requires time and the creativity that enables your canine partner to use his natural abilities. That's where it starts: finding a peanut butter-filled toy, antlers, any object of interest that both of you can get excited about. It's the together time, working to reach a common goal that develops communication and a resultant trust that will make you partners.

This first chapter has introduced five incredible canine partners, who solved our problems by using their survival instinct, aided by olfactory senses beyond our comprehension. The upcoming stories in the law enforcement chapter highlight the protective nature of our partners as another of their survival instincts steps forward to safeguard their pack.

In a rock pile, in a car tire – anything, anywhere – these two specialists know exactly where the drugs and explosives are. Here, it's only training as these teams reaffirm their trust, communication and bond with each other. On a real search, the drugs will be removed from the streets and the explosives won't detonate and kill ...

K9 law enforcement partners

Loving a living 'tool'

This chapter is dedicated to K9 law enforcement partners, working with their human partner to pay the bills – and keep him safe: finding illegal contraband and tracking/apprehending the bad guy.

Here, you'll find stories of the K9 still holding tight as a felon smashes his body against glass doors, and the bags and bags of elicit narcotics he locates and gets removed from our streets. The ever-present dilemma of putting a canine partner in danger is constant in every job he undertakes: intended to protect and serve our species, this is a 'tool' we have learned to love, making dangerous deployment agonizing.

The majority of police department K9s are generally trained for narcotics/explosives detection in addition to patrol/apprehension. Because these teams have two distinct and separate functions the dogs are referred to as 'dual-purpose K9s,' and train extensively in both specialties. A dual-purpose K9 obviously needs to embody those traits necessary to master and maintain two very different skill sets: maintaining quality of performance requires constant training and dedication, with a level of consistency that not many are capable of. All canine/human working relationships require there to be a strong bond of trust and loyalty, but in the field of law enforcement – where the potential for a life and death encounter occurs daily – this bond is especially vital.

Occasionally, the use of deadly force becomes necessary to protect the public or insure safety at an incident. The decision to deploy a law enforcement K9 is based on emergent danger: the immediate need to de-escalate a volatile situation and hopefully preclude the use of deadly force. Usually, the mere presence of a K9 brings immediate compliance, although unpredictable dangers give rise to a high degree of anxiety as the K9 partner takes the lead, making himself vulnerable, a situation both hazardous and, fortunately, rare. The reality of these risks, when combined with high-energy training, produces a strong, unquestionably unique bond, and the officer, constantly aware that his dog may lose

his life, develops reliance and respect for his K9 partner's abilities: the instinctual hunt and prey drives that facilitate determination, strength and agility. In an attempt to maintain a level of detachment – a professional 'arms length' – regarding the dog as a 'tool' allows the clear thinking that is absolutely essential in dangerous deployment.

The same hunt and prey drives that are necessary for law enforcement K9s to do their job can be mistaken for aggression. In nature, a dog's life depends on his ability to hunt, catch and dispatch prey, and it is these instincts that he uses when working – sensing through smell, hearing and sight: tracking, trailing, air scenting – to lead him to the 'prey.' Today's K9 partners eagerly track criminals, control unruly crowds, secure and detain dangerous felons, and 'hunt' all manner of illegal and dangerous contraband. Understanding their motivation – which must be both immediately available and totally controllable – is imperative, and achieved through communication in training. The refocused hunt/prey drive should be resilient, adaptable, fearless and tireless, a powerful combination which makes an apprehension K9 a force to reckon with, and quite possibly the most valuable partner/tool the officer will ever work beside.

The high drama present in deployment permeates every working moment of the partnership, and the need to utilize the tool the officer's department has paid for can be in direct conflict with development of the bond that will save his life. The intense K9 heart and courage observed in real, high drama moments constantly touches the emotions of their human partners, whose frequent inability to talk about their deceased partner indicates a deep internal struggle when trying to resolve the tool vs love dilemma.

Any canine partnership necessitates understanding a dog's drive characteristics and instinctual reaction to environmental stimuli, and good training can provide a basic understanding of potential reactions to environmental surprises, whilst also enabling the human partner to anticipate and encourage/discourage particular

requires solid control backed with respect and obedience. However, experienced handlers know that if they over-dominate, if they are the leader of their pack at all costs, it can eventually cost them in the drive and efficiency of their partners. If their bond is not based on trust and communication first, they can lose that extra loyalty, that do-or-die, that K9 'heart.'

Working canines must be thoroughly obedience-trained, and this is usually done at a separate time, and ideally away from their actual work environment. Saying 'NO!' in the middle of a deployment can seriously affect the outcome, and to over-give a command – 'NO, NO, NO' – can cause the dog to hesitate, affecting his efficiency. Implicit, detailed communication is required to achieve obedience – What; How; When – and this molding, like all other training, is done positively and repeatedly. The canine team must know and trust that a specific word will elicit the action delivered: simple, easy, positive, reward-filled

Left: Demonstrations and displays are integral to the commitment felt and shown by law enforcement.

The right officer and a very strong, vocal K9 partner helps our children understand the benefits of not getting involved with drugs, while seeing how a unique, reward-based system operates between these seasoned partners.

reactions. Encouraging development of hunt/prey instincts is essential in apprehension work, but will create a partner that requires a unique level of control and respect. The ability to direct these drives with a single verbal command takes intense training, communication and solid obedience.

Apprehension work necessitates bringing prey/fight drive (survival instinct) to the fore, and when this force is focused on man, it requires cautious, precise thought. Introducing the command 'NO' when the K9 is in full pursuit of his prey, or in the process of dispatching it, communication between partners, but not in the middle of an actual deployment. And even then, obedience must still encourage and allow natural drives to function unrestricted, assuring the best use of the K9's inherent abilities. When K9 heart combines with strong, refocused survival instincts supported by trust, communication, respect and obedience, the result is a dynamic K9 partner.

Kevin and Django
The key to Django's drive
"Working with K9s is a unique privilege, and being part of it not only takes additional time and commitment, it involves living it and breathing it. The extra responsibility that the family of the K9 handler has to cope with is intense: a dog specifically trained to bite is in their backyard or on their bed, and, as most officers are young with children, and have neighborhood children running in and out of the house, this is a serious consideration. But those who really love what they're doing, and appreciate the unique, awesome partner that has come into their lives, wouldn't have it any other way.

There are times when a hard-hitting, hard-biting partner is more valuable than any arsenal of weapons ...

"Dictating the handler's interaction with his partner, and maintaining high quality, positive training, is achieved via a reward system, but finding the right reward for an individual dog can occasionally require patience and creativity. Django required a unique reward, but fortunately the training program we received established and sculpted his training accordingly.

"Django was a Belgian Malinois, a breed known for its hard-hitting approach and agility, and Django was no exception. Built a little stockier than most Malinois, when Django hit, you felt like a big tank had run you down. Weighing only 68lb (31kg), Django became explosive when apprehending the bad guys. Having been raised playing with squeaky toys, apparently, he identified the high-pitched human squeal produced by the agitator (the person in a bite suit) as the same noise from his old squeaky toy.

"That squeal or squeak ultimately became Django's reward, and knowing how and when to use that squeak most effectively was a challenge at times. Django excelled in apprehension work, and after finding a way to incorporate that squeak into his drug work, I was able to make the whole experience a game, and when training is a game, the success rate goes up accordingly. So, when the agitator made a squeaky noise Django became a highly-motivated biting machine. The initiating bite with the subsequent squeal became his thrill and reward. He just kept holding on, especially if the person kept squealing. We had found the key to Django's drive.

"Django learned quickly to love bite work, but when it came to training for narcotics detection, he was initially ambivalent: there was no squeak, no squeal, no excitement. Finally, after locating the drugs, I let him pick up his squeaky toy, hitting and roughhousing with me, and this became his reward. Again, the right reward elicited the desired drive, and created my successful narcotic partner.

"Django didn't want to play with just any toy, however: he didn't care about retrieving toys, and chasing a ball was just not enough. But once I learned what *he* needed, I was able to help him understand what *I* needed and he became awesome, blossoming and achieving some great things.

"It helped to be open-minded and try different things, to discover just what turned on Django; the handler in a K9's initial training for detection work (finding drugs) must be open to options. In this phase of training only positive nurturing/developing of the K9's desires will bring out and intensify the drives which, coupled with the prerequisite scent skills, produces a great scent-source partner. It is absolutely necessary to find that exact positive reward your partner needs to elicit the reaction you are looking for. If the prescribed method for training causes frustration, a potentially good detector dog can be eliminated from the program, so several methods must be employed to determine which squeaky toy is the right one. Detection work is frustrating and exhausting, and requires methodical, focused attention. It must start out as a game and build proportionately to the training and experience of the dog concerned.

"My partner had several unique traits, other than his obsession for the squeaky toy. When there was a bite suit around and training was going on, Django's performance – his chase and take down – was the prettiest, by-the-book detain possible. He did everything he was supposed to do: perfect bite and hold or perfect detain (I've got a good detain story next), but when you took off the bite suit, when he sensed it was a real deployment and not training, he was the dirtiest damn street dog you ever saw. He didn't care how or where he got the bad guy, just that he did and he did not let go! Administrators and testing judges want to see that you train for 100 per cent, and at testing time need to see the control, the perfect detain. But on the street where the circumstances are way beyond your control, you just need the job done – and Django did the job.

"When deploying your K9 partner in pursuit of a criminal, force is only employed when the situation warrants it, so having a partner that will do whatever the situation requires is essential. The ability to distinguish a training scenario from the real thing, to understand and know the difference, is instinct brought to the level of instinctual intelligence: invaluable in the field and not something that can be trained. Like heart, it's just there.

"Okay, I mentioned a detain story. First, let me explain exactly what comprises a 'detain' command or an 'off' command. The variables are many, but initiating an apprehension command is done only when there's a need for force, and the K9 is deployed to apprehend, to bite. Other situations are initiated with the same command but without the necessity for the bite. So the same initiating process is used in a situation that looks as though the presence of a K9 could bring about a peaceful outcome, or when verbal negotiations are attempting to calm a bad situation and a little extra incentive is needed. Obviously, the first command to apprehend, when allowed to continue, does result in a bite, but in mid-run or mid-bite, if compliance is imminent and you give the 'off' command to prevent physical contact, your partner's response must be immediate: completely lie down, release the bite if initiated, and simply hold his position.

"In the second situation, however, you are not ready to have your partner use force: he is to just run toward the suspect but not engage while you are discussing the need for compliant behavior with the suspect. In this situation Django will come out and just lay down where I indicate and watch; contact is not initiated but his presence and appearance is used to calm the situation. To him apprehension is imminent, however, and he is in super-drive.

"I've described these scenarios because, initially, the same training is used for both; the final outcome being the only variable. With all that drive and all that energy going at high velocity, the proper response to this command can be difficult to teach, and comes only with dedicated training and a K9 partner who will respond to his handler with total compliance, which only comes with the development of a deep bond and devotion to each other as a working K9 team.

"If the situation is brought under control and Django's presence is not needed, being able to put him back in the truck, bringing him down and calming his drive without abusing it is essential.

"The following situation vividly demonstrates why teamwork under deployment conditions is so important.

"While still new, I deployed Django to apprehend a suspect. I sent Django across a busy downtown street and, at that same moment, a car pulled between the suspect and Django, immediately changing his visual target from the suspect to teenagers in the car, who began yelling and harassing Django. Ironically, earlier that same day, we had trained vehicle extractions, and Django cleared the median on that street, flying through the car window, jumping about 21 feet (7m). Django cleared the sides of the car window, and made a perfect shoulder bite, which just happened to be the shoulder of a young man who was innocent. Needless to say, within about 3 weeks I had the most solid call-off possible, to the extent it looked as though Django had literally stopped in his tracks the minute the 'off' command was given. It can be very important to have a sound partner who, when sent out, goes down and holds on one voice command if it looks as though the suspect will comply. If the dog needs to go further, he's still in position, and can either simply detain in a down position or continue and actually apprehend.

"Django was afraid of water. When we first tested him we simply threw the ball in the water expecting him to retrieve. Well, the ball wasn't his favorite anyway, remember, so adding the water issue (we were not aware of this then) meant he just didn't go after the ball. The ball was thrown in belly-high water and he just froze. He stood there, motionless. Apparently, he was so afraid that he really had a hard time even moving.

"We finally brought the ball out and Django actually bit the handler who had retrieved the ball: his frustration level was disproportionate and the poor handler with the ball was the recipient of his frustration. In subsequent searches and encounters with water we were to learn Django was really intensely afraid of water. In one particular instance when he was deployed, the sprinklers came on and Django froze. He really didn't like water, but he did like bite work and, after a moment's thought, his training and chase instincts came on and he continued out and around the sprinklers, ultimately apprehending his bad guy. With positive training and the right reward Django did learn to overcome that fear, or at least he worked around it.

"There are times when a hard-hitting, hard-biting partner is more valuable than any arsenal of weapons. The following instance was one of those times, and it's hard to believe in retrospect just how tough his jaws were and how determined he was to hold on.

"My office received a call requesting a talk with a suspicious person – an individual claiming he was on Utah's 'most wanted' list – who turned out to be a wanted felon. However, by the time I got there, he didn't want to be there, either. Being on duty, I was in my police uniform and police truck, and identified myself as a police officer, asking him to get off his bike. He complied. I then asked him for some sort of ID to prove who he was, and again he complied, producing a driver's license that was obviously fake.

"I made small talk with him until I could get a back-up officer to come. I was standing in front of him and informed him that it was time to take him into custody, a notion that he didn't like as he pushed me backward, turned, and ran toward Officer Ashton, the back-up officer (he didn't initially realize that there were now two of us). Turning around, he ran back toward me and then veered to the side. At that point he had assaulted two police officers, so, pushing the buttons on my belt system, I released Django from the back of my truck. The suspect ran toward a local tire dealership where Django caught up with him and they both went down, hitting one of those tall stacks of tires and rolling, with Django still holding on, attached to his upper thigh.

"I thought the fight was over, but as I approached the suspect, he actually stood up with Django still attached to his leg. In seconds he had positioned himself, with Django gripping tight, just inside some double glass doors, and was trying to dislodge Django by banging the doors against him. Django simply became more

agitated, and held on even tighter, despite the suspect banging the entry doors back and forth into his body. Pushing through the doors, Officer Ashton and I took the guy to the ground.

"This guy now has two officers on top of him, Django still attached to his thigh, and he's *still* fighting with us: he was actually doing pushups with two large officers on top of him and Django gripping on. I finally OC4[4] sprayed him, hitting his forehead. The spray ricocheted off and went directly into my eyes. I knew that the spray was going to take effect quickly, and, as my eyes began to close, I saw the suspect roll over and grab Officer Ashton's gun. Lying pinned on his back Officer Ashton was helpless, but, fortunately, the suspect was struggling with the holster, trying to get the gun. The spray was causing me to lose sight quickly and I went for my gun knowing I didn't have much time. I was bringing the gun up and forward to place it on the suspect's forehead and shoot: I knew he was getting a gun; I was

Django plunged into the water, instantly, without any hesitation, totally ignoring his fear of water.

going to be blind in seconds, and this time the pain from Django's teeth and jaws didn't seem to be getting the job done. I didn't feel I had any other option.

"Fortunately, just then everything came together and he quit pulling on the gun, rolled over and started screaming, 'I quit, I quit!' He was starting to go blind from the spray, too. The situation de-escalated as quickly as it had started, thankfully.

"Off-duty in shorts and tennis shoes, I responded to a stolen vehicle incident, grabbing my leash and gun belt and, of course, Django, showing up about 30 or so minutes late. We did a lot of training with our department police officers, who were told that if in foot pursuit of somebody they thought they could catch, they should, by all means, do so, but if apprehension was not possible to 'stop and go wide, marking mentally the last place the suspect's footsteps were seen. Let a K9 team track from there.' So I turned up 30 to 45 minutes after the incident to be shown a pristine track just waiting for Django.

"Django tracked toward the river. He was totally afraid of water, remember, and did not like to go in it for any reason. We had done a lot of training around and through rivers to try and overcome his fear, but he got to the edge of the river where the suspect would have gone in and just kept walking along the bank, back and forth, returning again and again to the spot at which the suspect had entered the river, not going in but making sure I knew where this bad guy had gone in. I turned and looked at my back-up officer, Officer Terry, and told him it was going to be him and me that got wet.

"Our first step took us chest-deep; in went our gun belts, radios, everything. Django was still walking on top of the reeds; I obviously hadn't realized how deep the water was. Fortunately, our flashlights kept working and we started along the river's edge. Django kept just a step or two ahead of us (on shore, of course). Suddenly, the suspect, who was quietly moving away while hugging the foliage, was lit up by our flashlights.

"Django had been given the command to 'detain,' which means watch and hold but not

make physical contact. The back of the suspect was partially visible, just the upper portion of his shoulders and his head with his face turned away. Given the verbal order to turn around, the suspect started to comply by taking one step toward us, lowering his hands to water level, an action that was immediately threatening as we couldn't see where he was going with his hands. Django saw the movement, too, as I gave him an override command and straight away he took hold of the suspect's upper chest – after he had plunged into the water, instantly, without any hesitation. The suspect's hands came up out of the water and we were able to take him into custody.

"Why and how at the crucial moment did Django overcome his fear of water? Did he sense the suspect's intentions, or did he respond to the urgency in my command? Time and time again he had been governed by his fear of water by detouring around it; this time he totally ignored those fears and went directly into the water for me, for his partner.

"A car-jacking incident at a busy downtown convenience store started violently as the bad guy – just a kid – approached a victim, held a knife to his throat, kicked him out of his car and took off. In pursuit, we found ourselves at a new transit track line, just being built so not in operation, and obviously empty of passengers, trains or any activity. Getting to the track line the felon was able to continue southbound on the tracks, although officers in two cars were unable to pursue. Having a pick-up, I was able to follow on the tracks.

"The car went about fifty yards and then wiped out. The suspect got out on the passenger side and ran off into the darkness, and all I could see of him was fluorescent Nike swooshes as he kept running into the night. I hit my electronic release for Django, who immediately responded and, in seconds, those Nike swooshes were airborne. Django hit the guy shoulder-high and stopped him about 100 yards down the track. I will never forget the sight of those swooshes as they went airborne.

"My first bite (I guess I should say Django's first bite) was a real bad guy who had just shot one of our police officers over a forgery. We were sent to a number of different places in the valley while we were still going through training. Django and I had just that day trained on release and stand still, and we now had a suspect cornered behind a restaurant in a narrow pathway between the garage and fence. The area was too narrow for me to fit through, and it was believed the suspect had wedged himself between the wooden fence and the garage. He had already shot a police officer, and nobody wanted to look around the corner to see if he was there. Handed a body shield by SWAT, I tried unsuccessfully to get a visual on the suspect, so sent Django.

"Django and I had only been together about 3 months, two months of which were spent in training. Now, suddenly, I heard this unusual whine, something I'd not heard before. I heard it again, a high-pitched whine, like he was being hurt. I was calling 'here, here, come here, now!' but Django wasn't coming. A more experienced officer on the other side of the fence was listening to my angst. 'Hey, dumb ass, try calling with the correct command!' he suggested. 'Fuss.' 'Stand still!' Suddenly, Django was next to me, which was exactly what we had trained for earlier that day (I guess class is for both of us, not just Django).

"Django had been on his first bite and the bad guy was back there, so I sent Django again, and this time the guy started yelling as Django attached to his hand. Another police officer had broken down the fence and was trying to pull the suspect through by the other hand. Django was on one hand and an officer on the other, while yet another officer kept yelling 'show me your hands, show me your hands,' as we were all obviously very anxious about that gun, the gun he had used in the earlier shooting.

"Duh! He didn't have a spare hand to show! I released Django, and the suspect was able to show one hand; we knew the officer had the other hand so it was all over. The suspect was apprehended and is still in prison for shooting a police officer. Django wasn't hurt and he had his first street bite. What was the unusual whine? I will never know, but I'll never forget my panic at the thought that my partner was hurt. Our partners

are at our side to enable us to return home to our family, but since Django was my family too, making the decision to send him into a dangerous situation never did become any easier.

"Though apprehension work was Django's first love he became a really good narcotics dog. Finding the correct reward made training exciting, and that same excitement ultimately transferred to narcotic work. On a specific SWAT call-out Django and I were to work rear containment while the initial search warrant was served and the DEA officers searched the house: no drugs found. Prior information indicated that a large amount of marijuana was present. The warrant was for the house but not any of the cars on the street. Understand, you don't need a search warrant to walk a trained narcotics dog past a car on a public street, as there is no expectation of privacy or violation of individual civil rights in searching the air space around a car.

"The DEA officer asked if I could walk Django around the cars, which I did, and about three cars down from the house Django gave a strong indication: he spontaneously turned (I had not told him to search) and hit the driver's side door handle, as if to say: 'Hey, are you sure we should be passing this car? There's something here I usually get rewarded for telling you about.' The driver didn't want to give us the keys to the car, so the attending officer called the attorney and got that car added to the search warrant.

"Inside the 4-Runner Django jumped over three seats to the rear of the vehicle, locating drugs in a safe under some blankets. Opening up the safe, which was unlocked, we found just under 4lb (2kg) of marijuana.

"Following a request by an agent, we were prepared to search for narcotics in a vehicle DEA wanted followed. Prior and current activity indicated the driver was a courier; probably carrying a large amount of cocaine or cash, or both. Not knowing which it might be a narcotics dog was requested. Following the vehicle for several miles, with him obviously knowing there was a police officer behind him, the driver was being very careful, and we needed a traffic violation to pull him over. Finally, he did forget to signal and I pulled him over, asking for his driver's license and registration. I explained to him that I was now going to give him a ticket for failing to signal and issued the ticket. I then asked 'Do you have any narcotics or explosives in your car?' to which he answered 'No.' I asked 'Do you mind if I search?' and his response was '"You're more than welcome to search,' and he put his car back into park (he had been in drive after I issued the ticket, ready to leave: now that he had given permission to search he shut off the engine and got out). At this point I asked 'Do you mind if my dog searches,' and again he replied to go ahead.

"Deploying Django, he immediately indicated on the passenger's side and went inside in the front of the car and indicated strongly on a blue cooler, one of those round coolers that usually holds liquid. I put the cooler on the roof and kept Django searching, but he kept coming back to the place where the cooler had been. I wanted to show him there was nothing in the cooler so I opened the lid. Inside were rotten tamales, and I can't begin to describe the smell that came out, it was so putrid: the unusual yucky odor was what Django had to be indicating on. Concerned the lid was not on tight I put the cooler down on the ground, placing it out of our way, but Django kept jumping out of the car and going back to the cooler.

"Finally, I had had enough of rotten tamales and decided I was going to throw the whole thing in a dumpster close by, but as I tried to put the lid on tight the blue part separated from the liner, and it all fell apart. Between the liner and the blue outer – supposedly camouflaged by the rotten tamales – was a kilo of cocaine.

"People sometimes just don't appreciate how sensitive our partner's nose is: it is virtually impossible to fool them, but, even knowing how good Django is, I forgot to believe in him this time. The cocky attitude of the suspect indicated he was pretty certain no one, not even Django, could locate those drugs. I knew there weren't any drugs in that cooler, just rotten tamales, but my dog kept telling me different: 'Hey, dummy it's right here' – and he was right!

"One frustrating memory in our early career is of a call that came in the middle of the night. A carload of individuals just returning from Mexico were suspected of having 10lb (5kg) or 10 bundles of marijuana. The amount wasn't known for sure but it was thought to be large. We were asked to search all of the cars in the parking lot, and Django hit on a van. We ran the license plate on that van and it came back to be our suspect's. Good first step.

"Django kept indicating near the gas cap. I was still fairly new in my career and I told the sergeant that while inside the van Django kept returning to the back of the car, trying to go to where the valve came through. When searching the outside of the van he would try to go underneath, back up to the gas tank.

"Visible on the underside of the van were new screws on an old car: all the evidence, everything led to the gas tank, but I needed a search warrant. Unfortunately, I didn't trust Django or myself. The DEA sergeant didn't want to drop the gas tank on Django's indication. We had enough for probable cause and to get a search warrant, but I wasn't confident enough to make the call on Django's indication, and my uncertainty probably transferred to the sergeant. On that particular night, I unknowingly watched probably around 100lb (46kg) of marijuana being driven off down the road ...

"A particularly interesting IRS request from Metro involved searching safety deposit boxes in a bank. Django was deployed to search one particular wall in the hope that he would select a specific box, giving additional evidence in an ongoing case. Shown a large wall of bank deposit boxes to search, Django went to work. Eventually he stood, actually on his hind legs, sniffing as high as he could reach. He actually scratched and barked at one particularly high box. I pointed out which box I would open and received a smile from the IRS agent. He knew the box he wanted Django to select, but to assure the integrity of the search I was not given any information or prior knowledge of the situation.

"On the following day, a subsequent search on a different wall produced a similar response and an even bigger smile, since the box Django indicated on was the exact box which provided the evidence that would complete the case.

"Unfortunately, real life gives us situations that are not ideal. During my K9 career Django had always been there for me, but I could not be there for him when he died. Dwelling on the particulars of that situation brings feelings of guilt that makes the grief over his death unresolvable. But like so many other things in life, time does heal, difficult memories fade, and the sheer wonderment of our experiences together fills the void of his absence."
Retired officer Kevin Hanson and K9 partner Django, Salt Lake City, Utah, America

Django was a high energy Malinois doing what he loved best, using his innate instincts to catch the bad guy and find the drugs, working in tandem with his partner. The trust between partners is directly related to field experiences, and requires constant fine-tuning via solid communication and training. The tension can become palpable during moments of crisis, but results in greater trust, communication, and an ever-deepening bond. Using Django as a tool at the right time, in the right manner, ensured that both of these partners returned home safely.

The duties of a patrol K9 require that he is intimidating on command: presenting a visual image that looks unstoppable actually prevents many situations from escalating. And looking at the pictures of patrol work in this chapter it is easy to understand the psychology behind that premise – the dogs are unstoppable; they look barely controllable because they *are* barely controllable: once initiated their dramatic display of jaws, teeth and growls is a force to be reckoned with. Amazing to see, these very same K9 partners go from fury to tail wagging as if at the flick of a switch when all of that real-life drama is over. Given directions to stand down they look immediately for their reward toy, a pat on the head, and a 'Good boy!' from their partner.

Jon and Bo and Drago
"I began my police career with the West Jordan

"When most people hear the word aggression they squirm. They don't like it in people and they don't like it in dogs. Healthy canine aggression is the essential instinct from which the dog derives its 'fighting drive:' courage and stamina to overcome an enemy ...

"When you buy a working dog, you have dynamite in your hands: a wealth of heredity and magnificence handpicked and packed for action. The features of working temperament include structure and stamina, temperament, instinct, drive, aggression, and most of all, nerve. Some of these traits overlap.

"Canine instinct is a complex system of drives, inclinations and propensities that propels the dog to accomplish specific tasks in response to external conditions and internal dynamics. Instinctual drives fuse into the potent force that throws the dog into gear in the presence of triggering stimuli, unless it has been trained not to react ... these instincts create the link between canine intelligence and the proper handling necessary to unleash the distinctive valor, courage and ability that make working dogs awesome. Balance is always a key factor.

"Learning to read this instinct [prey drive] is important in setting up a motivational program, and is more productive than forced training because it builds nature rather than fear of punishment." – Theresa Mancuso: 'Get to know your Working Dog,' *Dog World*

Utah Police Department in 1984, at 19-years-old the youngest officer in the state of Utah. After a one-year probationary period, I accepted an offer to transfer to the K9 squad.

"In West Jordan, Utah, at that time we had three service dogs. My dog, Bo, was a very intelligent black and tan German Shepherd who had had two previous handlers. It was a good experience for me to start with a trained dog: Bo taught me what I needed to know to get started, and I sought the assistance of other more experienced officers in order to make my dog successful.

"Most of us are aware that 'prey drive,' or the instinct to chase and catch and kill prey, is a key part of protection training. Prey drive provides the speed, the pursuit, and, above all, the confidence to fight the man."
– Jerry Bradshaw, 'Prey Train the Young Prospect'

"Bo was a dog with a lot of personality. He was very close to all of the staff at the West Jordan Police Department, but would not let anyone but me give him a command. It became known that if anyone other than me asked Bo to sit or to lie down or do anything, he would simply growl and go about his business of socializing throughout the office. Bo was very aggressive, and he loved to work, but crime in West Jordan in 1985 didn't give him a lot of opportunity. He was a very successful drug detection dog, and a strong deterrent during contact with criminal suspects.

"Since we had some downtime in West Jordan, I had an opportunity to develop some of my first dog training skills. I put a sock through the mesh door of the truck cage and knotted both ends. I could remotely release Bo at night to play, and then call him on the PA system when I was ready to go. Bo would jump back in his kennel and grab the knotted sock to pull shut his door. Most people thought that I was just lazy but I enjoyed learning about how to teach my dog. I didn't have much opportunity to compete with Bo, although he did win a gold medal in obedience at a local K9 trial.

"One snowy night, Bo escaped from the apartment where I was living. I woke the next morning to discover him gone, and found his footprints in the snow going out the back gate that I had inadvertently left open. I followed the tracks for nearly a mile across major roads, and finally to a canal, where it looked like he'd spent quite a bit of time. I was worried for a second that he may have drowned until I found his tracks continuing on the opposite bank.

"The tracks took a different route back to the apartment complex. I followed them to the parking area opposite my unit where one of my partners parked his patrol car, and that is where I found him. He was soaking wet, lying on the trunk of the only marked patrol car in this very large apartment complex! He must have felt embarrassed that he couldn't find his own home after coming so close, but at least he recognized the patrol car as something comforting (or at least promising) to him.

"I trained Bo at a local Schutzhund dog training club where I met Sgt Judy Dencker of the Salt Lake City Police Department, and trained with her dog, Rocky. Judy saw my passion for working with service dogs, and was intending to propose a new K9 program for the SLCPD, which started the first K9 program west of the Mississippi in 1958, sadly, disbanded in the late 1970s as a result of litigation.

"In those days, the dogs were very aggressive, and mostly used as a weapon rather than a search tool. Sgt Dencker proposed a new program where the dogs would be used primarily to search. Of course, the dogs would still protect themselves, their handlers and citizens, and they could apprehend dangerous criminals and do everything else that police dogs do, but the main objective was that they would locate people who were lost, disoriented or simply didn't want to be found.

"Sgt Dencker asked if I would transfer to the Salt Lake City Police Department, and, because of her influence, the opportunity to start a new K9 program, and the greater potential for K9 work downtown, I made the switch.

"I retired Bo to my partner at West Jordan who continued to work him for a few years. During several years of retirement, whenever I came over to visit, Bo would be in the window. He recognized the sound of my truck, and, as soon as the door was open, would just run right past me and circle my new K9 truck, trying to get inside. When Bo passed away, he received a full honors police funeral. He was a part of the West Jordan police family for 10 years.

"During my probationary period at the Salt Lake City Police Department, Judy Dencker – now a Lieutenant – successfully pitched her idea for a new K9 program, which, together with Sgt Don Campbell and others, I got started. We were ahead of schedule and ready to go before I ended my probationary period. Rules prohibited a transfer during this period so the implementation of the K9 program was delayed slightly.

"We then received a shipment of three dogs: Villo, Carlo, and Drago. When we picked them up at the airport, I wanted to pick my dog in that order as Villo was beautiful and vibrant, Carlo was large and stately, but Drago was little and mean. And who would name a dog Drago anyway? I hated it.

"Sgt Campbell assigned Drago to me. I got him out of the crate at the airport and he immediately spun and tried to bite me. After a little standoff, and then a televised [the dogs' arrival was considered newsworthy] fight with Carlo, I was able to get him back into the crate. Meanwhile, Villo escaped and took a tour of the airport, causing one jet to 'go-around' as its wheels descended toward Villo on runway 34R. The airport was shut down until Villo could be cornered and captured. Not a good start to our K9 program.

"Utah POST (Police Officers Standard Training) had just begun a K9 training and certification program as we started our program. The patrol and drug dog schools were imported from Germany, and emphasized control and discipline. Unfortunately, back then, each school only lasted four weeks before the team took its certification tests.

"During Carlo's certification, Chief Michael Chabries approached Sgt Campbell, and I heard him say 'I hope you have more control over your men than you have over your dog.' The Chief said this with a chuckle, but the words still carried a little sting. We worked our tails off and certified all of the dogs both in patrol work and drug detection work in just eight weeks.

"A short time later, we added another dog. His name was Ingo and instead of being a mean little dog like Drago, he was a mean big dog. Drago and Ingo went on to be two of the most successful dual-purpose (drug/patrol) dogs in the history of the Salt Lake City Police Department. Villo quickly became the most prolific drug detection dog in the state, and Carlo spent his time supervising the other dogs (he was the sergeant's dog).

"My inspiration as a police dog handler came from the civilian world. I belonged to a Schutzhund club (a civilian sport that imitates police dog work) that met once a week. From the start, I could see that these guys were training

their dogs to a level inconceivable to most police K9 handlers – and they held full-time jobs to boot. I decided that I would not be a full-time professional K9 handler and trainer outdone by a bunch of weekend trainers, so studied what little material existed at the time but mostly learned in the K9 School of Hard Knocks.

"I enjoyed competing with my dog because I could measure my level of expertise against my peers, and because it was a great opportunity to share and network with knowledgeable handlers. I became a state certified instructor and judge in both patrol work and drug detection. During this time I competed in every local, regional, national and international police dog competition that I could find, and before he retired, Drago had earned more police dog titles than any other I know of across the country, winning two international police dog competitions, five national championships, and several local and regional events. He lost several times, too, which is actually required coursework in the K9 School of Hard Knocks.

"When Drago retired after seven years of service, I went into the Narcotics Squad and started [began training with] a German Shepherd single-purpose drug dog named Lobo. I normally left Lobo in the office when we were out doing undercover work because he looked like the standard police dog, but one time I forgot, leaving him in a crate in the back of my undercover van. I invited a drug dealer to get in the van and Lobo let the guy have it with a barrage of barking, growling and fighting, trying to get at him through the cage. I told the guy that I needed an attack dog for protection which he believed and we made the sale, and we later made the arrest. I transferred to Detectives, and Lobo continued with other detectives until his retirement.

"After about eight years in the Detective Unit, I was promoted and sent back to the K9 squad. I had purchased a German Shepherd puppy – name of Oskar – from a two-time world champion sire in Germany some time before being promoted, and was training him in the sport of Schutzhund. Oskar passed his narcotics certification test at nine months of age, and at about 18 months won fifth place overall in drug detection, competing with about 65 other dogs at the Las Vegas Metropolitan Police K9 Trials. He went on to be a very productive patrol dog as well, but, unfortunately, was forced to retire early due to a disease called Degenerative Myelopathy. I went back into the Detective Division.

Drago

"I was on patrol and heard a 'Home Invasion Robbery in Progress' dispatched about three blocks away from my location. When the dispatcher broadcast that the suspect ran off on foot, I backed out my truck and slipped into an alley with my fingers crossed. I remember saying to myself that if there was a K9 god, I will see someone jump the fence into the alley in front of me.

"Well, there is a K9 god. At first I saw the arm and leg come over the four-foot fence, quickly followed by the rest of the suspect rolling over the top rail. I immediately opened the K9 door as I shouted warnings from my open window for the suspect to stop. The suspect darted across the alley and scaled the only eight-foot fence in the area: Drago jumped but was a split second too late (I can still hear the snap of his teeth as he tried to grab the bandit's foot). I quickly put Drago on my shoulder and he jumped the fence.

"The suspect, meanwhile, was scaling the fence on the opposite side of the yard. Drago jumped as the suspect was rolling over the top rail of the fence, catching the bandit's hamstring, completely suspended, as the suspect continued over the fence. Drago began to tug with all his might, and was finally able to pull the bandit to his side of the fence. The guy fell right on top of Drago, which did not make for a happy dog. The robber paid dearly until we could get him into custody. He later kicked an officer and broke the officer's teeth while being treated at the hospital.

"While driving down 900 West in the early hours of the morning, I glanced over and saw a man standing in front of and facing a closed restaurant. I stopped my truck in the middle of the road and turned off the engine. From about 35 yards, I could see the blinds moving behind the window where the man was standing: I had clearly stumbled upon a burglary in progress, but the restaurant was surrounded by fences, and I was not in a fence-climbing mood that night. I quietly exited the truck and got Drago out. I put him in a surveillance position until his attention was locked on the man. Right before the man entered the broken window, I quietly sent Drago with an apprehension command and, as he approached the man, I yelled 'Police, stand still,' which, to the dog, means don't bite, just go into a guard position, and, of course, alerts the suspect to my presence.

"Drago slid to a stop, lay down, and focused intently on the man, who was now two feet from him. The burglar spun around, completely froze as he focused on the dog, and realized what had happened. He complied very willingly and was taken into custody without incident. I didn't have to chase this burglar, nor jump any fences!

"My department received a call from a neighboring agency that a suspect had tried to run over one of its officers, and was in pursuit of said suspect. The suspect bailed out of his car and disappeared into a neighborhood block. I began to search the area with Drago and, as we approached the very first yard, could see in my dog's intensity and posture that he could smell the suspect. Sure enough, we entered that yard and the bandit immediately flushed from a bush and jumped over a four-foot fence. This is low hanging fruit for Drago, so instead of sending him over the fence and risking injury, I went back out of the front gate and deployed him down an alley where the suspect was running. I caught sight of an officer chasing the suspect in front of the dog, and yelled at the officer, who stopped just in time for the dog to rocket past him. The suspect looked over his shoulder, saw the dog chasing, and accelerated from extremely fast to breakneck speed.

"The alley ended in a T intersection with another alley. The suspect made a hard right turn at the intersection as Drago leapt through the air to grab him: I could hear Drago's teeth snap at the suspect's neck. He just missed his mark and went tumbling down the alley. Meanwhile, the suspect jumped a low fence and disappeared again.

"Drago shook it off and ran to the fence but there was a large patch of goat heads [strong thorny ground cover] in front of the fence that crippled Drago's paws. I cleaned off his feet and sent him through the open gate that no one had noticed. Drago tracked through the yard and located the suspect again hiding in the bushes on the other side of a 4-foot fence. The suspect flushed again, this time running laterally to the fence, Drago chasing along the other side. Fortunately, the homeowner had stacked his firewood along that fence and, after a little climbing, Drago was at the top rail. He simply dropped down from the woodpile into the yard where the suspect continued to run and grabbed the suspect's hamstring, bringing him to the ground in tears. At the hospital, we found what looked like a snakebite in the hamstring: just four small holes and no other damage!

"We teach our dogs to detain suspects who are not actively fleeing or attacking. Drago's first detaining capture involved chasing a stolen vehicle. The thief bailed from the car and fled on foot in an industrial area, and officers were 100 per cent certain that they had the suspect contained in a yard there, so I deployed Drago to locate him.

"We searched for about an hour but came up empty-handed. The officers assured me that the suspect was there, and even asked to call in other K9 teams to find him. I acceded to this request and put my dog over the fence of an adjacent yard because it was a quicker route back to my truck.

"There was a patch of tall vegetation in the center of this lot which I didn't think anything of until Drago ran over with his tail straight in the air. He began to run circles around this vegetation and then began to bark as he circled. Without me saying anything, I saw two hands appear over the top of the vegetation. I had Drago lay down and the suspect was arrested without incident. The other officers ate a little humble pie that night.

"Another time I responded to a report of

a burglar alarm where there were indications of forced entry on the door, which was also not completely shut. I called the business owner, who told me in no uncertain terms that no one had legitimate access to the business at that time of night: no one else even had keys.

"I yelled warnings through the door as loudly as I could, noting from Drago's posture that the building was occupied. After several more warnings, I released Drago, who entered, rounded a corner, and began barking. I hurried in to see a man working at a bench with his back to the barking dog. The man was wearing headphones and was listening to a Walkman. I finally yelled loud enough for him to turn around. He saw the dog and completely froze: it was clear that he was an employee. I recalled Drago, and after a while the man was able to catch his breath enough to tell me that he was working late without permission, that he had a key that no one knew about, and that the damage to the door was done the week before. He thought that he had successfully disarmed the alarm system before getting in some late-night catch-up work.

"Drago retired as soon as I saw his physical condition begin to deteriorate: I didn't want to push him to work in discomfort, even though he would have chosen to do so. He enjoyed a long, comfortable retirement with my family and me, and passed away from cancer at the age of 13.

"One of the many highlights of my years as the K9 sergeant was learning from Officer Mike Serio and his Bloodhound, JJ. I watched as he tracked criminal suspects one after the other under circumstances that would be nearly impossible for a German Shepherd to manage.

"JJ made it clear that the shortest distance between two points is a line. JJ's lines were not always straight but it was much quicker for him to follow a trail of human scent than it was for a group of patrol dogs to search yard-to-yard within a contained area that usually did not contain the suspect! It was more common than not for JJ to track right past officers holding containment positions to capture the suspect blocks – and sometimes miles – away.

"Bloodhounds were slow to catch on in

Utah, but a lot of eyes were opened when K9 units from different agencies began to leave their dogs in their vehicles and call for JJ's help. After a comprehensive study of the productivity of the patrol dogs which perform several functions, and of the Bloodhound which only does one thing, I realized that a 50/50 split of patrol dogs and hounds was the only way for supply to meet demand.

"Shortly, Bloodhound Chase and Bloodhound Moe began their careers with the SLCPD. I retired and went to work for the SL County Sheriff's Office. Prior to finishing my probationary period, I was back in K9. I picked a Bloodhound named Oliver from the same bloodlines as JJ's. Oliver has developed into a very nice tracking dog and received his first tracking/trailing certification at five months of age.

"While training in Colorado with both Oskar and Oliver, I got to know some of the dogs working in the Colorado prison system. One in particular caught my eye. His name is Cisco, one of the most productive hounds in Colorado. I learned that Cisco's retirement was imminent and that he was being bred to another very successful tracking dog. I couldn't help it. I picked up Molly, the pup most resembling Cisco in appearance and mannerisms. Officer Serio picked a male named Jr and the Los Angeles Police Department also took one of the pups. Most of the others are being trained for Colorado law enforcement."

Officer Jon Richet and K9 partners Bo and Drago. Lead training officer for the K9 program at the Unified PD Special Operations Division K9 unit, Unified police dept, Salt Lake City, Utah, America. Current K9 partner Bloodhound Molly

The strong play drive, resilient, steady, adaptable temperament, and a desire to be with people, are characteristics essential for good K9 partners, enabling quick, solid obedience in training, adaptability in variable working situations, and the development of a strong bond.

Law enforcement purchases some puppies, but mostly young adults who are ready to be trained and start work immediately. When

these new dogs meet their partners-to-be, the relationship begins with grooming (touch), calm positive talk, and a positive olfactory message sent by the human part of this team-to-be. There is simply no way to fool a dog's nose or his tactile senses.

K9 officers must project these positive aspects in order for the right type of bond to develop; one that leads to trust and communication, essential in law enforcement.

Reed and Olk
Being prepared for the 'whatevers'
"Olk was born in Germany in July 1992, one of a litter with names beginning with the letter 'O.' Oloff and Olga were a couple of others. His full name is Olk vom Karlmitblick.

"He was tested for police work by Jan Kaldenbach (supplier of police dogs throughout the world) and purchased, and spent the next

Mike Serio and Jon Richet with three of the Bloodhounds who are helping expand the face of Utah's K9 program.

several months at Kaldenbach's kennel in Holland. Kenneth Licklider, owner of Vohne Liche Kennels in Indiana, imports dogs from Kaldenbach, and Olk came to the United States in the summer of 1993. He was given his initial narcotics training and introduction to searching and apprehension at Vohne Liche Kennels.

"When the police department went looking for a new police K9, several vendors were considered and the Vohne Liche kennels chosen. Licklider was contacted and sent a video of the dogs he had ready for sale, from which Olk was selected.

"I had heard that when new dogs arrived they were taken to a fenced compound, and their appointed handler would slowly get to know his dog by feeding him treats through the bars of the crate before opening it. Licklider told me that Olk would be no problem whatsoever, and was due to arrive in Utah on 19 Oct 1993 at 6:30pm on United Air Cargo.

"I was both excited and apprehensive that day when I drove with my wife to United. I went to the counter and asked for Olk, and the clerk brought out a large K9 shipping crate to the dock. I looked in though the front door and saw the most beautiful face looking back at me. All anxiety vanished, and I opened the crate right there on the dock and out came the most handsome German Shepherd I had ever seen. Olk and I were instant friends. He was clean and healthy and happy to be out. He was 15 months old.

"Olk and I attended the Utah Police Academy Police Service Dog training school, certifying in both patrol work and narcotics detection, becoming a fully certified team in March 1994, and working together until his retirement on 7 January, 2000.

"During our time together we competed in many police service dog trials, and Olk always did well, winning 13 medals and two large trophies, along with ribbons. He had the second highest score in the International Police Olympics held in 1996, and in 1998 the highest score in the Utah Police K9 Olympics. He was a pleasure to work with.

"Following his retirement in 2000, Olk

came home to live with us, and spent the next four years there. At home he was my constant companion, and each night when I put on my police uniform he would follow me to the door, wishing he could go. It was hard to see. Olk passed away in October 2004 at the age of twelve, leaving a hole in my heart that will never be filled.

"Olk and I often assisted the local SWAT team, deployed on deliberate searches for suspects when appropriate, but mostly working close in perimeters to prevent escape.

"The first two stories are examples of Olk's apprehension work, off-lead situations that required a level of communication and trust between the two of us that I will never forget."

The standoff

"The Violent Crime Task Force and FBI learned that an escaped suspect wanted for shooting at parole officers was holed up in a trailer park in Layton. The Task Force had located the trailer at about 4pm on a hot summer's day, and, as several trailers near the target were being evacuated, the suspect appeared and opened fire with a pistol. Fire was returned, resulting in a grazing wound to the upper arm of the suspect, who immediately dropped his pistol.

"Standing in the street with a loaded pistol at his feet, the suspect would not back away from the gun, nor would the officers approach (the suspect obviously knew he would not be shot as long as he didn't reach for the gun, and the officers would not approach if he stayed near the gun). Stalemate. The Layton SWAT team was called to provide K9 support.

"Olk and I responded with the SWAT team to the trailer park, and were briefed by the SWAT Team Commander upon arrival. The plan was to put a ballistic shield in front of the SWAT file (a group of officers moving in a tight, tactical line, single file), the second officer armed with a shotgun containing beanbag rounds (non-lethal). As the line reached the trailer, half of the men would go to the back of the trailer and gain entry, denying the suspect an avenue of retreat. The remainder, including the K9, would approach the suspect. At about 20 feet (6m), the lead man with the shield would order the suspect to raise his hands and step away from the gun. If the suspect refused, he would be shot with the beanbag rounds, and the dog sent to pull him away from the gun. He would then be apprehended.

"The operation went according to plan up to the point the suspect was supposed to put his hands up and step away from the gun. Instead, he invited the officers to do things not possible from an anatomical point of view ...

"I had Olk on the 30-foot line in a tracking/pulling harness. While the suspect sounded off, I sent Olk around the front of the team. Olk knew exactly what he was to do: dogs are very good at reading body language and aggressive behavior. Olk knew who his target was and he was on the run to get him. The suspect saw Olk coming at him – he knew that the police could not justify simply shooting him, but they certainly could let the K9 get him with impunity – and this thought was enough to make him throw up his hands, yelling not to let the dog bite him! I had to put the brakes on Olk in the middle of his run (we were both disappointed), and the suspect then stepped away from the gun and was apprehended by the SWAT Team.

"Building searches provide a unique challenge. Officers of the Northern Utah Criminal Apprehension Team had intelligence information that a wanted fugitive was residing in a particular home, where they have tried several times to catch him. This particular night they had been watching the address for a time, and seen the wanted man in the house. Surrounding the residence, the officers made contact with someone inside, who allowed them in to search. A very complete search was conducted, but the suspect not located. Confident that the suspect had not fled, the team discovered a small door under an upstairs sink cabinet that looked as if it might lead to the attic area. Obviously, no officer wanted to go in there so K9 Olk was called.

"Olk and I responded, along with dog handler Robert Nace of Kaysville Utah as our back-up. The residence was an older, bungalow-type with a short and confined attic. I sent Olk in first, off-lead, with the command to search for

a suspect, then followed him. The attic rose to about four feet (1.2m) at the top down to nothing at the eaves, and was dirty, dark, and cramped. Olk was able to walk normally but I had to crawl from beam to beam, with a pistol in one hand and a flashlight in the other.

"I could see Olk working an area in the center of the attic that was walled off for the upstairs bedroom. He got real interested in a spot on the wall, and began to bark softly. I worked my way over to him and found he was at an area where the plumbing went into the wall. There was a small cardboard panel that I assumed gave access to some plumbing fittings, and Olk indicated that he wanted to get through it. I pulled out the cardboard a little and peeked inside.

"What I saw surprised me! The suspect was huddled up in a small compartment. Backing off and no longer able to see the suspect, I put Olk in his guard position, yelling to the suspect to come out, hands first or I would send in the dog. I waited and yelled again. Soon, I could hear scraping noises but didn't see the suspect. I was momentarily confused until I heard Officer Nace ordering the suspect to step out. I peeked again and saw that he had climbed out into a bedroom, and was being apprehended.

"Olk and I backtracked and got out of that foul, dark attic. Officer Nace showed us how the suspect had come through the wall: he had cut an access through the wall and built a small hiding place, complete with blanket and pillow. Whenever the police came to the home he would go up to the bedroom, crawl into his compartment, and pull the home entertainment center over the hole behind him. He had done this several times, defeating the would-be arresting officers.

"But not Olk.

"Drug searches were a big part of our job and Olk was good, very good. He and I tried to stop in at local hotels at night, for a little foot patrol. We always stopped and talked to each clerk, inquiring about suspicious activity or problems.

"On this particular night the clerk had been waiting for us to stop by because of a suspicious

Right: When the packages were opened, a large block of compressed marijuana in plastic wrap was found inside.

incident. It seems that a few hours earlier one of the cleaning staff had told her that he thought he could smell marijuana in one of the hallways. The clerk told us which hall, and asked if we would check it out.

"Olk and I went to the area described by the clerk; I put Olk in the down position at the end of the hallway and walked the length of it. I didn't smell anything suspicious, and thought that because the incident was hours old, our opportunity to locate an odor was well past. I returned to Olk and invited him to search.

"Olk went down the hallway in a good narcotics search, sniffing each doorway as he went. When he got to room 120 he spun around and put his nose to the bottom of the door. He took a very deep sniff and gave great narcotics indication by scratching and digging at the bottom of the door, hitting the door so hard that the occupant came to the door in his pajamas. I explained that the K9 had indicated the odor of drugs and asked if there were drugs in the room. The male suspect opened the door and admitted us. When the room light was turned on I could see a large amount of marijuana on the floor near the air-conditioner, and a Glock pistol on the table. Olk went for the dope and I went for the gun, whilst the suspect just stood there, half-asleep. Once the gun was secured I handcuffed the suspect and called dispatch to request the METRO narcotics agents.

"When the agents arrived they took custody of the suspect, the dope, and a loaded 45-caliber Glock pistol. The investigation revealed that the suspect had purchased the marijuana in Las Vegas, stopping in town for the night en route to the east. Needless to say, he checked out a little early in the company of his new narcotic agent friends, who took great pleasure in canceling his trip east.

"Olk and I were summoned to a US Post Office in Ogden Utah to assist the narcotics agents from Weber County. When we arrived we were met by an agent who explained that the police had been called by the postmaster, suspicious of eight or so packages that were insured for an excessive amount of money. He

felt that the packages might contain drugs. I asked the agent to hide the packages separately among the parcels in the warehouse. When he was finished Olk and I went to the warehouse area that contained the suspicious packages and a large number of other parcels. I put Olk in the down position and examined the area (I didn't know which packages were the suspicious ones). Returning to Olk I invited him to search, and he sniffed his way through the mail and located and indicated the odor of narcotics on eight packages. The packages were removed and taken into custody, and Olk and I were released.

"Later that day a narcotics agent called me and explained that the packages had been seized. A search warrant affidavit was raised which included Olk's narcotics certification information and his indication. Based on the circumstances and Olk's indication, a search warrant had been issued to examine the contents of the packages. When the boxes were opened it was discovered that they contained a quantity of glass meth pipes. It was speculated they had been shipped to be sold at a rock concert being held in Salt Lake City that weekend. The pipes were packaged in newspaper, and it was thought that when they had been packed, the packaging material had come into contact with drugs. Had the packagers been smoking a little weed while they worked, maybe? We'll never know but several thousand dollars' worth of glass meth pipes never made it to the concert, and consequently a lot of people didn't have the weekend they had hoped for. Too bad.

"Olk and I were summoned to a Postal Access Store that specializes in shipping boxes, and were met by a Narcotics Task Force Agent, who explained that several boxes had been shipped from this store some time ago, bearing shipping labels from a health food company in Utah County. The addressee was in New York City, and the packages had been shipped normally. When delivery was attempted in New York, the addressee had apparently become suspicious and refused to take delivery, so the boxes were returned to the Postal Access Store.

"The store manager had called the health food company in Utah County and advised that delivery had been refused. The health food store manager checked and said he had not shipped any boxes from the store: why would he use a store in Ogden when there were several shipping outlets in his area? The Postal Access Store personnel then called the police. The agent told me he had distributed the boxes among other parcels in the warehouse, and would we search the area?

"I put Olk in a 'down' and examined the area, which housed many boxes and assorted containers (I had no idea which were the suspicious ones). I returned to Olk and invited him to search: he found and indicated on three large boxes. The agent seized the boxes and informed me that they were the boxes in question. I accompanied the agent when he took his affidavit to the judge to ask for a search warrant, which was issued as a result of the circumstances and Olk's certification as a narcotics detector dog.

"In the agent's office the first box was opened. It held a large plastic cooler taped up with duct tape, which, when opened, contained two large, sealed packages, each weighing 24lb (11kg). The packages were vacuum-sealed in an aluminum and plastic polymer envelope. When the packages were opened, inside we found a large block of compressed marijuana wrapped in plastic wrap. The other two boxes contained packages wrapped in the same way. Total amount of marijuana found was in the region of 140lb (64kg).

"Some time later the narcotics agent told me that the investigation had resulted in the seizure of a large house, boat, autos, and a large amount of cash. The suspect lived in Arizona and was the subject of a DEA investigation. The incident in Ogden had given the DEA the link it needed to connect the New York contact to the Arizona target. It appeared that the New York connection had become suspicious at the time the packages were delivered. He thought that the police had been tipped off so refused delivery, and the packages were returned to Utah, which is where the caper came unstuck and Olk took over.

"Tracking involves a particular perspective: hunting bad guys on a long line, not knowing what is around the corner, especially in an outdoors venue, heightens every instinct, especially in the following case.

"The Davis County Sheriff's Office received a complaint from a property owner of a trespasser in a rural county area. On arrival there, the deputy was told that the property owner had observed a white adult male with long shaggy hair and a strange look about him, parked on the road near his home, at first just sitting in his vehicle. The subject then got out of the vehicle and opened the trunk, removing from it a wooden box about two feet long and a foot wide. The subject was approached by the property owner and asked what he was doing, to which he replied that he had just made a great sacrifice for the world, and that was all he needed to know. The subject then scaled the fence and disappeared into the brush. The property owner called the sheriff, but the subject and vehicle were both gone by the time the deputy arrived. The deputy requested K9 assistance.

"Olk and I were called out from home, as we were off duty. It was a wet April morning, excellent for tracking. The deputy briefed us: he felt that this might be some religious nut who may have committed a crime. What could be in the box – a head, an arm, a baby? I had heard about so many awful things, and seen a few, during my time on the force – what was today's search going to bring?

"I got Olk and a 30-foot tracking line from the truck. The property owner showed me where the subject had crossed the fence, and we began there. Olk and I located a scuff in the wet ground and set off in a southerly direction through the long, wild grass, wet from rain during the night.

"The track took us down a large pasture hollow and up the other side into the oak brush. The ground south of the meadow was clay, and occasionally I could make out a partial footprint, so was confident that we were on a good track. The track meandered up the other side, then down a gully. We crossed a wash and continued through broken brush and small trees. Finally, Olk tracked to an area of broken limbs and tree branches that had gathered in the bottom of a ravine where the water had washed them. He sniffed the brush pile and lay down. I examined the debris and found a wooden box as described by the witness. The deputy was called, and he opened the box to find it contained some small artifacts of unknown significance. The box was as described and was completely dry. We were confident that it was the box in question.

"I never did find out how this was resolved. The track was very good over some rough terrain and over a long distance. The anticipation, the emotional angst surrounding every step in a search for the 'unknown' requires focus, to be prepared for whatever might occur. There was no danger that day – no bodies; no bombs – but we didn't know that, and were prepared based on training for just this type of scenario. Good track, good find, and good to go home with images of small artifacts, not those my imagination had conjured up.

"We knew the conclusion of this next track would be very different to that of the foregoing story; there was a bad guy hiding somewhere. A local officer had stopped a vehicle in a residential area at night. Having obtained the suspect's identity (who was in his vehicle), the officer returned to the patrol car to do a records check and complete a citation. Whilst the officer was completing the check the suspect – a young adult male – left his car and ran. The officer gave chase on foot but lost sight of the suspect, so called for K9 assistance.

"As Olk and I were responding, other officers set up a quick perimeter that covered several blocks, and enclosed a pasture and barnyard area. After briefing, Olk and I went to the area where the suspect was last seen. It was a cold November evening, and it had been a very wet fall: good tracking conditions. We tracked through a residential area to a backyard that bordered a pasture to the back fence. When Olk came to the fence he crawled under the barbed wire and continued into the pasture at the center of the block. We could see other police cars on the perimeter with their spotlights on, and hear the radio traffic indicating the suspect had outstanding felony arrest warrants.

"The intention of the perimeter is to make the suspect feel trapped, and go to ground rather than continue to run. I felt the perimeter was good, and hoped it had been set up quickly enough and was solid enough to contain our suspect.

"Olk continued across a very wet pasture for its entire length, coming across several curious cows and dodging the odd steaming pile. On the other side we came to a corral and barnyard, the former containing liquid cow manure ... The track led up to this, which neither Olk nor I wanted to go through, so we skirted around it and got to the firmer ground of the barnyard, which contained some farm equipment, a truck, a barn, and a few outbuildings.

"I figured that the suspect must have entered the barn, so put Olk in a 'down' at the side of the open doorway, and made my announcement. 'This is the police, you in the barn call out or I'll send in the K9. You may be bitten.' I listened for a reply, and soon heard a quiet voice say 'Don't send the dog, I'll come out.' But rather than coming from the barn, the voice was coming from behind me! (dumb cop), as the suspect was under an old truck a few feet away. Olk was my back-up as I ordered the suspect out and handcuffed him, very glad to hand him off to another officer as he was covered in liquid cow manure from the knees down. Yuck!

"The call requiring Olk's tracking abilities for a violent, abusive, AWOL inmate was fraught with drama. The police dispatch center received a call from a female who reported that her boyfriend was AWOL from the Davis County Jail, drunk at her apartment. After becoming violent and abusive, he was currently asleep on her couch. Two police units were dispatched to respond.

"As the officers arrived, the suspect woke up and escaped from a back bedroom window. The officers gave chase but lost sight of the suspect as he left the apartment complex. The shift sergeant set up a quick perimeter and a K9 was called, to which Olk and I responded.

"Briefed by the initial officer, we were directed to the suspect's last known location. Attaching the 30-feet tracking lead, Olk knew that a track was afoot. He likes to track, and I'm sure he hoped that the track would end in a catch: given the suspect, that seemed quite likely, and no doubt Olk could read the tension in my body language.

"The locality was a large residential area, and it was evening: we would encounter pedestrians and vehicles. There were streetlights on the corners, but it was dark for the most part. I was told who the suspect was, and knew him from previous arrests and contacts. I knew also that he could be violent, and had used weapons in his criminal activities, so I was also really hoping for a catch, and Olk was hoping for a bite.

"Olk began to track in a driveway and across a lawn and into the street. He seemed to be on a good solid track. When he came to a corner Olk cut across a driveway and the lawn to a large overgrown evergreen bush. He put his head under the low brush then gave out a bark. I was close, so, with pistol in hand, I looked in the brush and saw the suspect hiding there, though could not

see his hands or a weapon. I ordered the suspect out from the brush and waited for his response. My lone back-up officer had advised the perimeter officers that we had located the suspect and were waiting for his compliance. The suspect didn't come out of hiding so Olk went in, grabbed him by the shoulder, and began to drag him out. I reached in and helped. Once the suspect was out in the open and I could see his hands, Olk was disengaged and ordered 'down' in the guard position.

"Olk's purpose then was to protect me in the event of an attack. My back-up officer and I began to search and handcuff the suspect, and all was going well when I heard a cry from behind me. When I looked, I could see Olk dragging away an unknown officer by the seat of his pants. I commanded Olk to release, which, rather reluctantly, he did, instinctively assuming a guard position, watching the officer, apparently unperturbed by the uniform. The handcuffs were on the suspect and he was out of commission, so I turned my attention to Olk and the unknown officer.

"I asked the officer what happened, and was told that, learning the location of the find, he wanted to help with the arrest as this was his case, so ran over to us, attempting to reach in over my back to get at the suspect. Not a sensible thing to do in the presence of a partner like Olk, who grabbed him by the britches to pull him away from me. The officer received only a short bite, with maybe a puncture or two, so no real injury, well, his dignity, maybe ... The suspect had been wearing a big, baggy, hooded sweatshirt and jacket, which meant that Olk had only grazed his shoulder, so all ended well."

Retired Layton City Police K9 officer Reed Heslop and K9 partner olk, Layton, Utah, America

It is important to know what to expect from a dog when you encounter a new situation. Nowhere is this more relevant than in patrol work, and training, training, and more training is the key. Remember, we are talking about an animal which we are going to put in a situation that requires the use of his survival instincts to protect his 'pack.' We can never completely know for sure what to expect, because every possible variable cannot be anticipated or trained for, but considering the obvious consequences of bite work, making every effort to understand a K9's actions is essential.

Working beside a partner that utilizes his cognitive senses – triggered by inherent survival instincts – to appreciate dangers that may not be apparent to us is always beneficial, and can even be life-saving. Once triggered, the prey/fight drive can prove formidable, however, and the human side of the partnership must maintain control over his K9's actions, usually achieved via the strong bond and without-question obedience, but which sometimes necessitates a degree of strength as the handler physically demonstrates to his partner exactly how something should be done. Mostly, the dog's own hunting instinct is sufficient to produce the desired outcome, since locating and detaining the bad guy will calm most volatile situations.

Unless apprehension is necessary, a non-physical detain is preferred, but this precludes the usual ending to a hunt, and persuading a K9 to switch off these instincts takes complete control. And as his senses mature and combine with his apprehension training, the force of centuries of inherent instinct can surface and prove challenging.

The K9 partner requires respect, and is both dynamic and legitimately intimidating; the human partner must maintain his respect whilst retaining control, carefully maintaining his dog's natural inclinations, and nurturing their bond. This is a fine line to walk while dealing with the tool he has learned to love.

When I first met the young officer who contributed the following story I had already heard about Joker lying dead in the street – everyone had. Joker's death caused a great deal of grief for everyone who had watched him work, and we had all enjoyed his high energy, 'move out of my way' attitude.

Joker's new handler (his former handler had been promoted), Officer Chris Bitten, started

"Defense training, even assuming that we are training a dog with good nerves, induces stress. Each dog has a stress threshold at which it will 'turn on' in defense (defense threshold), and a stress threshold at which he will abandon fighting as a strategy (avoidance threshold). The stress levels between these thresholds are the area in which we can work the drive without causing avoidance, and build confidence.

"It is important to remember that stress is a cumulative factor. If sufficient stress accumulates over time, the dog may abandon fighting as a strategy, and decide to avoid the confrontation. This is undesirable for a police service or working protection dog, for obvious reasons.

"Conflict is what dog trainers refer to as the confusion and resulting inappropriate behavior manifested by a dog during protection training, who is unable to change drives seamlessly during the dynamics of a confrontation with a decoy." – Jerry Bradshaw, 'Drive Channeling in the Working Dog'

working his partner with a quiet, calm, but determined attitude. Joker was a skinny, high energy young dog that needed and received patient guidance during a difficult transition to a new handler. Chris' personality traits were forged from life experiences, and the love Chris showed while bonding with Joker demonstrated a depth of calm determination not often seen in first-time K9 handlers.

K9 partners can become 'family' very quickly. They can be the reason officers make it home at night and, like so many of us with that one, memorable partner, Joker came into Chris' life and family at just the right time. The tender words on the picture at the end of this story, written by Chris' son, Trevor, express his feelings about Joker's death. Simply put, the words and picture of a young child, say it all!

Chris and Joker
Always on duty

"In October 1999, I had been in law enforcement for approximately 11 years. Early in the morning of October 16, 1999, a fellow deputy radioed for back-up to assist with a traffic stop: the driver of a pick-up was attempting to pull the first responding deputy into the cab of his vehicle, and drive off with him. A fellow deputy and myself responded to assist.

"The end result of this incident was that the driver lost his life. All of the responding deputies were placed on administrative leave pending investigation, and we finally returned to duty approximately four-and-a-half months after the incident.

"During this period I had time to reflect on my position as a law enforcement officer. The death of the driver not only affected me but my family, too, and giving up my position as a deputy seemed the only way to return some peace and happiness to my family.

"But my heart wouldn't allow it: being an officer is not just a job for me, it is who I am. Togother as a family, with commitments from and to each other, we regrouped, and I continued my career in law enforcement, now closing in on 19 years. A blessing in disguise was waiting just down the road when I was appointed a K9 handler with the Sheriff's office.

"Following the promotion of a fellow deputy – a K9 officer – to sergeant, I was fortunate enough to become the new K9 handler – Joker's

The chase ...

... and the detain. In the middle of apprehending a fleeing suspect, patrol K9s can be placed in a down posture and told to hold – detain – with one simple verbal command. If the suspect has decided to stop running, the need for physical contact with the K9 is over, but maintaining the psychological intimidation will also keep the K9 on high alert.

Right: Chris and Joker.

partner. Joker was a five-year-old Belgian Malinois who had been Chad's K9 working partner for three years. It was now my pleasure, my responsibility, to become his new handler, a task fraught with possible complications since an old bond had to be replaced without losing Joker's work ethic and drive. Chad explained Joker's commands, gave tips for helping with the bonding process, his eating habits, and insights into reading Joker's body language, his habits, his likes and dislikes.

"One important tip was the unusual manner in which Joker let you know he needed to be let out to relieve himself. He would begin turning circles in the rear of the patrol truck, at which time getting to a local park or field was important. I had been working with Joker for approximately 11 days, and part of our routine was to take him on patrol shifts to expedite the bonding process, even though we were not certified as a working team. This was helping both of us to understand each other, and allowing me a chance to appreciate how much time I had to get to a park or field when Joker started circling in the back of the truck.

"We were on patrol one night when a local security agency called in suspicious activity. I responded, as did four other deputies. The security officer had seen two vehicles move into the area, which were now located behind a storage unit with their lights out. Both vehicles had contained several people, and a check indicated that one of the vehicles carried license plates from a stolen vehicle. By this time the vehicles' occupants had fled on foot into a field containing several areas of trees, and we were able to check the vehicles more thoroughly, discovering that one contained what appeared to be stolen property.

"Being the only K9 unit on duty, yet not certified as a K9 team, I was unable to deploy Joker on any type of track. Frustrated at this, I was relieved when dispatch called saying that several people had been spotted by a passerby leaving the trees, going east from our current location. All the deputies cleared the area and responded to where the suspects were last seen, although I

remained at the scene to secure the two vehicles. Several minutes elapsed, and I returned to the two vehicles pending an update on the suspicious persons.

"As luck would have it, Joker began his ritual of running in circles at the rear of the patrol truck. I placed his tracking harness on him with a 50-foot line. and let him out of the truck to relieve himself and get some exercise while we waited.

"However, Joker was concerned with more than relieving himself, making a beeline for a group of fallen trees, barking and carrying on, behavior I had not seen before. I recalled him to me and he came. I told him to 'potty,' which was his command to relieve himself. Obligingly, he tinkled – and then again made a beeline for the fallen trees. Thinking there was probably a cat or skunk in the trees, I again called him to me, but this time walked him over to the trees to investigate.

"Then: 'Don't let the dog bite me, I'm coming out,' and, lo and behold, one of those driving the vehicles – the stolen vehicle, to be exact – had returned to the scene, having observed the deputies leaving the area, hoping to drive away, and had hidden when Joker and I returned. I notified dispatch and requested assistance. My sergeant soon arrived and asked how I had located the suspect. I explained to him that I had simply let Joker out of the truck to potty and he had done the rest. He laughed at this, and suggested that future certifications should contain hidden suspects in the potty break areas, unknown to the handler, to see if he could really 'read' his K9. The suspect was taken into custody and subsequently charged. My trust and confidence in my new partner began from that day.

"On January 15, 2004, I received a phone call at home from the other K9 handler with our Sheriff's office, who asked me to meet him around the corner from my home. As I walked to where he had parked his patrol vehicle, I saw Joker laying dead in a snow bank. My mind went blank and tunnel vision took over, and I could only stare in disbelief at my partner laying dead in the snow. I remember thinking 'this can't be happening.' My family had already struggled with the incident in 1999 when the driver was killed, and my return to law enforcement, now this, how am I going to explain that Joker was dead, hit by a passing truck? And how had he gotten out of my backyard and into the street? Many questions but few answers. This was more devastating than the earlier incident.

"Joker was buried in the local cemetery with many officers paying their respects. My two sons and the sons of Joker's previous handler acted as coffin-bearers. As my family and I were walking away from the cemetery the Sheriff approached and hugged each of us, and shook my hand. He told me that he had been allocated funds with which to replace Joker, and so, three weeks later, I drove to Arizona with several other deputies to select-test a new K9 for the Sheriff's office, knowing in my heart that Joker would never be replaced."

Sergeant Chris Bitton and K9 partner Joker, Weber County Sheriff's office K9 Unit, Weber County, Utah, America

"A different kind of Hero ... My hero has 4 legs ... 100s of tennis balls and 1 headstone." Joker became the family hero.

Protecting his partner, detaining a bandit, methodically locating narcotics, ultimately going home to his place on the couch was a full day, and Joker loved it. After working with a handler for three years, the transition to someonenew was probably difficult and confusing for Joker. If that was the case, his performance could have suffered, but the story seems to indicate he knew his job and would do it whenever or wherever. Joker's resilient, adaptable character, constantly in overdrive, his high prey/hunt drive seemed to enable a successful transition. This relentless, will not quit attitude, and spontaneous survival instinct that initiates and constantly motivates, this is the K9 heart.

Naturally driven to work, a dog with a good strong prey/hunt/fight drive instinctively reacts to stimuli to survive. 'Spontaneous engagement' and 'intelligent disobedience' are catch phrases that frequently describe activities initiated by the canine member of the team. Allowing the partner with the best nose to take the lead when possible is sensible, since he knows the direction of the scent and the intentions behind it. Dual-purpose dogs – those which have two jobs – frequently display a stronger ability in one or other of their working disciplines. Great sniffers are not always great patrol or bite dogs: it doesn't mean they aren't good at biting, just that biting is not their favorite thing to do; they would rather be using their nose.

"And some of the best patrol dogs that simply love to bite are probably wishing they were chasing a bad guy while finding drugs. Experienced handlers who allow for these differences enable the individual strengths of specific dogs to rise to the top and become the best of the best. Many of the dogs in this book have received high awards for their work, as the following story attests ...

Stan and Abby, Mike and Arrest
A lifetime with German Shepherds
"Probably one of the most important and interesting facts that I have learned in 22 years of working with dogs is that each has his own special strengths. Some dogs are great at scent work; some are great at patrol, so discovering and utilizing their strengths provides the team with the best potential for success, although this is not possible until you have actually worked a dog for some time.

We do extensive testing to understand their potential when dealing with their hunt/prey/fight drives, along with checking for basic olfactory awareness, but most dogs seem to be better at one thing in particular: either bite work or nose work, although this can be hard to determine if you have a good, all-round dog whose specific strengths might not be immediately obvious.

"The key, then, is to be flexible. A solid dog will be good at everything, but when his particular abilities surface it is your responsibility to encourage/discourage these, based on the type of work you want him to do. Fortunately, a good training program allows emphasis to be placed on training that compensates for the skill that isn't his favorite while allowing him to excel in his specialty.

"I had the opportunity to work with some exceptional German Shepherds, beginning with my first canine partner, Abby, a sweetheart of a German Shepherd who wouldn't hurt anyone. Abby and I worked in Search and Rescue, and later I was able to work with apprehension, protection and drug detection with Mike and Arrest, two great Shepherds. Abby found and looked for those who had lost their way, while Mike and Arrest found those who were purposely trying to be lost due to the mischief they had engaged in. We also looked for any paraphernalia or evidence they had discarded during a chase.

"Today, my canine responsibilities have changed. I do not have a K9 partner but continue to supervise and assist with securing canine partners for local agencies, and help with their training and certification.

"Throughout my life and career, the great German Shepherds that I have had the opportunity to work with have continually influenced my family and everyone associated with me, and the following short stories detail some specific moments and thoughts from a lifetime of walking behind and working beside those canine partners.

"I followed Abby, my SAR partner, into the mountains of Jackson Hole, Wyoming, looking for lost grizzly bear biologists, and into the heat of the Grand Canyon where we could actually feel the heat coming through the soles of our boots. We used some of our rappel training on that search, lowering the dogs ten or 15 feet (3-5m) down treacherous rocks swinging in a harness, which proved a good skill to have on that particular day. I remember digging out dirt holes in the mountain so that the dogs wouldn't overheat while we waited for the helicopter to pick us up – it was a long wait in hot, unforgiving country.

"Abby's particular ability probably surfaced when she was really, really young, and we would send her out to find our kids – a typical runaway – and she loved every minute of it. She became an excellent tracker because she was introduced to it as a puppy, and it was her family (my children) she was seeking.

"We trained for avalanche, learned how to rappel down cliffs with her balanced on a harness tied to my waist, and we did some lake searching for people who had drowned – it was amazing how her scent-discriminating abilities worked through obstacles like packed avalanche snow and water currents.

"Our search for a plane carrying biologists studying grizzly bears that came down in the Tetons lasted four days, and was one of my most memorable searches, even though we came home empty-handed. I vividly remember watching the dog teams work in the difficult, dense terrain, our energies focused on making sure we were at the designated pick-up spot so that we didn't spend the night in grizzly territory. Because we didn't know the area at all we spent some time making sure we didn't get lost. The fact that the plane went down while searching for a wounded grizzly bear did add to the excitement and intensity of that search.

"There are no pictures of that search nor, for that matter, of most of my searches because I was too busy watching Abby. The pictures I do have are of training scenarios, but I can still vividly

remember the places and the circumstances surrounding all of our searches.

"A small boy lost in a deep cave found and returned alive and safe to his family; a grandfather with two young children on a steep, snowy mountainside had all of our search and rescue teams scrambling that night. Fortunately, that mountain-wise grandfather was smart enough to bed down, and when it got light they all walked out into the arms of a delighted family.

"A callout for a child, lost somewhere in his rural neighborhood, set in motion a somewhat frantic search: ditch banks, swollen ditches and fields surrounding the home were thoroughly

Stan had the opportunity to work with some good Shepherds, such as Mike.

searched with a great deal of attention given to every possible hiding place. We returned exhausted and did one last search at his home – where he was found sleeping under a pile of clothes. Those were the good searches, where everyone was found alive. Abby passed away at the age of seventeen, an unusually ripe old age for a Shepherd.

"After studying K9 programs in Arizona and Texas it was thought that having a dog patrol the hospital property where I was employed may help deter escalating gang violence. So Mike became my next partner, purchased to provide a visual deterrent to the bad guys. And with Mike came an added bonus: he had a really great sniffing nose, and became a great dope dog.

"A big, dark German Shepherd, Mike's appearance did provide the necessary visual intimidation, and I never doubted that if he had been called on to bite he would have performed admirably. But Mike's nose was his best asset. He could and did find drugs anywhere the bad guys hid them. I thoroughly enjoyed watching Mike hunt for drugs, and seeing the disappointment on the faces of those who had adamantly denied having any.

"Mike was my first dual-purpose apprehension and drug detection dog, and probably one of the best multi-purpose canines I had ever worked with. He was called upon numerous times by local law enforcement to help with drug raids, and placed in many local K9 trials for his drug detection work, as well as his apprehension work. He also received Top Dog at the Utah Canine Olympics, and placed 5th at a K9 trial held in Las Vegas where agencies from all over the United States came to compete.

"But tough, apprehending, drug-finding Mike also enjoyed visiting pediatric patients in our hospitals, where the children immediately fell in love with him. His gentle personality made him very popular throughout the region for demonstrations, so he and I spent a lot of time traveling and demonstrating his apprehension and drug detection skills at schools, scouting and church youth activities. And Mike thrived on the attention and love from the children.

"Mike was deployed one time to apprehend a person who had been vandalizing cars in a parking lot. The suspect attempted to hide but was found in a matter of seconds, and pulled out by Mike from underneath a car where he thought he wouldn't be found, but Mike's nose had different ideas. His work ethic was sound and strong.

"Whether finding drugs, pulling bad guys from under cars or loving children, Mike was always steady and on task: he loved to work.

"Mike passed away at the age of nine – the average life span of a hard-working protection canine – from a condition called torsion or twisting of the stomach, which is a fairly common illness among large breed dogs that requires veterinary intervention within minutes or death is almost certain.

"Then came Arrest, a big, very big German Shepherd bought to work with Mike in his later years, and take over the patrol aspect of Mike's work. With almost all dual-purpose K9s, patrol work becomes difficult for them as they age: as with human athletes, the physical rigors of training and work can eventually have adverse affects on joints and muscles. Arrest's very presence – over 100lb (45kg) of pure, raw strength – prevented potential situations from even starting: his huge stature was immediately intimidating and very authoritative. But Arrest remained a puppy at heart all of his life when dealing with the people he loved.

"Both Mike and Arrest excelled at different aspects of their jobs – Mike in drugs, Arrest in bite work – but they were proficient in both; they were exactly what the hospital needed and we were able to capitalize on the strengths that enabled them to become some of the best dogs in the State.

"There is a saying that 'Shepherds leave their paw prints on our hearts forever.' My heart has indeed been touched and imprinted by some of my best friends – my Shepherds."

Retired Police K9 officer Stan Stark and K9 partners Abby, Mike and Arrest, Weber County Sheriff's office. Current Supervisor of Safety and Security, McKay-Dee Hospital, ogden, Utah, America

Sometimes, even the most experienced and trusting handler doubts his dog, and unique to the next story is the canine sense of humor. Nanto's handler, Sergeant Bob Nace, a field K9 handler for over 12 years, and a narcotics judge emeritus/trainer has an ability to know and understand the instinctual components of dogs. Fine-tuning field problems, Sergeant Nace excels in bringing out the best performance in each individual K9. Because of his years of experience, and the environment in which he usually worked – a world routinely filled with guns and handcuffs – Bob appreciated and encouraged Nanto's humor.

Bob and Nanto
A K9 with a sense of humor?

"Nanto was a 2-year-old sable German Shepherd who came from the Netherlands to Utah to become Kaysville City's first police service dog. He had been flown in from a vendor in Indiana after I had picked him as suitable for the job.

"Nanto sat in a kennel for a week or two prior to being shipped, and was air-sick on the long plane ride to Utah, which became painfully obvious to me as we set off for work the day after Nanto arrived. A police patrol car had been outfitted for K9 use and, to put it bluntly, Nanto smelled bad. After an unsuccessful attempt at a potty break, I took Nanto into the station to let him get used to where he was going to work. Much to my dismay a large puddle appeared on the carpet – so much for first impressions. The critical bonding time for dog and handler was not getting off on the right paw, so to speak.

"Nanto's first days on the job were sort of stressful for him and me. The long-awaited arrival of the 'wonder dog' I had fought for over the last five years was a dog who smelled bad and wasn't house (station) trained. The rest of the day didn't go much better as we went about our duties with all the car windows down to keep from being asphyxiated. Citizens wanting to see the new police dog were repelled by the foul smell. By this time, I was wondering what I had gotten myself into ...

"After an awkward first few days – and a much-needed bath – happily, Nanto and I began

Nanto: Kaysville City's first police dog.

to bond, and in time, with a lot of patience and hard work, we became a team.

"But Nanto had a unique quirk: a sense of humor, and a cop sense of humor, no less. Not immediately obvious, the first time this showed itself was the garbage can caper.

"Nanto loved to run into the police station and visit with the gals up in the front office, who would give him treats and attention. Next, he would visit other officers at their work stations, and then return to me, lying under the desk until he was ready to resume his patrol duties.

"One particular officer loved dogs, and always gave Nanto extra attention. Just before leaving this officer, every time Nanto would tip over his garbage can and run off. No other officer was subjected to this joke, and even after the officer was assigned a different work area Nanto would come into his office and tip over his garbage can, day or night. If the garbage can was there he would tip it over. The officer would chuckle about it and ask how I had taught Nanto

Taking a turn in the 'bite suit' keeps perspective fresh on exactly what happens when you deploy your K9 partner, and he apprehends a fleeing suspect.

to tip over just his can, but the secret was never revealed.

"The next joke, so to speak, happened during a public demonstration. A bunch of traffic cones were set out with a small quantity of narcotics concealed in one of them, typically the end one. The dog performing the narcotics demonstration would go along and sniff the line of cones, and indicate on the one that had the narcotics concealed inside, after the handler had given an explanation to the crowd about the keen sense of smell that these highly-trained dogs have. After the usual long-winded explanation of what to expect, it was time for Nanto to impress the crowd. Instead of sniffing along the line of cones, however, Nanto promptly took off, tipping over the cones one at a time, and looking inside. Finally reaching the end cone with the narcotics inside, he turned this over, too, and started barking at me. Caught completely off guard, I could do nothing but laugh at Nanto's antics. Satisfied with his joke, Nanto simply grinned.

"His quirky sense of humor was obvious not only around the officers but the suspects, too. Nanto usually slept in the back of the patrol car when he was not needed to effect an arrest. A particular suspect was clapped in irons without incident, and placed in the front of the K9 vehicle, where he became rather vocal. Nanto, awakened from his nap by the jabbering suspect, took immediate exception to this interruption, and growled at the suspect, swatting him through the cage with his paw. The suspect had been unaware of the sleeping Nanto, so began screaming like a little girl, trying to hunker down on the floorboards of the vehicle in an attempt to get away. Needless to say, this reaction caused amusement to the observers and satisfied Nanto, who promptly went back to sleep.

"Nanto also liked to sucker in people and bark at them, making them jump back in fright and scream. His first victim was the poor cleaning lady. The patrol vehicle had tinted windows designed to keep the interior of the car cool for Nanto, and these were very dark and difficult to see through. The cleaning lady, wondering if Nanto was in the vehicle, walked up to the rear

side window, cupping her hands on the window in an attempt to see in. Nanto jumped up and started barking and baring his teeth; all that could be seen was a flash of teeth through the window, which was extremely impressive and not just a little frightening. It looked as though the cleaning lady might have a heart attack as she jumped back from the vehicle, a growl of satisfaction emanating from the back of the car. Nanto's timing was impeccable.

"After the sedan was replaced by a pick-up truck, Nanto would lay in the back in the shadows. Should an officer look in as he passed, Nanto would lay there, unconcerned, but if an officer walked by without paying him attention, Nanto would be up, barking and barring his teeth at the startled man.

"Nanto loved to meet new people, especially women in dresses or skirts, which he would promptly put his head under, much to the embarrassment of both me and the victim.

"His ability was put to the test one night when we were asked to search for two car-jacking suspects who had run over their victim. An officer from the neighboring agency had attempted to pull over the stolen vehicle, which had been driven off. The suspects then abandoned their vehicle and fled on foot into a farmer's field. A containment was set up, with the suspects somewhere within, and another K9 team was called to assist with searching the buildings located in the area. The search was conducted off-lead so Nanto could cover more ground.

"Using the wind to our advantage, Nanto

Funeral for a dog. A K9: a living tool who left a void in the hearts of many. He, like all the other heroes in this book, will never be forgotten or replaced.

and I began the search. I directed Nanto to the left into an area that would offer the suspects good concealment. Nanto checked the area as directed and broke to the right. Somewhat frustrated, I redirected Nanto to the left. Again, Nanto broke to the right, working a scent cone. I allowed Nanto to continue, promising that if Nanto led me to a raccoon or a cat, he would pay. To my surprise Nanto had located the suspects concealed in an irrigation ditch hiding under running water.

"Nanto held the suspects with his signature detain – bouncing up and down on his hind legs and barking – which, since Nanto was a large dog, was extremely intimidating. I held the suspects at gunpoint until other officers at the scene could respond and assist in effecting arrest. As a result of this incident, I developed great trust in Nanto's ability to search, both for narcotics and suspects and, subsequently, Nanto was credited with several captures of wanted suspects and several narcotic finds."

Retired Sergeant Bob Nace and K9 partner Nanto, Kaysville Police Dept, Utah, America. K9 adjunct narcotics instructor and judge, Utah Police officers' Standards and Training. Current consultant for police agencies

and private businesses in the training and deployment of service K9s

Closing this chapter with a touch of humor seemed appropriate, considering the drama these teams face every day. Nanto was proficient in narcotics and apprehension, but will also be remembered for the smiles he brought to the faces of many. As well as the uniform, tasers, handcuffs, nightstick and gun, today's crimes demand intense preparation and intelligent, calm responses: professionalism at moments of crises is crucial. K9 partners lovingly and protectively walk at the side of their partners, and regularly save their lives, as well as facilitate daily tasks that might not otherwise be possible.

"I will remain ever silent, ever vigilant, and ever loyal.

"And when our time together is done, and you move on in the world, remember me with kind thoughts and tales.

"For a time we were unbeatable. Nothing passed among us undetected.

"If we should ever meet again on another field I will gladly take up your fight.

"I am a police working dog and together we are **GUARDIANS** of the **NIGHT**." – Unknown

That others might live

Simply one of the best descriptions of nose work – the basis of all scent work – is given by William G Syrotuck in *Scent and the Scenting Dog*: "The point source oriented dog is more characterized by the head up and sniffing the air currents posture. He is seldom ground oriented, and is cognizant that the source may be anywhere above or below ground level. The basis of training is to follow the increasing level of odor intensity until the dog has 'honed in' on the source. This type of animal has the highest discriminatory potential as he must constantly discriminate the pure odor from the surrounding environment, and then determine its point of strongest concentration."

This is the method most search and rescue dogs use, inasmuch as taking in air molecules as fast as possible will enable a quicker find. If that tiny scent molecule is not present, the dog will continue his search, but if it is present he can quickly locate the source.

"Numerous hours of training by these search and rescue dogs and their handlers occur throughout the world every day, and yet no one focuses on these dogs and their handlers.

"So what motivates these people to train themselves and their dogs in rain, snow, and heat of summer?

"In the years I have been associated with this strange group of people, the only answer I can find is: they care. They care about the victim, they care about the family of the victim, and they care about their community."
– Michael W Mitchell: 'Search and Rescue Dogs,' *Dog Sports Magazine*

Volunteer search and rescue teams (SAR), coordinated through local law enforcement, are called in in the event of a lost individual, without regard to weather, terrain, or time of day. Time is of the essence. Preparation for any situation is vital and the ability and willingness to 'drop everything and go' is essential. Dedicated individuals use their time, money and energy to train their canine partners to reunite people with their loved ones.

The five stories in this chapter are representative of the issues facing SAR teams as they respond to call-outs, whenever these are received. Notable comparisons to the canine partners in previous stories are their physical endurance, and the determination that enables them to work hour after hour on the mountains, in the desert or on an avalanche.

Coupled with olfactory skills refocused on the scent they have to locate, and strong communication with their partners, SAR canines actually dictate the flow of a search. Strong physical attributes and spontaneous reactions to environmental hazards are absolutely necessary for these SAR partners, and intelligent disobedience can only be developed and nurtured with the aid of trust and communication. The strength of character and determined attitude that allows the dogs to lead their human partner is absolutely essential when searching a mountain for a lost person.

Trained to locate with the scent they are given, the dogs work tirelessly to find its owner: maybe someone on a mountain, under the snow, in a lake or up a tree. Through training – which uses a verbal command in connection with the scent to initiate the desired search action in the field – these canine partners learn to focus their discriminating noses on a specific scent provided by an article belonging to the lost individual.

On an actual search, the dogs will utilize their olfactory hunting skills and track or air-scent with single-minded determination to locate that specific scent for their human partner. Most of the SAR partners are working breeds which inherit herding instincts, an ability they take very seriously, rounding up and protecting their 'flock'

"Night searching initially involves the use of hasty search techniques. It is difficult to search at night and particularly slow and inefficient to attempt to do a close, thorough search from the start. Hasty techniques allow the handler to gather information about his area – the size, trails, barriers, and terrain features.

"Normally, dog teams work well at night, but if it is a hazardous area with cliffs or old mine shafts, night searching becomes unsafe.

"Most search call-outs seem to come at night. The subject gets lost during the day; friends and relatives look for him, then call in the sheriff. When the subject isn't found by dark, the sheriff expands the search and calls in the dog teams and other searchers. The decision then becomes whether to leave immediately and search the rest of the night or wait until first light. Much depends on the urgency of the situation: whether the subject could survive the night out; the weather, and the dangers of the terrain. Searches for small children and the elderly usually go on all night as these people are at greater risk."
– Marcia Koenig: 'Wilderness Strategy for Dog Handlers'

Her only goal locating the lost, this search and rescue dog's determination drives her on over any terrain or hazard.

"... the search and rescue dog team (if well trained) will do the job of twenty searchers on foot. This is a conservative estimate." – Michael W Mitchell, 'Search and Rescue Dogs,' Dog Sports Magazine

Right: Bart was a hard-headed black Lab – literally. At one water workout he actually broke one of Erica's front teeth with his head. But that's another story ...

with total dedication. This characteristic is integral as they search the mountainside, locate the scent, and run back and forth between the lost person and their partner until the two are reunited.

Searching in the dark for a child is a real-life drama, filled with a level of urgency and emotion that propels every footstep taken by both team members. The seasoned team in the following story knew the search was real simply by the emotion in the air. Erica obviously knew when she received the call-out that this was not a training activity, and there was no doubt that Bart – 95lb (43kg) of muscle and drive, with enthusiasm to spare, and the perfect partner for Erica while she searched the night for a lost child – knew, too, in the following seconds or maybe even simultaneously.

We have discussed trust, heart and 'living tool' in depth, and the following stories highlight the intense communication that exists between partners who have trained many long, hard hours for just this type of emergency.

Erica and Bart

The sun rose and illuminated a perfect footprint

"Bart and I crawled into bed; I closed my eyes and said my nightly prayer. 'Please keep us warm and safe ... and please don't let there be any searches tonight. I am so very tired.'

"Thirty minutes later my pager, which I kept under my pillow, began to vibrate. I grabbed it and walked into the kitchen to return the call. A ten-year-old girl was missing in Carbon County, just south of Price, Utah, and had been since 11am when she had had a fight with her mother. I glanced at the clock: it was now 11:30pm. That was just about right. It seems that once a person goes missing the family searches until dark, and then calls in the local sheriff, whose deputy drives to where the individual was last seen to look around. It always seems to be close to midnight when we get these call-outs.

"I rang the call-out coordinator to advise I would be able to respond to the search, and she told me that Rhonda would also be going with her dog, Diva. I gave Rhonda a quick call and made

arrangements to meet her at a local parking lot so we could make the two-hour drive to the search area together.

"The minute I touched my backpack, Bart was at my side, dancing and leaping with excitement – three foot vertical leaps. He'd make any basketball coach proud! He was ready to go, although I still had to check through my gear and add fresh water to my pack. I left a note for my husband and loaded Bart into the back of my truck.

"We met the local sheriff's deputy at the convenience store and followed him more than a few miles down a dirt road until we arrived at the place the missing girl was last seen. We gathered around the deputy for our initial briefing. Apparently the girl had had a fight with her mother earlier in the day and walked out of the camp, refusing to return when her parents called her. Her parents began to look for her and, when the sun set around six that evening, felt they had to get help.

"This is the part I don't understand. Instead of just one of them driving to get help, they packed up their entire camp, so that even if their daughter had decided to return now that it was getting cold and dark, there was no place for her to return to. It was all packed up in the truck and heading into town.

"The search area ran parallel to a river to the south, which was partially iced over, especially near the banks. There was a dirt road that also ran parallel to the river, and north of the road was a line of bluffs.

"Rhonda and I were working together. Diva and Bart seemed to make a good pair: Bart worked very fast, and Diva worked very slowly and methodically. Our assignment was to work along the dirt road to make sure that the missing girl hadn't crossed the dirt road to the north and headed into the bluffs. Rhonda and I scented our dogs on the scent article and started working down the dirt road. 'Do you want to go to work? Let's go find Sandy.'

"The full moon rose, making it unnecessary to use flashlights for all but the closest of work. The dogs' glow sticks bobbed back and forth as they ranged ahead of us, and we kept in touch by radio with the other teams as they worked along the riverbank. All of the action seemed to be down by the river. Teams were reporting footprints, and one or two areas where the girl had stepped through the ice and into the water itself: not a good sign. Reportedly, she was very lightly dressed in only jeans, a sweater and light canvas sneakers. Not nearly warm enough for the 28 degrees F that the little thermometer on my zipper pull currently showed.

"As Bart and Diva continued to work along the dirt road, it was fairly obvious they just weren't getting any scent. The only places they were showing any interest in was where the tiny washes were flowing from the dirt road and running toward the river. The scent was rising up along the washes. As we crossed each of these washes, we would radio down to folks along the river that we were still getting indications that the girl was following the river, hoping that she hadn't gone into the river.

"Up ahead we could see a dark mass to the left of the dirt road. A body? A bush? Or a rock? Whatever it was, Bart and Diva were incredibly interested in it. We switched on our flashlights to find that both Bart and Diva were literally vacuuming a large rock with their noses: a fairly good indication that Sandy had been sitting there. She wasn't there now – where had she gone?

"We worked throughout the night, grateful for the light of the moon and the glow sticks on our dogs. We could see that they were working; there just hadn't been anything to find in the area we had been assigned to. But that was our job, to clear our area.

"As the false dawn broke, we came upon several of the local search and rescue personnel, sitting in their trucks, getting warmed up. They had been following the progress throughout the night by listening to the radio chatter, and told us that we were coming up to a big wash that would head down to the river. They suggested we cut down through the wash to see if we could find anything that way. Rhonda and I decided to wait and let the dogs rest a few more minutes until the sun began to rise, and then we put our dogs back to work and walked east towards the wash.

"As we reached the bottom of the wash, the sun rose and illuminated a perfect footprint of a very flat sneaker. At the same time that I saw the print, Bart took off, following the footprints. I called in our position to the command center to advise we had a footprint and Bart had taken off: a very good indication it was the scent we were looking for. The center said it would send searchers on four wheelers down the wash from the road toward the river. A few minutes later we heard the searchers say they had found her.

"Bart had run all the way to Sandy, the missing girl, then returned in a classic recall, and

Avalanche training is exhilarating, exhausting, and can be dangerous. And it always separates those who should be on the mountain from those who should not!

we headed back down the wash toward the river. He and Diva had worked very hard all night long and deserved a long drink and a rest. And, of course, a reward for a job well done.

"After the dogs had drunk their fill, and had a short play period, we began hiking back up the wash toward the dirt road. We had several miles to hike before we made it back to the command center. Everyone was there waiting for us as we came in to cross our names off the list. I was also happy to see that the ambulance was still here, sitting with its engine running. The back door was wide open and we could see Sandy sitting on the gurney, cloaked in pre-warmed blankets with her arms already wrapped around Bart's neck. As she hugged him, she smiled up at me and said 'I saw him! I knew you were coming!'

"Sandy was cold, but otherwise unharmed by her adventure."

Avalanche La Salle Mountains, outside Moab, Utah

"We trained each year for avalanche work, although there were not many opportunities to put our training to use: not because there were no avalanches or people caught in them, but because of the short survival times of those who were. Consequently, all of the avalanche searches that

we were called on were for body recoveries, where the victim was already dead, but we were going into a dangerous area where our first priority had to be our own safety.

"One such search was an avalanche recovery on a Thursday night in the LaSalle Mountains, just east of Moab, Utah. The sheriff flew us down to Moab on Friday morning, where a helicopter was waiting to take us to the deposition zone of the avalanche.

"We unloaded our dogs and gear from the helicopter, and covered the dogs' faces as the helicopter took off again. The incident commander met us at the toe of the avalanche. Seven people had skied into this mountain bowl, decided that they probably shouldn't be there and, while turning to leave the area, apparently heard a thunderous 'WOOMP' (the horrifying sound of an avalanche). I don't know if they had time to realize what was happening before they were caught in that wall of snow.

"When the snow stopped moving, one of the survivors found himself totally buried apart from one arm above the quickly settling snow pack, and was able to dig himself out. Glancing around, he noticed a flash of color from a jacket,and quickly dug out a second man. Using their Pieps [sound-emitting sensors] to locate the others, the two men recovered the other five skiers, laid them carefully on the surface of the snow and performed CPR on each: unsuccessfully, as it turned out, despite working until nearly dark, when the pair skied back to the trailhead for the long drive back to town.

"It was close to midnight by the time the two reached the sheriff's office to report the avalanche.

"A massive storm moved in the next morning and, by the time we arrived at the foot of the avalanche, dynamite charges had been dropped to bring down any snow that could produce another avalanche in the area we needed to work, which recovered the victims in 15-18 feet (5-6m) of new snow.

"We began working up from the toe of the slide, and quickly discovered that the snow was so deep and densely packed that no scent seemed to be getting through for the dogs. Changing tactics, we began working our dogs behind the people working the probe lines, allowing the dogs to catch the scent rising up through the snow holes the probes created. The sheriff called into town for longer probe poles, and they wound up welding two 10 foot (3m) poles together. On that first day we recovered two bodies located by Bart and Kallie.

"The second day Bart kept intently working one particular path, starting up near the top and working down twenty yards or so. I called over some probers. Another searcher walked over as we began working behind the probers, and introduced himself as one of the skiers who had been caught in the slide. He pointed up the hill, showing how he was carried down to where we were standing, exactly the same place Bart had been so intently working most of the morning. He explained how he was able to dig himself and the others out. Bart was very happy to see him and did a short recall back and forth between us. 'Look, Mom! Here he is!' Bart's olfactory senses told him that this was the person he had been scenting, in that exact spot, and he was thrilled to know he was no longer under the snow.

"It was Saturday afternoon by the time all five bodies were recovered. Sitting at the debriefing that evening, I was struck by how small and close the community was. A woman caught in the slide was the fiancée of one of the searchers; all of the searchers were friends and relatives of the victims: all somebody's brother or somebody's son. Although, of course, every victim we search for is somebody's brother or son, those who search the mountain with us are not usually directly related. This circle was tight, and raw emotion hung in the air.

"Although we had completed our search for the victims of this avalanche, it seemed our search for a ride home was just beginning. The county sheriffs were always eager to get us to their search site as quickly as possible, but occasionally we were left to find our own way home. And this was one of those occasions ...

"The sheriff told us he would send a Suburban to drive us back to Salt Lake, but when it pulled up to the door of our hotel room, we quickly realized that this wasn't going to work, as the vehicle was from the coroner's office, and was carrying the recovered bodies to Salt Lake for autopsy. The sheriff thought we could squeeze in up-front with the driver, which wouldn't be a problem, but our dogs riding in the back with the bodies certainly was! I was afraid that such prolonged exposure to the scent of dead and decaying bodies would ruin Bart's ability to pick up a scent. It just wasn't worth taking the chance.

"We finally managed to hitch a ride with another searcher who was headed back to the Salt Lake valley. It was another job well done. What a good dog!

"If we are really lucky, each of us will have one very special dog in our lives, and, for me, that dog was Bart. I purchased him from a backyard breeder. Both parents were on site, and they seemed calm enough. I didn't know much, but I knew I wanted a confident dog: not skittish or wary. Bart was just six weeks old when I took him from the litter. He may have been old enough to be weaned, but he was in need of some boundaries. I have come to believe that this is something that a dog can teach to a puppy in a way that may be more difficult for people to convey, which is where his dam and littermates would have come in.

"Our first urban rescue workout helped me understand Bart a bit better. Just before lunch one day, I was feeling extremely frustrated by his behavior: he was so very excited, and would not sit, stay or lie down. All of his basic obedience training seemed to have evaporated; I was almost in tears – of frustration or embarrassment, I'm not sure which.

"We were fortunate to have a special guest with us that day, Dr Ian Dunbar, who noticed my frustration and pulled me aside. He told me that, of all of the dogs working on the rubble pile that day, Bart would be the first he would choose for search and rescue work, as he had the drive that the work required, and would keep working until he was tired, then work some more until the victim was found. And this he did, time and time again.

"At this workout (a long, 8-hour day) Bart was the only dog that did the required three minute bark on the bark-box [a box containing a person that the dog must indicate is there by barking for three minutes] on the first try. He would get so excited about finding his victims in the rubble pile that he would bounce up and down as he barked, causing the entire section of the rubble pile to shift. Although he had the drive to do urban work, I was afraid he might injure someone hiding in the pile with his enthusiasm if the pile shifted too much, so Bart happily returned to wilderness work where he could run to his heart's content.

"As part of our wilderness training we did a lot of tracking work. Part of our certification involved having our volunteer 'victim' lay down a track, a second volunteer following to cover the victim's trail. The test was to see if the dog could correctly track the victim up to the point where the two tracks split, and then follow through to find the right person.

"One day I was fortunate to have my 'victim' head off away from me down an open slope (as opposed to dense terrain, so I could see Bart working). I brought Bart from the truck and showed him the scent article and, In typical fashion, he took off running right away with his nose to the ground. He never did wait for me to give him the command, 'Track!' He knew what his job was, and he just did it.

"I stood on that hillside and watched him work along the track. I could see when he reached the point were the trail split, and he doubled back to alert on the scent article. He then continued on until he reached the right victim. They called on my radio to let me know that Bart was already there. At that point, I headed down the hill to meet him as he came racing back to tell me that he had found his person, and he also showed me the article that he had found. I think that was the first time I realized he really was alerting on the articles. I had never been able to see that before, and always thought that he was just kind of blowing by them in his hurry to get to his victim. Bart led me back to the 'victim:' what a good boy!"
Erica

The foregoing account illustrates the need for a partner with a drive like Bart's, which is the key to success. A mountain search and rescue dog who doesn't let the dark, the depth of the snow or the length of the search slow him down is essential when someone is lost. Bart needed a partner with the skills, patience and love to care for him when he wasn't searching, and Erica has those qualities in abundance, directing all of Bart's working drive into a productive outlet, and patiently nurturing that drive when he wasn't on the mountain. This dynamic worked, and provided a great search and rescue team for eight years.

To assure a quick find, the information Erica radioed in in the first story concerning the location and direction of the footprint enabled other searchers to move quickly to locate Sandy. While Erica radioed the information, Bart continued, pinpointing Sandy and coming back to let Erica know, 'Hurry, Sandy is waiting.' Bart had found Sandy, but his task was not complete until he got Erica to Sandy. So back and forth he would travel, quickly, repeatedly, until he succeeded in uniting the two.

This back and forth action – a 'recall' attributed to herding instincts that requires exceptional communication skills between team members – can be absolutely essential if the individual is hidden from sight or unable to respond to calls from the searchers. Throughout the search Erica and all the other search and rescue personnel had been continuously calling Sandy's name, hoping to hear a response from her. In the event that the aircraft or four-wheelers out in front, acting on the information Bart and Erica had supplied, still couldn't locate Sandy, it was important that Bart continue, to finish and unite Erica with Sandy. This was Bart's 'heart.'

Four-wheelers or small aircraft usually make the 'find' based on the direction given by the dogs, quickly taking the lost one back to base camp for help and care. It is extremely important that everyone on a search works as a team, expediting the 'find' in case of injury or potential health concerns.

However, this successful wilderness recovery prevented Bart from completing his job, and they were apparently returning empty-handed. Fortunately, the ambulance containing Sandy was still there when the partners returned,

allowing Bart to feel his success: Sandy's arms around his neck. Undoubtedly, Bart's trust in Erica and their level of communication enabled him to understand his job had been completed. A quick pretend search of a volunteer victim would have given Bart a positive end to the search (his reward) had Sandy not been at base camp, although Bart would have known the difference: after all, he had searched for her all night. It is always important to even a seasoned canine to feel success at the end of a search, and every effort is made to ensure a positive finish.

Every search is obviously unique, comprised of its own set of environmental conditions. Unforeseen environmental elements and lack of a specific starting point (the track) make searches more conducive to a search dog than a tracking dog, as a search dog can start off with no scent and search until he locates either a ground scent (track) or air scent. He then uses either or both to locate the lost person, preferably forsaking a ground scent to check out the fresher,

"Reward in the field is a must when dogs have worked long hours ..." – Paula Mackay, 'Working for Wildlife,' Bark magazine

faster moving air currents). One search dog alone cannot usually do the job; it takes several and they must be strategically placed.

The need for the trust and communication between partners developed during training exercises intensifies and heightens as each hour passes while searching for a lost child – as in the case of Sandy. Suppressing feelings of foreboding as time goes on, the handler won't quit, and tries hard to prevent negative emotions from affecting the search. Occasionally calling the child's name, trying to prevent the emotional transfer of impending doom to her partner, the search continues, the team remaining as positive as possible to facilitate searching at peak efficiency.

This situation is similar to the emotional struggle that K9 officers experience when deploying their partners in dangerous situations. Shielding a canine partner from emotional angst is virtually impossible, however, so realistic training scenarios and experience working around similar emotions are essential to prepare the dogs for real crises. A mature, seasoned team learns and understands the emotions surrounding

"For scent discrimination training, the scent article is important. It is the item used to let the dog know what to find." – Susan & Larry Bulander, Ready! Training the Search and Rescue Dog

a life-and-death situation, and will continue working effectively under all circumstances. When work ethic and training combine with team bond, an SAR canine assumes an almost fanatical but absolutely instinctive state, their need to complete the job all-consuming.

In the next story, Ashley undoubtedly knew of Margaret's concerns, even before Margaret could verbalize them, but she also knew the search was vital, and that they needed to continue.

Margaret and Ashley
Search is an emergency; search is a mystery

"March 1988: a three-year-old boy missing in the Tonto National Forest, Arizona initiated the second largest search in the history of Arizona, second only to a criminal manhunt.

"A large family group was staying at a cabin in the forest, and everyone was having fun. Randy's mom thought he was with dad; Dad thought he was with mom, when Randy and a young cousin wandered off. The cousin came back but was too young to say what had happened. Where was Randy?

"When Rocky Mountain Rescue Dogs, Inc[5] was called, Randy had been missing two days and it had snowed. Randy had never seen snow before. Six dog teams responded to Payson, Arizona by small plane, and were taken to the mountains by helicopter, where everyone searched into the night. We slept for a few hours and then went back out again in the morning.

"Ashley and I were dropped off at a gravel pit area where three drainages came together at the far side. As we started out Ashley picked up the scent in the south drainage, but the wind changed and she lost it. We worked our area, moving up the mountainside that was thick with trees and brush. Ashley was working only a short distance in front of me, much closer than usual, walking very purposefully, and kept looking at me over her shoulder. It was the strangest thing I had ever seen, but this is what an alert is, a change in behavior.

"Ashley climbed out the steep side of the drainage onto the hillside, and I had to scramble

on all-fours to follow her. She circled back downhill and jumped over a large log. She had found Randy.

"Ashley put her head down and sniffed the boy. The stub of her tail went wag-wag slowly. The forest was silent. The boy was curled on his side, snow lay around him, and his jeans were down a few inches in back so I could see the action figures on his underpants. His blond hair was bright in the early morning sun, and his blue eyes stared straight ahead.

"We sat down hard, drained of energy, even though we had only been working for an hour-and-a-half. I put my coat over Randy just to be able to do something for him. This was our first dead person and he was so small. This was why Ashley had stayed close to me rather than running ahead.

"I called over the radio that we had found Randy. It seemed like it took forever for deputies to arrive, but in reality it wasn't long at all. The body bag they put him in was huge for his three-year-old frame.

"Somehow, Ashley and I made it off the mountain to the truck that would take us to the airport. Ashley always usually jumped immediately into the back of a truck when I told her to kennel, but this time she couldn't do it. She put her front feet on the tailgate and had to have a boost to get up. We were taken to the airport, flew to SLC, drove home, made it into the house, then both collapsed on the living room floor.

"It seemed like that little spot of sadness should have taken over the whole world but it went on like nothing had happened.

"Ashley was my Bouvier des Flandres girl dog, my fairytale 'Best in the Land' dog. I didn't know anything about Bouviers, but the ad in the paper said the breed was quiet inside, lively outside, and non-shedding, which sounded perfect. A co-worker who lived by herself got a dog for protection after someone broke into her house. I lived alone and thought maybe I should get a dog as a deterrent rather than a response.

"I went to the address listed in the paper to check out the pups, just to look. The pups were eight weeks old, and looked very fluffy and all

"People in search and rescue for years claim their dogs could remember from year to year the scent of specific individuals (names are used when searching), when re-sent to search an area for a long-lost person. Smell is a long-distance and long-lasting sense. It is more persistent and far less time-dependent than either sight or sound. Odours linger, providing information after the event and offering hints of things yet to come ..."
– Lyall Watson, *Jacobson's Organ*

"I called over the radio that Ashley and I had found Randy." – Margaret

tummy. Ashley crawled into my lap and into my heart.

"I was reading the paper one morning as I spread it on the kitchen floor while paper-training Ashley, when an article about Rocky Mountain Rescue Dogs that included a couple of quotes from guys I knew from ski patrolling years ago caught my attention. It sounded like an interesting thing to do with a dog.

"While waiting for my application to be considered I read the recommended search training books and did some practice problems with my dog. For example, when raking leaves I hid toys and articles in the piles, which Ashley

"We have all been touched by the stories of a family being reunited with a loved one, either a person missing as a result of natural disaster, or the victim of senseless crimes by people who feel the need to hurt others.

"Closure with the find of a loved one is needed and, in all cases, this is the job of a search dog team."
- Michael W Mitchell. 'Search and Rescue Dogs' *Dog Sports Magazine*

would find and then hide for me to find. We did simple search problems when I could get friends or family to help us.

"The first group workout we attended was an avalanche workout at Powder Mountain. Holes were dug, victims buried to simulate an avalanche, and the area mucked up. The dogs then entered the area to work the problem. It was amazing! I couldn't believe what they could do; I couldn't believe what Ashley did!

"Ashley had long, gray brindle hair, a powerful chest and thighs, and a full beard and mane. At first others couldn't see her expressions, but her big brown eyes, pink tongue smile, pointy, stand-up ears that caught every sound, and stubby expressive tail, Ashley could convey it all. When she hit a hot scent and took off on a track, her beard would blow back in the wind. She would sit at the top of a ridge and pick up all the scents around with that big nose of hers.

"She normally didn't care about other dogs or other people (unless they had food), and had no patience for jogging, though was happy to hike forever. When the pager went off she was ready to go, working in the heat of a desert day or the cold of a winter blizzard night. She travelled in helicopters of all sizes – snowmobiles, four-wheelers, and was hot-loaded into a C130 – no questions asked. She worked in all the western states and Venezuela, from the headwaters of the Kern Kawia Rivers to the border of Venezuela and Columbia. In Merida, Venezuela, the sister of the girl we were looking for said, 'Ever since you brought that dog to this country the people haven't stopped petting her.'

"At Echo Reservoir, searching for a drowning victim, Ashley and I were sent on a Park Service boat. I was at the back and Ashley was in the front of the small craft. The Ranger asked me how I knew when she had the scent she was looking for, just as Ashley ran to me and grabbed the scent article sack out of my hand. 'That's how,' I told him. An alert is a change in behavior, and this time it was very clear. Rusty was working along the dam and got the find, but Ashley knew where the victim was."
Margaret

Extensive training in dangerous environments enables these unique teams to go anywhere to help anyone in trouble.

Extensive training in dangerous environments enables these unique teams to deploy their skills anywhere to help locate those in trouble, and the next three stories are examples of that type of training.

The emotional rollercoaster that volunteers involved in search and rescue experience strengthens resolve, and develops strong, determined personalities. These SAR volunteers are obstinate, obsessed people who get the job done, regardless of who or what gets in the way, possessing very similar character traits to those of their canine partners. Emotional and physical strength, olfactory prowess, and determined, intelligent disobedience – whatever it takes to find the lost person – is exactly what these teams give, but the emotional cost to both partners can be huge, requiring a unique strength of character.

All members of the search and rescue team share the family's grief: their personal investment in a search is real, and they carry those emotions for a lifetime.

After Ashley died, a second Bouvier named Diamond walked with Margaret for many years until her recent death. Notable from Diamond's many searches was that she located a snow-covered airplane in the western desert of Utah. For over 20 years Margaret's work with Ashley and Diamond exemplified the unity and strength that is possible when a canine team reaches that extraordinary level of oneness to become partners.

What unique skills did Ashley possess? Why did she keep working through the snow, climbing over the deadfall, ultimately locating the lost child, only then to react quietly, subdued and seemingly depressed, after finding a child who had died? Being a Bouvier des Flanders, Ashley came from a strong working background. Incredibly stubborn, physically strong, but intuitively sensitive to her handler and the emotions in her environment, Ashley was born to work. Fortunately, Ashley found herself walking at the side of a high-energy partner, who carefully, lovingly taught her the hows of team searching. Margaret's training abilities refocused Ashley's innate skills, and enabled communication through body language, ultimately allowing these two to work together as a team. A dog's tracking skills are legendary, so man need only work with a canine, connecting vocal commands with actions in the field. Given the command to 'find,' Ashley combined tracking and air-scenting skills, and with a scent article provided by Command, Ashley found that one scent on the mountain that belonged to Randy. Margaret correctly read Ashley's body language and followed.

Training doesn't prepare anyone for the emotions experienced on a real search. But when reasoning and understanding conquer the fear of that dark night, the team begins working as one.

The study of body language is fairly complex concerning the canine species. Because our partners don't actually verbalize their intent, it can be confusing to know exactly what they are saying. Obviously, animals don't speak; at least not our language. However, relocated anywhere,

> **"No dog handler has come of age until he is out there in the middle of the night stumbling around in the mud, the rocks, the rain, looking for a little girl who is going to die if his dog doesn't find her. Or he is creeping around, gun out, searching for a murder suspect who is armed and ready to shoot him or the dog, whoever makes the first mistake.**
>
> **"The fear and the understanding come at the same time. After that, the professional dog handler works to read his dog. The key to success is the power of observation and timing and common sense. Read your dog. Effective communication with your animal is everything." – Sandra Bryson, Search Dog Training**

without benefit of language books, a guide or interpreter, our canine partners would obviously do just fine – an ability that most of us will never develop.

Canine language is based on inherent senses that cross all geographic borders: in Africa, England, China, and the United States, canine body language is the same. Man is able to learn and understand his partner's subtle body cues, but trust in what it says doesn't happen overnight. In the middle of a very dark night, searching for two small girls, surrounded by dense mountain deadfall and rushing water, thoughts of the fear and dangers affecting the girls bring home just how essential it is to read your dog and to make the right response.

As Susan Bulander, co-author of the great SAR training guide *Ready! Training the Search and Rescue Dog*, puts it "… the tone of your voice is critical. With body language, tone makes up the primary means you use to communicate with your dog. You must make your tone of voice directional, and no-nonsense, rather than questioning, dictatorial, hysterical, and loud.

"A dog has an acute sense of hearing. A lack of response is not because the dog does not hear you; it is because he chooses not to listen to you. Do not yell at your dog. Speak in a soft-to-normal volume."

On one of my first searches – looking for those two small girls – the emotions in that night air could have been cut with a knife, and knowing and trusting the body language of Katie, my SAR partner, was one of the few things that kept me going. A fisherman found the girls early the next morning: it was a very good morning.

The following story highlights the emotional challenges a new team can experience when the handler forgets to trust (even for a few minutes) in the communication skills of her partner.

Judy and Frita
I knew the moment I met her I would never leave her side, nor she mine

"I shivered as I stared at the brilliantly lit, star-filled sky. The vastness of the Uinta Mountains was even more evident at night, and the cold seeped into my many layers of clothing. How long could an elderly woman dressed for a warm, fall day hike survive in the bitter cold of night? All I knew for certain was we had to find her quickly.

"Frita and I were a level II search dog team with Rocky Mountain Rescue Dogs. Our

These two search teams are prepared for a long, cold search in extremely challenging weather and terrain.

group had been called to assist Summit County Search and Rescue to find a woman who had failed to return to her car after a day of looking for mushrooms. As a level II team, Frita and I were assigned an area near a veteran team consisting of Margaret Gregory and Ashley.

"I was anxious to begin; I didn't want the woman's family to see me shiver from the cold. I knew we needed to do something quickly, and was not yet accustomed to the planning required prior to sending teams into the wilderness. As Margaret left us in our assigned area, I felt a rush of adrenalin, warmth and optimism. I had a great dog; we were assigned an area of high probability. People had survived far worse: we would find this woman quickly and get her to the loving embrace of her family and a warm fire.

"Even better, Frita seemed to be on to a scent! My heart raced as Frita lifted her nose and worked what must have been a scent cone. As she crested a ridge, she took off with a bound, and I ran to keep pace with her. She ran back with a perfect recall, and took me directly to Margaret and Ashley. My heart sank, but I thanked her for showing me Margaret, and asked her to go back to work, which she dutifully did.

"Once back in our assigned area, I watched Frita's every move. She wandered, sniffed, chased a chipmunk or two, did everything but try to find the person I so desperately wanted to help. I tried being patient – I knew I had a very good search dog – and did my best not to lead her, pressure her, talk too much … but I really needed to find our missing woman! As my frustration grew, Frita seemed to sense that she should be working. She put her nose in the air and got immediately on task.

"Once again my heart began to race as I could see Frita was on to something. I marked her alerts, but mostly watched the beauty of my dog at work. After a half-mile or so, Frita took off and came flying back with a textbook recall. I asked her to 'show me,' and with pride, she led me back to Margaret and Ashley. How could this be happening?

"Years previously I had read an article in the newspaper about Rocky Mountain Rescue Dogs, and, before even reaching the end of the article, I knew this was something I wanted to be a part of. My life already consisted of trail running, hiking, backpacking and adventure sports, every moment of it spent with a dog. It was a perfect blend of service and living my passion. At the time, however, my canine companion, Ginny, was 12 years old, too old to search, and I did not think it fair that I leave her in her twilight years to go play with another dog. Instead, I spent time learning the skills I might need for search and rescue, volunteered as a 'victim' for search dog teams, and knew my time to join them would come.

"At the age 14, Ginny suffered a stroke, and I held her in my arms and watched her pass silently to the heaven that I know exists for dogs. Through my tears, I managed to tell the veterinarian my dream of raising a dog for search and rescue. I wanted to search with a German Shepherd, but knew nothing about purebred dogs. She asked me to call her when I was ready. I knew I would never be ready – replacing a beloved dog is not possible – so I said I was ready then.

"She took me into her office to show me a picture of a beautiful, young, skinny Shepherd, with brown eyes that looked as if they could see into your soul. Gale, my veterinarian, bred German Shepherds! Frita had recently been returned to her as a 'bad' dog, and Gale offered to give her to me if I promised Frita a life of companionship and search work.

"A few days later I went to meet Frita, and she came home with me for a trial period, although I knew the moment I met her I would never leave her side, nor she mine. We traveled across the United States and Canada; we hiked, skied, played hide and seek, took obedience classes, agility classes, and learned the basics of search work. Frita was a playful but serious dog. She wanted to please me more than anything else, and I could not have asked for a more perfect companion. I was definitely the weak link in the team, taking longer to learn how to read a map and compass than she did to solve the most difficult of search problems.

"So what was going on now? At a time

when I most needed her to show her skills, Frita was goofing off! How many times was she going to take me to Margaret and Ashley while a woman was freezing to death in the wilderness? Margaret, sensing my frustration, reassured me, explaining that sometimes the best way to find a person is to eliminate all of the places they were not: the person we were searching for was clearly not in the area assigned to us. We returned to base camp to report that our areas had been covered. Then, I trusted Margaret more than my dog, although, over the years, I would come to trust them equally.

"Each team returned to base camp to report the probability of the missing person being in their area. After reporting, Margaret – who was acting as our search commander – met with the sheriff. It was decided that I would join Margaret and Lane to search an area that Lane's dog, King, had shown interest in. We set off for a particular area where we would spread out and begin searching. The dogs followed, waiting for the command for their favorite game: 'go find!'

"As we neared the designated area, all three dogs took off as if chasing a deer. I looked at my dog in frustration – she had never chased wildlife – although Margaret and Lane watched a little more closely: their experience had taught them to know and trust their dogs. As the dogs ran back to us, I could see Margaret's smile, and followed her gaze. Off in the distance was a person; could it be the woman we were looking for? Frita caught my eye, and ran back to the figure in the distance. It was our missing person, and Frita knew it!

"The woman was cold, suffering from frostbite, and very ready to have her ordeal end. She had survived by staying positive and on the move throughout the freezing night. At the time, however, I'm not certain who was more excited, the 'victim' when she saw the dogs, or me when I saw the pride in my Frita's eyes.

"I would see that look many more times during our search and rescue career. Frita was a great search dog, and seemed to take tremendous pride in her abilities. I learned to trust her, and to appreciate that great teams develop as people learn to read what the dogs are telling them.

I would not trade the experiences I had as a member of Rocky Mountain Rescue Dogs for anything, and regard those I shared that time with as family. But the greatest gift of all was the relationship I was able to share with the best dog in the world."

Judy

My first field experience, in SAR training, was following Judy and Frita on a very steep mountain. Depends on your point of view of what steep is, of course, but I remember thinking I couldn't go one more step! This was just a training exercise: why push, what was the rush?

Reflecting on a long, successful job, search and rescue partners, Judy and Frita, share the moment

But Frita went straight up and Judy followed, because she knew that Frita was following the scent, and her responsibility at that point was to support Frita. I was yet to learn that, in SAR, as in police work, a training scenario that properly simulates reality is key. Adrenalin and emotions should run high, and unite team members in an objective, nurturing and developing trust and communication: essential factors in a real search. Training should also test the team's physical limits.

For a team to be of genuine use, not only is a properly trained canine 'nose' and sound communication between team members essential, but both should be capable of handling the rigors of a mountain, a desert, an avalanche field – or whatever physical barriers come between the team and search success. Training enables an understanding of capabilities, and allows the human team member to know exactly where he or she is proficient and what their limitations are.

Most of our canine partners become different creatures in the field; they are in charge. Filled with self-confidence and determination, they expect their partner to trust them, to follow them, to know that their nose knows. They also sense our pride in accomplishment when they succeed, and our pain in defeat.

You've read firsthand accounts of exceptional actions driven by training, and that extra – the canine 'heart' that steps up, takes over, gets done what needs doing, regardless of training or previous experience. When our partner's ability to learn is focused for work at our sides, he responds with the absolute knowledge and expertise necessary to accomplish trained tasks.

Self-confidence also promotes intelligent disobedience, strengthening a personality that empowers the canine hunt drive. Now, combine instincts that sense the atmosphere of an uncertain situation, and our partners will provide whatever action the situation requires. All searches are filled with the unknown; training can only provide for some potential scenarios, and our partners fill the gaps with their innate senses and instinctive intelligence. Somehow they know,

and find whatever extra is needed to get the job done.

All of the people in all of the stories in this book benefited daily from these partnerships, and the unique intelligence and insight a dog brought into their lives, and into the search field, nurturing that special bond and connection.

In 'Wilderness Strategy for Dog Handlers,' Marcia Koenig gives great advice for canine search teams:

• Searching with dogs requires an awareness of wind and scent and how to best utilize them
• Know what the wind will do
• Do what you can to take advantage of the wind. The highest percentage of coverage comes with letting the wind bring the scent to the dog
• Non-thorough searching (hasty search) gets the handler into the area quickly to see what it's like, and provides information to the operational leader to aid in the search planning. It gets the SAR team into detection range of the subject – either with the handler's voice or the dog's nose. Hastily searched areas must be mapped as they will contain holes in coverage that may need to be searched later
• On a search, the decision on how to search various areas depends on what the sheriff wants and on what other resources are available to him
• However, hasty search techniques are necessary for subjects who are likely to be moving out, such as hikers and hunters. And more people are found from opening up search patterns than from staying with a tight pattern
• With a non-thorough technique you take a chance that you will miss a subject on this pass, but you greatly increase the chance of finding the subject alive. It is easier traveling up high where you can see, yell and hear
• The skills of thorough and non-thorough searching, terrain searching, and night searching are only developed through experience

Jodi and Winnie
Winnie and I had seen enough
"I really never wanted a dog … that's what I thought. I had had them in the past, and I wasn't

any good with them. I would wind up giving them away, or letting them get hurt or something worse. I had learned to shut down my emotions early in my life because I always had to leave my animals, or they would leave me.

"All I said was maybe I could think about getting a dog, and with that we were off. My close friend Judy, a Rocky Mountain Search and Rescue member, and the one responsible for dragging me to all of the training there, had scoped out possible breeds, and already had some located. We left a University of Utah against the University of New Mexico football game to head south to Draper.

"It was almost like a farm within the city – many dogs, cats, horses. I saw a bunch of puppies and I went to sit down in the middle of them. Some stayed, some left, but one followed

me when I left. I bent down and picked her up and looked in her eyes … Hello Winnie. Only I didn't know she was Winnie yet, of course: that wasn't until I had paid the $20 and put her on my lap. We were driving home when I first called her Whoopi, except we had a friend whose dog was already using that name, so out came Winnie. It was close enough and she responded, so there she was.

"I had no intention of joining a Search and Rescue group. I was initially at training sessions because they were always looking for someone to be the pretend victim: hiding in trees, ditches, tall grass, behind logs and rock – anywhere that would present a challenge for the 'working' dogs.

"My dog, Winnie, usually stayed at home, and I don't really remember how I got started taking her to the sessions, but once I did she loved to find things, just like the 'real' dogs.

Heads up – on high alert and on the run – these two determined search and rescue dogs are taking a direct line to the scent of the lost individual.

Winnie's agility proves that in tough terrain her size and breed are a bonus. But for now this little Border Collie – pictured above as a puppy with Jodi – rests in the shade behind a big German Shepherd, waiting for her next assignment.

Winnie probably wanted to be a search dog long before I thought about it.

"She made great progress and seemed to love everyone in the group – both two- and four-legged types – and they seemed to like her, so I thought Search and Rescue might be fun. Winnie would love the workouts: climbing, rappelling, rafting … it didn't matter what it was, both of us were having fun. We were called on our first search … both nervous, wondering 'What are we doing?' Winnie would take control and I would follow and, as long as I remembered who was in charge (and it wasn't me), things worked out.

"Things went pretty much as I thought they should, and then we had our first 'find:' a terribly distraught young man who had a mental illness and had decided to end his life. Thinking back, I think Winnie found him right away, but allowed me to take her away from the scene. We continued most of the day searching beautiful country only to return to where we were first dropped. Margaret's wisdom convinced the group that we should begin again, as she had seen signals from the dogs indicating that something was there.

Finding nothing but stillness and calm the first time, Winnie and I started again, and this time she led me directly to the young man's body, hidden in a tree.

"More searches, more bodies, which neither of us had expected. Although we never had another official find, we were beginning to think that this was not what we had bargained for, and subsequently left the group for a while.

"On rejoining (though I'm really not sure why we did), we found that the people had changed; dogs had come and gone; policies were different, and everyone had a cell phone, so no longer any need to search for those who wanted to be found. Those who didn't want to be found – alive, anyway – were still there, but Winnie and I had seen enough.

"Thinking back on some of the best and worst memories with Search and Rescue, I am certainly very glad that I decided to get a dog, and that Winnie shared her life with me. I met some wonderful people who have come to mean a great deal to me, and for that I will be forever thankful."
Jodi

This type of work can be exhausting, frustrating, and desperately disheartening, demanding every ounce of your dedication and emotional strength as, hour after hour, you call the name of the lost one, and then listen for a response. Jodi's story paints a vivid picture of the pain of a Search and Rescue handler who saw too much, too soon: images forever seared in her heart and mind.

Statistics indicate that most canine Search and Rescue personnel work an average of five years, usually the working life of their first canine partner. Considering the emotional trauma of every search, those five years could seem like an eternity, but when their pager goes off, the team will be found on the mountain, partners attempting to locate the lost and reunite families.

On my very first search with my partner, Katie, I remember wondering the same thing as Jodi: "What are we doing here?" In most cases the canine part of the team is thinking precisely the opposite: she knows what she is doing there, and if her training was successful, and she sees the result of her nose work, it becomes almost impossible to keep her home once the pager goes off.

Shirley Hammond of *Dog Sports Magazine* discusses some of the finer points of keeping a dog motivated:

"There are several things involved. One is that dogs need to be trained that searching is a game, and you need to keep it a game. And a game has to be fun. It isn't that you're not going to put time in and work the dog hard, but the dog has to get a fair wage for doing that work. And each dog has its own gauge of what a fair wage is.

"If you work for a company and it demands a certain amount of work from you, and then, at the end of that period of time, says, 'Well, that was good, see you next year,' and that's all the response you get and practically no paycheck, you're going to think, 'I don't know if I'm going to do this work any more for this person.'

"Whatever the paycheck for the dog is – food, a favorite game, a romp where you just roll around the grass and play – the dog should choose the reward system that is the best thing in the world for that dog. Dogs need to be appreciated, and for a dog that really works, there must be something special, a payoff, for that dog to continue to do that work."

On my very first real search, I was solo, without my canine partner, as, apparently, I wasn't ready to work with my dog, although I thought I had learned my skills while my partner was passing one proficiency test after another.

First, I left my water in my car. And second, when asked to give directions I replied "Next to the big tree," on a mountain full of trees. I didn't use my compass or GPS, but told the entire search party this! Not funny then, and still embarrassing eighteen years later, but I learned a lot that day. Leaving my partner home seemed outrageous that morning, but before the day was over, I understood why. A real search creates a different level of anticipation and my anxiety took over and threw out any semblance of intelligence I possessed.

We had been training for eight months for this day, and now it was here. Probably the most important lesson I learned was to slow down, think, be totally prepared so that deliberate, rational thought would motivate each and every action in the field. Erratic, unplanned actions cause everyone problems. Clearly, that was the last time I ever left my water in the car, and never again was I unprepared. Jim, one of my SAR instructors, did not share his water with me that morning, but did laugh when I gave my directions. I still consider him one of my best instructors, and the following story will explain why.

Jim and Rusty
Understanding beyond search work and part of everyday life

"We have always known that there is a communication link between man and dog, who have worked in partnerships for hundreds of years. As a person who has had long relationships with various dogs in my lifetime, I wasn't aware of how deep this connection could be, but in 1990 I began training my one-year-old Golden Retriever, Rusty, with the Search and

While others were afraid to go over the edge, Rusty loved to rappel. He proved fearless: a unique character trait which made him invaluable in dangerous terrain such as this.

period, we tested and qualified to participate on searches.

"Shortly after, we were called on our first search, which involved looking for a three-year-old boy who had been missing in southern Arizona. We left Salt Lake City, Utah, and arrived at the Command Post at dark. After being briefed, we were taken to our search areas and left. Being out in the dark, searching for a missing three-year-old boy with my dog, really emphasized the importance of being able to understand what my dog was or was not telling me. Would Rusty have an 'alert' that I would miss? Would a three-year-old not be found because I couldn't effectively communicate with my dog?

"As a new handler, I was given search areas of lower probability, but this still didn't ease the pressure. Rusty and I did have some alerts in a wash that helped to narrow down the search area, and, after being missing for three days, happily, the young boy was found alive by another dog team.

"Via continuous training over the years, Rusty and I deepened our level of communication until we could read each other almost subconsciously, and I felt more confident on every search we went on that we were clearing our area effectively.

"We had a call out for a missing elk hunter in northeastern Utah. The area was very mountainous, and bordered a 1500 foot deep canyon. While searching areas with the County Search and Rescue teams, I was asked what my dog was 'saying,' and was able to answer that he was alerting on animals, or other hunters or searchers in the area, but that I was confident he was not alerting on our missing hunter. We had been given articles of clothing that had only our missing hunter's scent on them, and I knew Rusty would tell me when we hit that particular scent.

"Rusty finally gave an alert that I knew was from our missing hunter, telling me that the scent was coming from down in the deep canyon. I called over other dog teams and they were able to confirm Rusty's original alert. Later the next day, the body of the missing hunter was found in the bottom of the canyon. He had chased an elk

Rescue group Rocky Mountain Rescue Dogs, and, over the next ten years, discovered that it was much higher than I thought.

"As a new team, the first thing that Rusty and I worked on was building that communication link, by setting up situations where I knew where our 'victim' was, and learning how to read Rusty as he worked to find him. Over a six month period we strengthened the communication bond between us, and, at the end of this initial training

"At present, there are over 150 air-scenting search dog units around the country from Alaska to Georgia, and from Maine to California. New units are continually being formed. While specific training methods and operating procedures may vary from unit to unit, the basic concept of searching with air-scenting dogs is quite uniform (based on the pioneering work of Bill Syrotuck). Such uniformity enables SAR-responsible agencies to know what to expect when they request search dogs, and to know how to best deploy them in the field. It also enables teams from different units to work together on large-scale searches.

"Handlers work their dogs downwind of the section assigned to them, or cover the area in a way that provides dogs with the best scenting coverage. Handlers map the area they have covered and report their POD (probability of detection) to the plans section or operations leader upon completing their assignments." – National Association for Search and Rescue (nasar.org): SAR Dog Fact Sheet[6]

Directing Rusty with touch, voice inflection and hand signals for a FEMA (Federal Emergency Management Agency) test. Jim indicates the exact direction Rusty is to take to reach a simulated disaster.

Rusty was able to filter out the various animal and human scents on the mountain, and help pinpoint the scent of the missing hunter.

"Not all scents are easy for a dog to pick up, as numerous factors – such as how fresh the scent is, wind conditions, how dry the air is, and where the scent is coming from – come into play. Scent from a live person, with a steady, light wind in perfect terrain provokes a much stronger alert from Rusty, such as a change in direction, ears perking, increased intensity in tracking, and tail wagging. Scent coming from deep in a compressed snow pack after an avalanche, or from a body in water where currents will diffuse it, might only cause Rusty to twitch his nose as he catches just a little of it. I had to learn all these signs in order to figure out what Rusty is telling me, deciding then whether it is a valid alert and something we should check out, or if he is just sniffing the scenery. It is also extremely important for me to be able to tell Rusty things when he was still in sight but out of hearing range, via hand signals and body language.

"Over the course of our ten-year career in Search and Rescue, Rusty and I participated in hundreds of searches, looking for lost hunters, missing children, misplaced Boy Scouts, skiers caught in avalanches, drowning and disaster victims. We searched through all types of terrain, from high mountain peaks, and steep brushy or rocky slopes to deserts and urban sites, and we searched in all kinds of weather from bitter cold and snow, to hot and dry.

down into the canyon, couldn't get back out, and died from a pre-existing medical condition before the search for him had even begun. Because of the communication bond between Rusty and I,

"Over the years, Rusty and I developed a deeper understanding of each other than I have ever had with any of my other dogs, which went beyond search work and was a part of our everyday life. It was an indescribable joy to be so in tune with him and work toward a common goal."
Jim

Fide canem – Latin for 'trust your dog' – is the creed of canine SAR organizations, and is essential on a mountain search in the dark as it can mean the difference between life and death. When trust and communication are built on that strong bond, this enables the dog to focus above his natural hunt instincts (hunting man, not food). Like detection specialists finding illegal and

"In the last analysis, intelligence in animals may not be so much a question of mental ability as of communication, the establishing of mutual interests and mutual understanding." – Patrick Lawson, *More Than Courage: Real Life Stories of Horses and Dogs, and People Who Have Loved them*

dangerous contraband, and the K9 holding tight to a felon, SAR canines utilize survival instincts to bring the lost home.

Note: All of the names of the victims have been changed or written out to protect the families and the memories of their loved ones.

Vital to the safety and peace of mind of the blind or partially-sighted is the sure knowledge that wherever they are led they will not be in danger. Independence and safe mobility can be only partially provided by a white stick, which, whilst a great tool, requires slow, deliberate movement, and can even be a social barrier in some cases.

A tool is usually an inanimate object, but one type of 'tool' allows safe movement at a faster pace while maintaining independence, simultaneously eliminating the barrier created by a cane, and that is a dog – known as a Seeing-Eye Dog or Guide Dog. Pack instincts – similar to their hunt and protect instincts – allow them to guide those without sight. Intelligent enough to take into account distractions and react accordingly, in this context the canine partner becomes an indispensable living tool.

That canine heart, discussed for decades in fables and legends, can seem elusive – difficult to describe with words – but more deeply develops through bonding, and the confidence of the dog to say 'No' when a requested movement or action is not safe or wise.

The following stories encapsulate the essence of this amazing inter-species relationship, revealing a unique synergy. Guide Dog teams develop a symbiotic partnership wherein both parties benefit: the blind are able to live and function more naturally, accomplishing basic, daily tasks which those with sight take for granted, whilst their canine partners get to do what they were born to do – work – at the same time leading, nurturing, protecting, and loving their partners.

Brad and Tommy
There are no words to describe that type of devotion, that type of connection, and that type of love!
"I had been waiting three days now and I still didn't have a dog. I was ready for this before I flew to California, and now the wait was excruciating.

"For the first five months of being blind, almost every moment was filled with excitement and preparation for the arrival of our first child. As my wife and I eagerly made the necessary

arrangements, I didn't even take the time to start any rehabilitation or services; it just wasn't a priority during that time. Shortly after the arrival of our daughter, however, I started rehabilitation. In the state of Utah, rehabilitation is both physical training and adjustment training, and I learned cane mobility and some Braille. Just being around other blind people and learning how they do things was a large part of adjusting to a new lifestyle.

"As a very young, newly-sightless person, becoming comfortable with the slow pace essential for safety was beyond difficult. Walking with a cane requires a slow, cautious gait, and becoming fairly sedentary, unable to walk at a 'let's go' confident pace, can be a physical and psychological challenge. Restricting physical movement for safety reasons is, obviously, logical, but I was too young to accept restricted, confining, inhibited movement, and could not – would not – allow my blindness to take my mobility, too, possibly causing depression that could affect my whole life. I was determined that my blindness would not make any other changes in my life, in my wife's life, or the life of our new daughter.

"I had been using a cane for about a year when a good friend proposed a different option: he handed me an application form for a Guide Dog. Before my blindness I witnessed how a particular Guide Dog had enabled independence and mobility for his partner, and remembered how simple, basic movements seemed effortless at the side of that Guide Dog. My whole family adjusted as we began preparing for our first Guide Dog.

"First, though, I needed to excel in cane mobility before moving on to a dog. I wanted – no, needed – to be able to go out, and I needed to maintain my independence. But the cane came first, and learning good orientation skills with it is essential to working with a Guide Dog, and had been my focus for some time. So, I was ready. After a successful interview concerning my needs and abilities, my application was filled out and I was off to California.

"But three days! True, they had to assess my needs, my personality, and mostly my pace to

Right: The importance of selecting a partner with a complementary gait became apparent on Brad's very first walk.

ensure a good match, but come on! I had carefully made the decision to become a Guide Dog partner, and taken the necessary time and steps for preparation, because if there was one thing I absolutely didn't want it was to be confined to my immediate surroundings.

"Finally, 'Dog Day' arrived and I got my hands on that leather harness with Tommy, a real dog, at the other end. I'd been told it would be like lassoing a jet airplane, and that was about right, as Tommy almost pulled me out of my shoes the first time I took that harness. But holding on to that leather harness, walking with Tommy, I knew I would be able to walk without my cane; a brisk walk, if I wanted, and I would be okay!

"Things had moved in slow motion that first long year; it was all a blur: blindness, a wedding, a new baby daughter, physical and adjustment training with rehabilitative services, orientation work with a cane – a year of life-altering events. What a time! And now Tommy was at the other end of his leather harness which I held. Just yesterday that harness had held my instructor – pretending to be a dog – on a 'Juno walk,' checking my pace and balance, discovering the physical issues each person brings to the impending partnership.

"This last step helps the instructors select a good field match, and, for me, that was Tommy: a large, strong Golden Retriever, 26 inches tall and weighing in at 80lb (36kg). Tommy was full of drive and initiative, and I was twenty-four years old and ready: we were a good match. And we would become great partners.

"The next four weeks, 28 quick days, were spent learning a new way of life. What a real thrill for me; I had only been blind around a year-and-a-half; much of that time without independent mobility, not able to go where I wanted, when I wanted to, making each day seem like an eternity. Once I got Tommy, memories of that settling-in, becoming safely blind, those sedentary days, quickly faded.

"However, there was a lot of work ahead before Tommy and I reached a comfortable pace, and not everything was smooth or idyllic. We began working in a residential area, learning

what it's like to operate as a team, building up to business areas, and gradually all types of obstacles and environments: sidewalks, different pathways, inside and outside of businesses, busier street areas, and eventually downtown San Francisco. The school tries to provide scenarios similar to that of your home base; you train on BART [Bay Area Rapid Transit] buses, all types of public transportation, customizing for the individual needs of each new team.

"Most ready-to work Guide Dogs are around two years old, having spent the first year, year-and-a-half of their lives with their puppy raiser for socialization, and then three to six months at the training center. The time at the center is where they learn to lead, to guide someone who's blind, and there are two phases of training. The first is the 4-H socialization and, within that process, any of the dogs can wash out and make a career change: distractions, sensitivity to gunshots, cat chases, car backfiring, activity that might distract or make questionable working situations are grounds for a career change. The guidelines are very strict, requiring exposure to virtually any and every external stimuli that might be encountered.

"Since there is no way of knowing where the dogs will ultimately end up, a wide variety of scenarios – from crowded intersections in downtown San Francisco, to the Podunk, Kansas hayfields – are introduced to each potential guide. This type of exposure – apparently excessive – de-sensitizes a sound dog to most external things. This is also when any emotional insecurities come to light which would make being a Guide Dog not the right career choice.

"With a ratio of one trainer for every four teams, the pace at the center is fast and furious, and training occurs both morning and evening. The canine gait is pretty much set and individual like our own, but it can be slowed, and you will eventually establish gait harmony. Starting with a partner that is a little faster works best, as he will adjust and slow to your pace, whilst a slower partner might never be able to keep up.

"A first vivid memory of leaving the center was walking down a very large sidewalk with Tommy at my side. That was the day I realized Tommy's physical speed and strength, and appreciated the importance of those three days when the instructors had watched and analyzed our every move, their diligent observation resulting in Tommy in my harness, and a perfect fit! Those in training at the center can be 18 and getting ready to go to college, or 81 and preparing for their first Guide Dog. The center never knows precisely what the experience of those people receiving one of its dogs is going to be, but does know that it needs to pair the dogs so that a sucessful team is the result. Achieving the best possible fit is the highest priority, so being diligent and utilizing years of experience, strict, proven, step-by-step guidelines are followed.

"Our final instructions in California were to stick as closely as possible to the directions given, review them often during our daily routine, stay textbook where possible, and not cut corners. If and when things weren't quite right, we were told to take the time to go back and correct issues immediately (indicate the correct way and praise, praise, praise). Simple, but important guidelines designed to keep the team working together smoothly.

"Finally, in April I brought Tommy home, and together we began going to places I had frequented with my cane, moving faster and with a level of confidence I had almost forgotten. It was great. A time/distance factor – an estimate of how long it would take to get from one location to another – was a concept I had learned during rehabilitation training, which supplies another tool for smooth movement, providing a sightless person with an approximate time frame based on the distance to be traveled, which eventually becomes second nature.

"Having to recalculate these time/distance factors, now that I had Tommy, gave me a great deal of satisfaction. The new calculations gave me a good idea of where Tommy would need to make a left or right turn, keeping me involved in the guiding process, an important ingredient in successful, independent travel. My independence and our safe arrival depended on the focus and attention of both of us: one driving, one leading.

"Eventually, I wanted to walk further distances and, on one particular day – a really big day in my life – I took a different route to our veterinarian. What I didn't know, however, was that one of the sidewalks was under construction, presenting a total barrier. A hedge came out all the way to the curb, and the sidewalk discontinued temporarily, making it necessary to go out and around, into the street, picking up the sidewalk on the other side of the street

"This was already a fairly busy road on any day, and being under construction made crossing it difficult for any veteran team. At the curb, Tommy hesitated, stopping as if to check things out. Not appreciating the changes in the area, I gave him the 'hop-up' command, 'get closer,' and 'show me,' which means as I probe out with my left foot, I need to check the curb for a drop-off, any obstacle, feeling out to the top and sides, checking for an overhead obstacle or a side obstacle, anything that justified Tommy's actions. Again, still looking for the reason we had stopped, I said 'hop up, get me closer.' Tommy responded to my second request and moved forward, slightly, but I still wasn't close enough.

"Feeling frustrated I gave a leash correction with a third verbal 'hop up,' and again, he moved slightly forward. This time I could feel the curb, just the end of the sidewalk, as Tommy sat down; he sat down altogether, as if to say 'that's it, I'm not going any further.' Still unable to feel anything but the edge of the curb, I told Tommy again to go forward, and again he refused; just sat tight.

"Tommy just wouldn't go, so I did – right off the curb, into the gutter, and directly into a six-foot hole! Instinctively letting go of the harness as I fell, for just a split-second Tommy was undoubtedly looking directly down at me. Was he grinning? Instantly, he and his wagging tail were all over me in that hole, licking, wagging, checking me out: 'See, I told you, I told you.' At that moment I felt I could trust Tommy with my life, and this changed the depth of bonding I developed with him and all future guide partners.

"However, in time, I again found myself not totally trusting that Tommy would or could protect me, fairly certain that I knew better than he. When I was down in that hole I was certain I could completely trust him, but doubts re-emerged: after all, went my reasoning, I'm a member of the superior species, how can a dog know more than I do? Around then, I bumped into an overhanging tree, which seemed to confirm what I felt: Tommy let me bump into that tree, he hadn't warned me.

"But – and here's the big lesson – that's simply the way of blindness, and I needed to learn that I was still blind, and I was still going to bump into stuff, because Tommy could not protect me from everything. We were partners, it wasn't down to just one of us, we were a team. Yes, Tommy did facilitate a new, safer vigour to my life, but no one thing can make life totally safe for anyone.

"It took some time and some bruises to

put those two facts together. Standing in the hole that day, I did finally laugh, though my heart skipped a beat or two when I realized how badly I could have been hurt. I lifted Tommy out first and crawled after him, very thankful I hadn't broken anything, and glad that I was twenty-four, strong and healthy.

"I finally stood back on the curb and we made a right turn, going out around that obstacle, allowing me to praise Tommy for his good work: after all, it was not his mistake that had put me in that hole. Tommy had refused my commands, so we reworked the scenario, allowing me to reward him for doing it correctly. Intelligent disobedience, training, it all came together that day. I'm sure Tommy had it together long before that day; it was my learning curve that was slow but I did have the good sense to backtrack and praise him and love him for being my partner.

"When you have a foul-up in communication it is absolutely essential to rework the situation and correct any confusion, in order to leave your four-legged partner clear on future tasks. When showing your partner what to do after bumping your head on a tree limb, for example, you back up a few steps, show him the obstacle, telling him to yield – a familiar command – repeat and praise until understood. Dogs have poor depth perception which, when an uncharacteristically high obstacle such as a tree branch is encountered, makes the task difficult to learn, but the concept of show, command, repeat, praise, is always the same, and repetition in regard to developing height judgment is particulary relevant as dogs don't automatically see the danger.

"Never knowing what's ahead, you need absolute trust in your partner, even in preference to other people. For example, well-intentioned people who indicate that it's okay to cross a road if the light has changed are unaware of the unique needs involved when my partner and I reach a busy intersection. Only complete focus between the two of us, and a new light sequence will enable a safe crossing, preventing unexpected issues with surging parallel traffic and traffic making right-hand turns. So I've learned to trust my partner and his innate senses and instincts which take into account all of the surrounding activity that could potentially affect a street crossing. Our needs are unique, our timing very specific, and in that instant, we must be completely focused on each other.

"The day I learned to trust– or began to learn to trust – was just the beginning of a lot of new things I had to learn. I had no idea that Tommy, my partner, would extend the bond we shared to include my family: after all, what could Tommy do for my family, it was me who was blind?

"Shortly after the sidewalk hole incident, I was sitting with Tommy at the bottom of grandma's cast iron curvy staircase. Unleashed, not working, completely off-duty, Tommy was relaxing with me, and chewing on an old toy. Suddenly, from the top step, Lyndie, my daughter, began to fall down the steep stairs: open, cast iron railings suspending each floating step and leaving large, open-air, leg-breaking gaps. In an instant Tommy had positioned himself to gently but firmly support Lyndie, preventing her from falling more than two steps. I guess he was watching after all while chewing on that toy!

"Lyndie was only 15 months old, and Tommy became the family hero, that day, not just mine. I was amazed at Tommy's actions, and wondered how he knew what to do? Obviously, he hadn't been taught that at school or in his year learning socialization, but here he was, preventing a disaster.

"It's now twenty-one years since I began living with canine partners, and I am still amazed and without many of the answers. Since my partners contribute to my daily safety and my very existence, their influence makes them an integral contributor to the wellbeing of my whole family.

"Tommy retired at nine, returning to the people who had loved him as a puppy. The initial trainers of our Guide Dogs, the family which introduces them to the world, preparing them to be our partners in life, are excited to welcome home these old timers. And, whenever this is possible, it's a great way for them to enjoy their retirement years.

"A unique opportunity to visit my old partner after his retirement was an unusual experience for me, giving rise to feelings still difficult to explain. When I first saw Tommy, he excitedly jumped up, right there on the car seat, right next to me. My immediate response was to say 'Hey, wait just a minute, get down, that just isn't allowed,' and Tommy started to comply and respond to me, his old partner. 'Yes, it is allowed in this home' came a quick, firm reply. His old/new family reminded me that Tommy was done working for me, and here and now, he was allowed on their car seat. 'Oh, okay, you're the

After crossing a busy intersection, his partner's pause, telegraphed through the harness, lets Brad know the curb is ahead. He signals 'hop-up' and they safely complete the crossing. (Courtesy Jim Dowling)

boss,' and I quietly pulled back. My ever-present handler thinking, which forestalls bad habits, was and is a constant in all of my canine partnerships, and prevents interference with a work-associated focus. This day, Tommy was simply being a dog, wiggling and greeting his old partner, which seemed wrong somehow because it's essential to our safety and therefore our very existence that our partner's focus is directly on us. I forgot that Tommy wasn't my partner anymore.

"We spent some time on a riverbank throwing toys, and Tommy just loved the outing with all that attention. Old and new family, he was excited and really having a great time. Seeing if he would still respond to my calls, I was quietly pleased to note he would come back to me first. His attention and actions that day showed he would always care for me, always respond to my needs and wishes first, probably until he could no longer respond. Tommy and I had 'lived' a different level of bonding: bonding born of necessity. Words are totally inadequate when trying to explain a connection of that depth.

"Did he still know me? Obviously! Did he still feel a connection, a need in me so deep that he would leave someone else that loved him and that he loved, to respond to my need? Without question! Words cannot do justice to that connection and that level of love!"
Brad

Two of the most important elements in a good partnership are trust and communication, without which the team has no chance. It was obvious from Brad's story that he did not trust initially, and it was fortunate that his experience of falling into the hole didn't have permanent consequences.

Without doubt, trust has to be earned and learned by both. Communication – non-verbal, to a large extent – takes time and practice. Brad learned a lesson some never do: you can trust your life to your partner, and your level of communication is absolutely essential to that trust. The resultant bond, strengthened by daily work experience, was completely responsible for the development of Tommy's canine heart.

The story of Buddy, America's first Seeing Eye Dog, has been told and retold over the years, but at the time of her arrival in the the United States in 1926, canines assisting man in any way apart from hunting or during war was virtually unheard of. Unbelieving New York newsmen were convinced that Buddy could not do any of the things that her partner, Morris Frank, claimed, but the reporters watched in amazement as Buddy competently guided Morris across West Street, a busy, broad New York thoroughfare. Today, similar stories are commonplace, and tell of everyday tasks and the gift of independence which Guide Dogs provide. But on that day all those years ago, it was Morris Frank's confidence in Buddy that helped him across that street. (Apparently, only one of the reporters made it across – and he took a taxi!)

There are always challenges for pioneers, and Morris Frank and Buddy had their share. On one occasion, a train conductor challenged Morris about his dog, whereupon he calmly removed first one and then the other painted, prosthetic eyes that he always wore to prove that he was, indeed, blind, and that it had been Buddy who had calmly led him onto that train and into his seat. Morris probably grinned at the thought of the look on the conductor's face for quite some time.

Whilst in Switzerland where Morris and Buddy trained together, on one of their usual walks Morris experienced his first of many rescues by a dog. A runaway team of horses careered toward the pair down a narrow street with high embankments. Aware of the obvious danger coming their way, Buddy did the only thing she could, and pulled Morris (her pack), up the seven foot bank. Down on his knees, arms around his new partner, her cold nose in his neck, the bond between Morris and Buddy was obvious.

Morris first met Buddy after a long and difficult boat trip to France, en route to Fortunate Fields in Switzerland, which left him physically and emotionally exhausted. When he finally arrived at his destination, however, as his arms went around Buddy, he knew immediately that they would be a great partnership, and she would be so much more to him than his eyes. Their partnership – Buddy's level of devotion and love, coupled with her ability to allow Morris to live an independent life – was the beginning of a general awareness and appreciation of how dogs can help people.

Dorothy Eustis, Buddy's trainer, had spent several years schooling dogs for police work, as army messengers, for sentry duty, and for the Red Cross in Switzerland. But it was in Potsdam, Germany that she had the opportunity to work with a school which provided Guide Dogs for the blind, and her experience in Germany led to an article being published in the *Saturday Evening Post* that brought together Morris, Buddy and Dorothy Eustis.

Two years after uniting and mentoring this unique team, Dorothy heard of their success and joined them in America, starting the first Seeing Eye School in Nashville in 1929. Morris and Buddy were already recruiting sponsors and funds, and together this team of three opened a school to train Guide Dogs, its first class graduating that same year. Due to the visionary efforts of Dorothy Eustis and Morris Frank, life for Americans with visual impairment was about to change forever.

After twelve years of walking at the side of her partner, Buddy died, leaving a legacy that lives on every time you see a dog in a harness for the blind, at the side of a wheelchair, with a child's arms wrapped around them, or on the trail of a lost person. Hailed a national hero, Buddy's legacy extends to every single working canine partner.

Possessing all the poise, beauty and charm of the dignified German Shepherd, restaurants, railways, and even United Airlines allowed Buddy and other certified Guide Dogs to use their facilities: indeed, one of Buddy's last duties was to be presented with United Airlines' formal consent to allow Guide Dogs to travel on its planes. Unsteady on her feet because of age and its accompanying debilitation, Buddy stood proud at the award, somehow knowing that she led the way for others to follow. Her example and service started the world thinking about what these

incredible friends wanted to do: be at our sides; happiest when working to help us.

Buddy helped the blind to see and regain their independence – to move into the world, onto the streets, trains, and airplanes: places they thought they would never get to alone were once again attainable as their world opened up. With a dog at their side, even the seemingly impossible became achievable!

Like all the other canine heroes in this book, Buddy was simply doing her job. Her excitement and pleasure at helping Morris live a safe, normal life is mirrored in the actions of all of the partners mentioned here. Buddy never quit, on duty 24/7, just like all the others. Her total commitment did not allow anything less than this.

Facilitating quick, safe, precise movement is the Guide Dog's goal while keeping his blind partner from danger – which can come in many forms – using perceptive senses and diligent observation. A speeding car is obviously dangerous, as is a tree branch that hangs over the sidewalk, or a construction hole in the crosswalk, but how can these canine partners be expected to anticipate the various dangers, constantly guiding their partners to safety? How do they know when it is necessary to disobey an insistent, direct command?

The answer is partially through training, but ultimately by refocusing their protective, nurturing instincts on the individual holding the harness. A confident personality, and physical strength and balance allow them to bodily support their charge when necessary, and guide or move him or her when imminent danger threatens. With this refocusing, a unique collaboration results; their partner becomes a member of the pack, protected and nurtured as one of their own. Pack wellbeing is the very essence of species survival.

> "I can't put into words what my personal friends and the people of Nashville did ... Nashville accepted the dog into restaurants, on streetcars, and everywhere I went ... It was glorious: just [Buddy] and a leather strap, linking me to life." – Morris Frank, *Through Buddy's Eyes*

Forming a deep connection with people at an early age establishes the groundwork for later development of the strong working bond described in these stories. Early imprinting on humans allows us to become members of the pack; as such we are afforded more than basic friendship and companionship – we are nurtured and protected with survival instincts essential to life.

The blind face a daunting challenge as they attempt to navigate and negotiate physical barriers, and a Guide Dog in their life brings confidence and independence while restoring basic mobility. Consider the time spent at training school where these partners become one in movement and thought, and the everyday exercises that maintain and strengthen that relationship. The involvement that most canine teams experience cannot be compared to these partnerships: the moment-to-moment, life and death, give-and-take between dog and person.

Quality time is essential, and is proportional to the bond and level of trust that will develop and result in a better partnership. Whether a six-week-old puppy or one of the thousands of rescue dogs waiting for a forever home, it's vital to begin laying a foundation of trust from day one by spending quality time, and making gentle physical contact. Nurturing; playing; loving: the building blocks of a permanent bond.

Suzanne and Coral and Martina

My lost independence returned with Coral

"I didn't want people to know I was blind, so I didn't use my cane until I was in trouble or lost. For five years I tried to fool people about my sight. I had some side vision [peripheral vision] that enabled me to discern light, and I was able to see some large objects and movement, but it was all very blurry.

"When I finally started using a cane, I was still attending college at the University of Utah. Using a folding cane that could be easily concealed in my book bag, I would produce it

only when absolutely necessary, otherwise I simply traveled slowly from class to class. I felt this enabled me to maintain my independence for a little longer: something that was extremely important to me.

"After finishing school at the University of Utah, I spent two years working with abused children as a licensed clinical social worker with the Family Support Center, and then three additional years in private practice.

"While attending the Blind Center, I kept hearing more and more about the advantages of a Guide Dog. I really wanted a dog but had mixed feelings about using one as a guide. I wanted to be independent for as long as possible, so waited until I could hardly see before I finally applied for a Guide Dog.

"At school I kept hearing about a gentleman named John who had his first Guide Dog, and was eager to share his experiences. John had recently become blind, too, and with his first Guide Dog – a lovely black Lab named Traveler at his side – he offered his time, advice and encouragement to anyone considering this important step. John had a reputation for being kind and sociable; someone easy to relate to. I really needed advice from someone that had recently gone through such a life-altering experience, and who had survived with a positive outlook, and John proved to be that person. We took classes together at the Blind Center, where we learned mobility, Braille, and daily living skills along with karate classes that taught enhanced listening, and how to maximize your feeling senses. But the most important thing John and I learned was each other's name, and we soon became man and wife.

"Before I went blind I had this beautiful, bright yellow Vega, my first car. I loved that little yellow car, and waiting at traffic lights I was always the first to leave the intersection. I could beat anyone! I loved moving out in front, the speed, the independence and the freedom. So when I lost that, when I couldn't drive any more, I really missed those feelings; that independence, that speed, that sense of freedom.

"Coral – a beautiful, black Lab, my first Guide Dog, my first canine partner – gave me

Suzanne's Guide Dogs always go everywhere with her, sharing her successes; enabling her successes.

back some of those feelings. I remember holding onto that harness the first time and we just flew: to me it felt just like flying as Coral was fast, very fast. When I first started walking with her after using a cane for mobility, it took every ounce of physical and, yes, mental reserve to keep up with that beautiful girl. Those feelings of freedom and speed did come back because of Coral. And that sense of independence I thought I would never feel again, well, that came back, too.

"Having the companionship of Coral allowed me a sense of freedom, which opened doors I hadn't used for a long time. A simple walk in our neighborhood became a pleasure again, and I did a ton of walking. I would walk to church every week in all types of weather, and, even though the snowy sidewalks are particularly difficult to navigate, with Coral I just followed.

"The texture of the ground's surface seemed especially important to Coral, and how she chose to navigate us depended a lot on the condition of this. Coral sensed slippery or dangerous conditions, and even with a foot of snow on the sidewalk – which before would have been paralyzing with just my cane – Coral safely led me down the middle of the sidewalk. Snowy

conditions created a blanket of fog that shrouded the few remaining blurry shapes I could still make out, taking away all of my depth perception, leaving the environment a one-dimensional piece of paper: totally flat.

"After one particularly bad snowstorm when I was trying to get to my office, snow banks created physical barriers all over the sidewalks and in the parking lot, but I simply told Coral 'forward,' and held on as she slowly navigated around the snow drifts. Coral patiently made her way to the house where I worked, winding around and away from the physical barriers of snow, which she knew I could not physically conquer. We had been to my office many times, but this time it was necessary for her to find a new, safe, previously uncharted route – and she did!

"The serious purpose of our partners is so evident in a situation like the one just described. Most young dogs will be rolling and running and jumping in new snow. Not a Guide Dog, not Coral. Her job was to lead me to safety and she did just that.

"Safety is one of the most compelling reasons for working with a canine partner, second only to the freedom and independence that returns when you place your hand on that leather harness. With the new-found confidence that this brings, it becomes a pleasure to go for a walk, secure in the knowledge that you will return home without the previously usual bumps and bruises. Uneven sidewalks or over-extended tree branches had been impossible to navigate with just a cane, but with Coral they were no problem.

"Walking with Coral one day we got to an area that was especially noisy, and Coral stopped. I told her to 'hop up,' which means continue, but she refused. I stood there thinking I'd better listen to what Coral was telling me: at times like this a dog's training, wisdom, genetics, intelligence, acute hearing and innate sense of danger combine, and given a command to 'Go' Coral decided to disobey this.

"Like most people, I like having my commands followed, so learning to wait and listen, to trust my partner, did not come easily. But I did wait, calling on *my* training, *my* intelligence, and putting my trust in Coral, and within seconds a car came zooming out of a driveway. The surrounding noise had prevented me from hearing the car engine; I didn't even know it was there. Coral did, though, she heard it, she saw it, and, understanding the danger, did what was necessary to make me wait.

"How do they train a dog for intelligent disobedience: in other words, when you say 'Go' they say 'No'? I believe it's in the initial selection of the dog. All of the training is done by positive reinforcement, showing them when they make a mistake, but only with love, not destroying their 'heart' but actually building self-confidence. This type of interaction (training) nurtures the already present intelligence that registers and responds appropriately to each situation.

"Coral even did things she wasn't asked to, in most instances I didn't know there was even a need for a command until after the situation had occurred.

"It's not every day that I face life-threatening situations, of course, but frequently encounter new locations to navigate. It is my responsibility to maintain Coral's initial training, and this is a daily, ongoing process, done with positive reinforcement – praise-praise-praise. If she makes a mistake, I immediately re-enact the situation, showing her the correct way, reinforcing and then praising when she gets it right. Being consistent keeps us as a team on top of our skills, maintaining our bond, our faith, and our trust in each other's responses and abilities.

"In my first years with Coral I was constantly amazed at how unique her skills are, how her instincts had been rewired to meet the daily needs of my life. One particular time, while visiting my first husband in the ICU at the University of Utah hospital, a friend took Coral and I to his room. The next day, however, Coral and I were on our own. Navigating the hospital would have been a daunting task for anyone, but not for Coral. Up on the third floor we went right and then left: the floor number and the first two turns comfortably remembered from navigating without a canine partner. But now where? Coral was on her own, but after taking me around more turns, down more halls without help or cues (I didn't have any to give!), through all the hospital confusion, long halls, turn after turn, and those strange smells, she took me directly to my husband's side, where she had been only once before. I never could have done that on my own.

"A necessary skill for blind people using a cane is an incredible memory, but all Coral needed, apparently, after the first time when she did have directions, was the verbal command 'Go.' In a familiar location (the third floor just off the elevator), her confidence and training meant she knew exactly where to go (she probably could have navigated from the car). Her memory, her instincts were awesome, and time and time again I would use these to get me safely to my destination.

"I could 'read' Coral's body language via her harness. She was a very sociable dog, and when her tail began moving just a little, I knew someone had made eye contact with her, and her next move would be to elicit a scratch or a hug from them. At the university, finishing my bachelor's degree and working on my master's degree, we would often be walking down the hallways, and Coral would search out eye contact, looking for a smile, and then her behind would start to move. I had to really watch her, and frequently told her 'don't you dare wag that tail!' It was heartbreaking to prevent her from giving the world the love she had, but vital for me to keep her focused on me and her work; my life depends on that focus. I knew she was trying to keep her mind on her work, but she was such a lovable, wonderful dog: a real 'people dog.'

"A big part of the continuous training aspects of a Guide Dog is maintaining their focus and concentration. Sniffing and exploring when working has to be corrected so that their focus is on you. It is vital to stay tuned-in to your partner, whose responsibility it is to get you whereever safely, but it is *your* responsibility to help them maintain their focus, staying in touch with every minute body change. Understanding their body language in the harness, and immediately correcting any deviation from the norm – always with love – helps maintain focus.

Attentive to Suzanne's need for a gentle pace, her partner calmly guides her through life, providing constant companionship and love.

"It's important that Guide Dogs have the right temperament. John and I take our partners everywhere we go – into restaurants, stores, schools, hospitals, airports – anywhere we are, they are. Frequently, little kids walk right up to their faces without us being aware of their presence, so the right temperament is very important. No growling, no barking, hopefully no licking! While walking in the mall we would always stop and talk with the parents and little kids, trying to convince the kids that they need to ask before petting. We met a lot of people that way. But we obviously had to keep our partners from being too social most of the time in order to stay focused on us and their work. I actually got to where I would just use my new command 'don't you dare wag that tail!'

"A sense of humor is vital to anyone with a disability, and John and I would laugh when trying to correct our partner's social forays. We know and appreciate the focus and dedication our canine partners have for us over ninety-eight percent of the time, and it is never easy to oppose a strict limit on their people-loving. It is partially their people skills that bring them to our side and endear them to us, so we walk a fine line, allowing them to reach out and receive loving attention whenever possible, while still keeping them at our sides, observant to our needs.

"We know how important the positive aspects of their personality are. Coral was a sweetheart, so sweet and wonderful. Maintaining her focus and allowing her to enjoy life was a responsibility I took very seriously.

"Coral worked with me until she was almost ten, and then I got her replacement, Martina. Even though I had loved and laughed at Coral's social temperament, this time I asked for a more serious partner. My health was giving me more trouble, and a partner that was easier to handle with a personality that wasn't quite so outgoing and loving seemed like a wise move.

"I knew Coral was perfect and my heart was so full of her dedication and love, but when I got Martina, I just knew I now had the second most perfect partner."
Suzanne

Right: John and Traveler at graduation: a smile on John's face and a serious "I'm ready" expression on Traveler's.

John and Traveler and Mick
Simple, unbridled movement
"My first dog was a black Lab named Traveler, and when he and I first took the harness together I clearly remember my feelings of exhilaration and freedom. I am diabetic, and had been using a cane to get about, so was confined to the restrictions this imposed, moving fairly slowly. NOW, I was actually unable to keep up with Traveler; it felt just like I was riding a motorcycle, the air rushing by me. I experienced an exhilaration that hadn't been present for so long! Traveler gave me back my old self, my active me, my independent me.

"I had been getting around using a cane fairly well for about four years, apart from in snow because, when the sidewalks are covered, a cane just can't push through everything, or help with the total lack of depth perception that a white-on-white fog – the result of a snowstorm – creates.

"Because of my diabetes, three times a week I needed to spend five hours on a dialysis machine. For some time my health kept me from applying for a Guide Dog, because having one does require that you are healthy enough to provide proper care for your partner. In addition to basic daily care, working with a Guide Dog to develop that coveted relationship takes substantial time and energy, especially initially. Making that Guide Dog your partner requires even more, a lot more. But finally, when I felt that was possible, I applied and was accepted.

"When I took Traveler's harness for the first time it was an incredible feeling. For years, using a cane brought necessary restrictions, but now with Traveler those feelings of simple unbridled movement were back and everything changed; Traveler gave me back *me*.

"I was amazed at how much better I could navigate with my new partner. With a cane I'd been constantly feeling my way down the sidewalk, bouncing the cane back and forth to locate obstacles, but Traveler did all that in such a speedy, trustworthy way that I could just *go*, and at a speed that was initially more than a little challenging. Using a cane for some time meant that my physical condition was stuck on slow, so it took some doing to get up to Traveler's speed. But the freedom and feelings of confidence and independence that came with that speed adjustment proved boundless.

"And one of the fringe benefits of a Guide Dog is good health: I became much healthier after getting my new partner because of the exercise I now took, so when I said 'Let's go,' I could, with a confidence of movement that had disappeared along with my sight. Being able to just step out is a simple ability for those who can see, but lost to the blind for obvious reasons. Now, after I learned to trust Traveler, that ability was restored to me, together with a quality of life long since lost.

"Moving freely at this new pace was only possible if I could completely trust Traveler, however, so now it was my turn to learn how to do this. At the center we were taught basic commands, but believing that the commands would be received and acted upon as given was a very difficult concept to accept, regardless of what the center trainers assured. Getting about in darkness for some time, I had become hesitant, slower, and cautious about all movement, so letting go of those feelings happened slowly. How could I know, I mean, really know, that this new creature at my side was going to safely navigate me through all the obstacles that I knew were out there? I had spent four dark years, carefully insulating my physical self from the dangers around every corner, and it was difficult to adjust.

"My training took place at the Guide Dogs for the Blind center in San Rafael, California. We had been working all over San Rafael, and I had a pretty good idea of the city's layout. One of the first things we were required to do was cross a street, and in a controlled scenario, a car comes right at you. In this instance, the dogs are trained to stop and back up, to stop you in your tracks, and in this exercise Traveler did well, very well. This alone might provide sufficient evidence of a partner's ability, but you know, I'd been getting along alone for some time, and just one example, though impressive, didn't do it for me.

"More exercises followed, and about the third week we took a bus ride downtown and were dropped off, one team at a time, and asked to find our own way back to the training center, and it was this particular exercise that finally made me realize how valuable Traveler was. As I was on dialysis, the center had a nurse follow me without my knowledge, so I really wasn't alone, and Traveler was there, of course, so I really, really wasn't alone. Trained to walk to the nearest corner or light and ask the first person who comes along what the street signs said, I proceeded accordingly. Receiving two co-ordinates, it's possible to determine direction, and be on your way.

"The center had given us two hours in which to return, but when I learned the co-ordinates, I knew it would take us just five minutes as we were just around the corner from our pickup spot. The nurse probably didn't want to go for a long walk, but I gave her one anyway: I didn't know she was there, remember, and I really didn't want to get back in just five minutes and wait for everybody else. So, I went shopping! I went to Macy's and See's candy store without realizing that this woman was walking just behind me, up and down, and down and up the streets of San Rafael. I had had dialysis the day before, so now and then had to stop and rest, to get my blood pressure back up to where it needed to be.

"Finally, after about an hour-and-a-half of shopping I returned to the center with bags full, and a great experience. Navigating in and out of the stores, between and around people, going just where I wanted, as I wanted, without hesitancy or concern, made me appreciate Traveler's worth as never before. Traveler kept me safe, yes, but this added benefit – the sheer joy at the freedom of simply 'going' – was an unexpected treasure.

"It was also amazing how many people approached with Traveler at my side. The cane had always been a deterrent, it seemed to keep people back, but with Traveler, well, it was just the opposite. I was moving freely now, making

This courageous couple spent years together with their Guide Dogs by their side, living life to its fullest. (Courtesy Olan Mills Studio)

new friends, too, both unimaginable just a few weeks ago, but making friends and acquiring confidence came easily with Traveler at my side. His personality was similar to Coral's [Suzanne's dog]; he was very sociable and friendly, and when he made eye contact with someone his tail got going and his whole body would wag. He loved people and he loved kids, probably kids most because he associated them with food, and he was always looking for a foody lick or a treat of some kind.

"Working in a harness day after day is difficult work, requiring strength and physical stamina, so when that dreaded day comes for retirement, making that change should be logical, but it's not! The emotional bond and partnership that has developed has become so intimate that it defies description, making it hard to accept that your partner no longer has the physical strength needed for the job.

"Wanting to protect Traveler's aging back, Mick came into our lives. Young, strong and eager to go, Mick gladly stood for the harness that had been Traveler's. Traveler's cries to go [with me] were heartbreaking. That quality, that heart, that strength of soul which made Traveler my first partner, one of the teachers in my life of blindness: it seemed so cruel, as he stood wanting to wear his harness, wanting to be at my side. When it was finally time to release Traveler from this earth, I was determined that any future partners would be retired to a loving new friend who could give them their retirement years away from me, away from their job, a job that Traveler would have continued to do, even if it meant his life.

"The partnership of a Guide Dog – a relationship that enables the radical life changes I have described – should instil confidence when a new partner becomes necessary. But complete trust, well, that would take longer. And with my new partner, Mick, there would be a trial period of bonding and learning each other's ways.

"One day, as we were crossing a very busy street, having made the necessary stop at the intersection, the light changed and I gave the forward commanded for Mick to 'hop up.' One

John and Suzanne

Sadly, John passed away shortly after this interview, leaving a hole in the hearts of everyone who knew his smile and kindly character. Norton, John's canine partner at the time, returned to California to spend his retirement years with his puppy trainer, Louise. Suzanne still smiles at the mention of John: a gentleman and her sweetheart.

Both Suzanne and John became blind at the age of 23 due to diabetic retinopathy. Previously sighted, both chose to use canes before finally applying for their canine partners. After getting their first dogs their general health improved significantly because they were now able to get about and walk, a simple activity that changed everything. Even their blood pressure went down and consequently everything improved.

Sounds rather ordinary, but basic, everyday life would not be feasible without their 24/7 partners. Just this past year Suzanne's partner alerted a cleaning lady to a deadly insulin reaction threatening Suzanne's life. Knowing something was wrong she began going between Suzanne, who was unconscious, and the cleaning lady two floors away. Back and forth, back and forth she went until the woman realized there was a problem. Immediate attention to this life-threatening condition enabled Suzanne to be here to tell the story.

For John and Suzanne the impossible was made possible every day because of their canine partners.

instinct that the blind rely heavily on is hearing, and at this busy intersection, with non-stop noise, it wasn't easy to filter sounds and determine direction, even taking into account the location and speed of vehicles in relation to myself. I had still been practising this, even after receiving Traveler and now Mick, so I felt confident in stepping out. Even though I knew Mick was trained to use all of his senses, here, today, with all the sounds at this intersection blending together, I gave the 'hop up' command because of my senses, just as a car to my side pulled out.

"The driver must have been watching the other cars ahead for the light change, not looking for pedestrian traffic. I did not hear the sound of the car's engine as it accelerated and the driver apparently didn't see us. Mick jumped back, pulling me back, disobeying my command to 'Go,' saving us from being hit head-on, although the wing mirror of the car hit my forearm.

"Sometimes blind people experience phantom sight, a relatively unique situation similar to the feelings experienced by someone who has lost a limb. The memory of this incident and the feelings it prompted are still vivid in my mind, and, whenever I talk about it, I can actually feel that blow, the startling pain, the fear, even twelve years later. I will always remember how close I came that day. Fortunately, Guide Dogs are taught to utilize all of their senses, and Mick's instincts and training served us well that day, proving how valuable my new partner had become, undoubtedly saving my life. That day, Mick was necessary to my very existence; my life.

"But in the case of Suzanne and I the life-saving instances are not the whole story. The real story, the really big story, is the fact that we live and function on a daily basis just like our neighbors or anyone else. Together for 16 years, we have traveled using regular, commercial services; we have flown to Canada, Florida, Hawaii, England, and New York. We have Christmas lights and a Santa on our roof that I put up myself. We enjoyed the 2002 Winter Olympics, and are always looking for new restaurants that serve Italian food or some of the other dishes that are our favorites. Because of our experiences with our canine partners we give frequent talks about our lives and the dogs at our side, an interaction that increases our sense of being, bringing us out into the world so that we can interact more fully with people. Because we have unique canine partners we have a quality of life that allows us to live more fully, every day of our lives.

"Our partners are so intertwined with us that, without their ability and desire to guide, be our partners, offer love and consolation when our souls are wounded, make us laugh and lift us, we truly would be blind."

John

Every species has defining characteristics and specific traits unique to each individual, which genetic-manipulation can influence, in some instances successfully. The process of puppy selection for Guide Dog use is one of the most important, troublesome, and unpredictable aspects of becoming the human partner in this special relationship, and has been fine-tuned by the experts who supply Guide Dogs.

Beginning with the genetics of each puppy, to the day that the animal's harness is placed in the hands of a blind person, each step, every little detail is choreographed: genetically (breeding) and socially (training) engineered for success. Ultimately, of course, it is a dog's desire to work at our side that matters the most – not his physical strength, not his intelligence, but his need to be with us and the innate senses that enable him to facilitate a good life for the partner he walks with.

In 1947, after spending time with Dr Paul J Scott, author of *Genetics and Social Behaviors of Dogs*, Clarence Pfaffenberger introduced a gigantic change in Guide Dog training. Research indicated that initiating puppy socialization at approximately seven weeks, a time when canine social relationships shift, enhances the human bonding process. With the realization of the importance of early human contact, changes were made that eventually rippled through the canine community as a whole. Man's partnership,

his bond with the canine species, is directly proportional to early human involvement in the animal's emotional growth and his bonding potential.

Clarence Pfaffenberger, while formulating a timetable still in use today, left a blueprint for successfully raising a puppy. When selecting a puppy for guide work, search and rescue, and therapy, many religiously follow Pfaffenberger's advice that socialization begins when the pup is seven weeks old – the optimum time for a positive human/canine relationship – which promotes a strong bond of love, trust, and communication. While some organizations cannot afford this time investment, the strategy has successfully provided Guide Dogs for the blind for many years.

Today, there are so many dogs who find themselves in shelters or on the streets, that the current push to adopt unwanted adult dogs is the socially and morally responsible way to go: it is the right thing to do when choosing a dog to become a family companion. Most shelters will give as much information and help as they can, and allow extra time to decide which dog to take home. They desperately want this match to be forever.

Doing your homework about breed traits, understanding instinctive behaviors (the need to hunt/run/chew/work), as well as physical characteristics such as eye color/size/shedding/drooling, to name only a few, will help with deciding which dog will work with your lifestyle, and can offer a forever home to, be he or she hunter, lap dog or agility specialist.

LaDoris and Remca
She gave in every way to everyone

"Freedom comes with fur and lots of love. I had always loved animals, especially dogs, and never wanted to be without a dog in my life. It was my dad who pushed me into getting a dog guide: he feared for my safety, knowing that I had no intention of staying still or having someone lead me around.

"It was the summer of my twenty-first birthday when I boarded a small prop plane in Lewiston, Idaho headed for San Rafael, California.

A few days prior to leaving for the trip I was nearly hit by a car whose driver decided to jump the light a bit too fast and quick. I was very happy to be leaving to get my dog when I did, even though I was sure that this dog would make me look more blind.

"Her name was Remca and, to this day, I have never seen a more beautiful Golden Retriever, or one that came with the wings and halo she did. No, she wasn't perfect but she was my angel. Remca was afraid of balloons, but if I needed her where there were balloons, then she worked there. That was only the beginning.

"When you go to the school to get a dog guide, you do what is called 'night routes,' which are an important part of our training. They're called this because we load up on the bus when it gets dark and go work different routes with our dogs.

"We do this for several reasons, but a big one is that things look different to dogs at night, and we need to know how to handle that situation, becoming comfortable working at night as well as in the day. For some of us with some sight, this can be very scary, because during the day we depend on whatever little sight we do have, and at night it is gone. In fact, it is worse, because instead of the blackness that a totally blind person experiences, we get an indistinct world of shadows.

"I can still remember the fear in my stomach on my first night route, and how silly that seems now after twenty-two-plus years of having wonderful guides by my side. I remember how confidently my little beauty stepped out in her harness, the handle clenched tightly in my sweaty hand. When we left the hotel lounge the lights of the little town were still bright, but as we walked to the courthouse there was almost no light, the businesses all were closed for the evening: lights off! I didn't trip on the sidewalk cracks, though, or hit anything and have to say 'excuse me' to walls! I knew our trainers were out with us as they said 'hey' as we passed by them.

"Gradually, my feet got lighter and my smile got bigger with each step as I realized Remmy was not going to let me fall, or run into things or get

hit. I cannot explain how free I felt, and how elated and happy. I spent the rest of the time at the hotel lounge afterwards hugging Remmy, and thanking her for my new-found freedom.

"Within about a year after school, I was married to Joel Laffite, my first husband. We met while I was getting Remca, and eventually had a healthy son in November of 1986. My husband said he only married me for my Goldie, meaning Remca, of course. Since I would not give her to him, he took us both. Remca was an incredible guide, but she thought my new son, Donvier, was her baby. She went to every doctor's appointment during my pregnancy, and every time I visited the hospital to get rehydrated and medication, Remca

LaDoris' beloved companion, Chips, always tries to take center stage, probably knowing that when Annie, a wheelchair Guide Dog, starts her work guiding, his job of loving and comforting will be temporarily lost.

LaDoris was born with bi-lateral cataracts, a complex, congenital rubella syndrome (CRS) called Hallermann-Streiff.

She eventually required a wheelchair to remain mobile, and with it came Annie, a white Lab trained as a wheelchair guide. Born the youngest of a large family, LaDoris was lavished with love from her siblings and parents, and her strength of character and their guiding love has created a strong, tender woman who embraces all who meet her. Not totally blind, LaDoris wears thick glasses, and with the aid of her jewelers loupe magnifier, maintains contact with the world via her computer.

Undoubtedly, her canine partners – tender companionship and compassion by her side every moment – have been pivotal to her quality of life, providing more than basic, safe movement. These strong, gentle giants mirror the tender, loving woman they live with. Somehow understanding their importance in her life, they eagerly anticipate her every need.

was there, too. When the big day came, both Remca and my hubby's dog, Honda, the sweetest darling little Shepherd, were waiting with Dad and Grammy.

"It was Remca who got the very first kiss when baby Donvier was brought into the room.

The nurse held him for Remca to see, and she gave him a very gentle lick to seal the deal that he was her son. Remca made sure I was right on top of anything the baby might need, and when he needed something done or threw something out of the stroller, such as his pacifier, Remca picked

Guide training for a wheelchair taught LaDoris to direct with her foot. Protecting their working trust, she knows how important it is never to kick her partner, though navigating the chair whilst giving verbal, hand and foot gestures can be challenging.

it up and carried it. A man stopped us one day to tell me that my dog had something in her mouth: Donvier's pacifier. She had it nipple end in her mouth, just carrying it like it was what she was supposed to do; it did belong to her son, after all. She didn't change diapers, though; she drew the line at that!

"I'm sure you've seen young children use large dogs to pull themselves up to learn to walk. I didn't think that was a good idea, so my son learned to use the furniture, but Remca would let him balance with her and walk slowly, so he could learn to walk with her. I just don't know how she knew this stuff, but she did.

"And it wasn't only the baby who came in for her attention. When my husband became ill with heart problems that eventually led to his passing, Remca would go to him whenever she felt he needed her. She gave in every way to everyone who ever knew her.

"She had a silly side as well, and would do anything for a tennis ball. She may have loved those balls as much as she loved me; I never really wanted to push that to the limit to find out. When we met I could not get her attention because of a tennis ball. She also loved to go down slides … yes, I do mean children's slides. A park in Kingman had a low slide that was wide and the ladder was more like steps. She started going up all by herself and kept it up until we left the park. She also loved swimming and diving for rocks. I know that a lot of dogs don't like to go under water but she loved to go get the rock when it sank to the bottom, and she was a very strong swimmer.

"I think that Remca and I had a bond that was instant and eternal. I didn't have any friends then, apart from my husband, and she was my best friend and confidant, as well as my shopping buddy. She was one wonderful girl, and will always be missed. Remca loved everyone whose lives she touched – and she touched a lot of lives."

LaDoris

Long before LaDoris and Remca became partners a great deal of thought and preparation went into Remca's upbringing, and one of the most influential elements of this process was her puppy raiser.

This responsibility is initially placed in the hands of a volunteer, who does not receive a penny for the hours and hours of gentle love, feeding, and step-by-step shaping of some of the most critical elements in a Guide Dog's development – trust, communication, and resultant bond – that he or she invests.

During these months the puppy is gently and positively introduced to any and all possible environments and activities. Encouragement to explore and become confident will ultimately result in a personality strong enough to develop intelligent disobedience. Positive exposure to all manner of experiences, from barnyard hens to airport terminals, usually precludes the presence of fear and anxiety in a sound candidate, ensuring that all future experiences will be calm and uneventful.

Of course, we can't take our own dogs into all of the places that potential Guide Dogs are allowed, but it is extremely beneficial to take them to as many as possible to habituate them to these experiences. Socialization at a young age will create self-confidence, helping to develop a calm respect for your leadership, and expected behavior in new environments. Wearing their distinctive vests, these in-training pups can be seen in grocery stores, restaurants, malls, hospitals, libraries, and any place their young trainers deem important to their socialization: anywhere that life happens.

So, who better to teach patience, love, and gentleness, whilst introducing an eager puppy to the world, than an eager youngster with no preconceived fears or angst? The Carines family raised 18 canine partners – 14 puppies for Guide Dogs, Inc, and four puppies for Canine Companions for Independence. Supported by a loving family, youngsters Rachel and Melissa took on this huge responsibility, which they regarded as an opportunity, to ready the puppies for their life as 'lead dogs.'

This is where that all-important human/canine connection begins, establishing the groundwork for which becomes the responsibility, joy and pain of a puppy raiser. Rebecca Carines, the girls' mother, wanted to involve her whole family in a project that would help others, and in this she was successful, changing lives forever.

Here are their stories ...

Rebecca Carines
We loved them, too

"It was our responsibility to raise these puppies with the ability to calmly and confidently approach any and all situations they may encounter, whilst allowing them to develop their own innate decision-making abilities.

"We all approached this responsibility seriously but with a level of tender nurturing. Our daughters were the prime care-takers, spending untold hours playing, loving, teaching obedience and talking with strangers as they escorted their current puppy from one unique environmental situation to another. The experience of sharing this type of responsibility, and the feelings of accomplishment when we succeeded in turning over a puppy that became someone's lifeline, was one which has had a lasting impact on our lives.

"People frequently ask how we could possibly turn over a puppy we had raised and loved for that long, 'I just couldn't do that, I would fall too deeply in love immediately, how could you just give it away?' they would ask. I can assure everyone who asked that question, or even thought it, that we loved them, too, and it was not easy! But we saw the faces of the people we helped, and we heard their words of thanks, and saw their tears as they expressed their gratitude. There was no question that we had changed someone's life. Being able to help someone else, that is always a great lesson, but doing it together as a family, that had a lasting affect on all of us.

"But still, it was the hardest thing to watch those kids going up to this big industrial cold truck and give back their puppies, turning their dog over to a stranger, and walking away with an empty leash. I have a lot of admiration for my girls, it was hard, but everybody tried to focus on the end result: this puppy was going to be helping

Right: On their last day together, Rachel is with Treasure as she receives a 4-H medal: an award from this national youth development organisation.

somebody. This puppy was going to change someone's life."
Rebecca

Rachel Carines Walton DVM
They were all dear friends

"When the day came to send back our puppies for formal training, it was bittersweet. Of course, it was never an easy thing to do; even though we got a new puppy to raise at the same time, the goodbyes were always tearful. Like my mom, I remember walking away with the empty leash in my hand.

"After our puppies returned to school, we would get periodic progress reports on how they were doing. I believe they used to say that only about 50 per cent of puppies would complete their training and become working guides. Of the 8 dogs I personally raised, four became working guides.

"When a dog was paired with a blind person, they would undergo formal training, and puppy raisers were invited to formally present their dog to their new partner at graduation, which was such an amazing experience. Even at a young age (I was ten when my first dog graduated, and

16 or 17 for the last one), I could appreciate what a difference a Guide Dog made to these people. They would often speak of the freedom having a dog granted them, and were so appreciative of the work we did with the puppies, and our personal sacrifice in letting them move on. Some of these people continued to keep in touch with our family, sending updates and photos. This day was the culmination of the entire experience, and, when you saw how much it meant to someone else, made all the sadness of giving away your friend worthwhile.

"I can honestly say that I never wished for one of my graduated Guide Dogs to come home. While I know I missed them, I realized how much more their partners needed them.

"To me, they were all dear friends and companions, but to their partners they were so much more. The dogs that didn't graduate were a little harder, but we were able to find loving homes for all of them as well."

Rachel

Melissa Carines Ellis
Thanks for giving them their eyes

"My first puppy came to me when I was six years old. One of the questions we were often asked was 'How can you give up the dog after a year?' Most people thought that this would be just be too hard to do, and, while it was hard, I was somehow comforted by the fact that this dog might be able to help someone else because of me. My response would often be 'I love animals and I love helping others, so this seems like a good way to combine these things.'

"I think one of the things that training Guide Dogs did for me was to help me feel comfortable talking in front of people, as we would very frequently give demonstrations to different groups about what goes into training these dogs. I used to be a very, very shy little girl, but to get up in front of people with a dog by my side seemed to make it easier. The dogs were often a great conversation-starter, too; they seem to have a way of breaking down the walls that we seem to build.

"I was always amazed at how thankful and grateful the people were who received the

Suki and Melissa visit a working farm for exposure to one more unique and stimulating environment.

Guide Dogs I raised. They would frequently thank us for giving them their 'eyes' again. Many a time we had the opportunity to go to our dogs' graduations and meet the blind people they were paired with, and in that short time it was very clear how grateful they were for what we did to help train their new partner. It was also good to see if your dog remembered you. While I believe mine all remembered me, it was fun to see which seemed surprised to see me after so long. I sometimes wondered if the dogs ever thought 'why did my mom drop me off here?' though I think once they were paired with a blind person they understood why I did.

"It was also lovely to see how happy the dogs were with their new owners, and the new partnership they had formed. Going to the graduation ceremony was a great way to come full circle, see what you did and how it would change someone's life."

Melissa

Several different Guide Dog programs exist throughout the world, which raise and provide guide and service dogs for individuals who need help, all with different parameters and time frames for their programs and training for specific jobs. All successful canine programs develop their training around the specific dog they are working with. So, with some variation, 12 to 18 months of a Guide Dog's early life are spent with volunteers, and it is this early love, socialization and obedience-training which prepares them for their profession. After this period they begin their formal training: 2 to 3 months spent preparing, step-by-step, for their life in harness, leading their partner.

Guide Dogs learn intelligent disobedience at a younger age than most working dogs, because their job is to safely navigate their partner around and through potentially dangerous situations, regardless of the command given. Their role requires that their already present pack/nurturing instincts are encouraged: they absolutely must put their partner's safety above all else. Man shapes their instincts, their desire to please, their need to work, in such a way that they can best help their partner.

Clint and Libo and Sachmo
Canes are for blind people ... and I wasn't blind!

"I never allowed the loss of sight to take away my dreams or my vision for my life. Admittedly, I was a little (or a lot!) cocky, and I still have an attitude and high level of assertive energy that has served me well. For many years, I did not want to admit I was blind or limited in any way, and would stumble about like I was drunk rather than allow a cane to guide me. Canes are for blind people, and I was *not* blind!

"The stigma sometimes associated with blindness tends to prevent a lot of people from accepting the inevitable, initially. The fact is most of us run from the inevitable, not wanting anything to do with any of the paraphernalia associated with blindness – a cane, Braille reading and writing, a Guide Dog or just someone's helpful arm – because, when that happens, everyone knows what you aren't ready to admit. Accepting yourself as you are, with all that life has given, *and* taken away, requires a degree of maturity and

calmness to allow someone with my attitude and determination to move forward.

"Maturity comes at different times in everyone's life, and dealing with glaucoma made me grow up fast. When occasional bursts of juvenile attitude emerged, I'm sure those around me wondered ... Ultimately, I did realize that asking for help, accepting an extended arm, and especially walking with my Guide Dog, my partner, would enable me to accomplish anything I chose to do, and I did eventually accept all of the trappings of blindness – except for a cane.

"Bungee jumping, rock climbing, biking, skydiving, skiing, golfing: all were part of the vision I held for my life, and all were possible because of my attitude, my assertive energy, and my ultimate maturity, but not because of any cane. Total acceptance of a life-limiting disability can inhibit living: there's a fine line between acceptance and compliance. 'Oh, you can't possibly hit a golf ball if you're blind,' well, maybe not like Tiger Woods, but I can and did hit a golf ball, and I rode bikes, not like Lance Armstrong, but I rode them.

"And finally, after settling down and finding what I really wanted to do – be a good father with my partner, Libo, at my side – I also tried wrestling, singing and speaking.

"When people ask about my Guide Dog, my partner, naively they exclaim 'Oh, how great he is, he must be like your right arm,' or 'I'll bet he's your best friend.' But a Guide Dog is not my right arm or my left arm, he's me and, as such, is so much more than a best friend: he completes me.

"Libo and I reached the point where verbal commands were mostly unnecessary; he just knew what I wanted and needed, and our relationship reached an even deeper level. Little could I know or even dream of the support that this unique relationship would provide.

"It is possible to get a dog when you are 16, but I never really wanted one then. I thought both dogs and canes would be a pain in the butt, and back then I didn't want either; I was sure I could manage without them, which I pretty much did. I was born with glaucoma – an insidious, creeping disease – but for my first twelve to thirteen years

I was partially sighted, and could distinguish colors. Knowing I would eventually lose my sight completely, I was taught by an itinerant teacher that came to my school. Kindergarten began preparing me for the inevitable, and here I learned to read, write, and, of course, physically navigate my environment just like sighted children. My second itinerant teacher started with me in the third grade, and stayed with me all through school, which was a really great thing for me. Unfortunately, she was really just like my mom, and so easily manipulated. I really got away with a lot!

"I did eventually lose most of my sight to glaucoma, despite having a great doctor and numerous surgeries (which seemed to make it worse). Glaucoma is an awful disease, what with the medication and the pressure in your eyes, the pain, and the knowledge that blindness is imminent. Some days I am able to tell if the light is on, and I can usually differentiate a window from a wall, but not always, and that might be by feeling the colder air that comes off of a window.

"I had taken up wrestling in the 2nd grade, and when I eventually lost my sight, I thought that would be the end of wrestling and all sports activities. However, my coach explained that there are special rules for a 'blind guy,' and taught me how to do what is called a touch start, whereby my opponent touches my hands constantly whilst we are on our feet. If we should lose this contact, the referee blows his whistle and we reconnect. This enables a blind wrestler to know where his opponent is, making it totally fair.

"I was and still am very thankful for that rule. Actually, blindness is an advantage in some ways when wrestling. When you're sighted and wrestle you use your eyes constantly, and don't 'feel' where your opponent's balance might be off, but being blind you can feel this, and may be able to lever him off of you: advantage blind guy! Because of that advantage, I continued to wrestle, and as an 8th grader I came in second and in the 9th grade I came in first in the state. Establishing and then maintaining a sports activity throughout my junior high and high school years was extremely important in the development of who I

am, my self-confidence: you know, that male ego testosterone thing.

"Still, I was really stubborn and didn't want to admit I was going blind. Learning mobility meant using a cane, so I told my itinerant teacher that that was not going to happen. We eventually compromised and she drove me far away from my neighborhood to learn how to use a cane. I got the general idea but never used it; I didn't want anyone to see me with that thing in my hand.

"I graduated from high school and went to college at the University of Utah, and still didn't use a cane (the only time I use a cane now is when I'm doing a school assembly, and talk about failing the test: I still hate that thing). I was literally falling down the stairs at college, probably giving the impression I was drunk. There are actually worse things than being blind, but at that time, I really didn't care if they thought I was drunk.

"One day, while watching the *Sally Jessie Raphael Show*, guest Tom Sullivan was talking about his Guide Dog, and how he had just retired one and had a new one. Well, that changed everything for me, and I began thinking that if my hero, Tom Sullivan, could do that then I could, too.

"Tom Sullivan authored the book *If You Could See What I Hear* which was made into a movie. He was a wrestler, a musician, a commentator on *Good Morning America*, and the guy I wanted to be like, so when he wrestled, I wrestled; when I heard that he coached, I knew that I could coach; when I heard that he had a Guide Dog, I wanted a Guide Dog. He was really my role model, and thank goodness he awakened me to the value of a Guide Dog, probably one of the most valuable lessons I would ever learn.

"An incredible fun, scary chance opportunity arose which brought *Good Morning America* to my doorstep. (The program shadowed me for a week, culminating in a wrestling match I was coaching, and a meeting with Tom Sullivan, and a good-natured one-on-one with Sullivan.)

"Thinking that the initial call from the program was a joke, I gave the producer an incredible schedule of activities for the upcoming week. Consequently, my first ever singing 'gig' occurred at a local restaurant (which did me a big favor) but it got a mention on the progam so quid pro quo! I was shaking like a leaf: a very nervous little boy even though I was twenty-four. When *Good Morning America* asked me who my heroes were, of course, Tom Sullivan was top of that list. I explained the connection and how I had patterned much of my life after his, how because of him I got my Guide Dog, coached wrestling, and sang. At the end of the week, on the last day, the progam surprised me by bringing Tom Sullivan to my wrestling match. My hero! It was an awesome experience.

"I called the Guide Dog school after watching that show, and it sent someone down to give me a test. A test! Okay, I can take a test. I thought they were going to give me a verbal test or a Braille test, and had no clue they were going to give me a cane test, so I didn't practice, I hadn't been using a cane – had never used a cane, not really. I guess I was lucky I even had a cane around.

"The tester told me to cross an intersection I used to get my bus to school, which I usually navigated by following movement, and dark and light shapes that I could see. I crossed that street every day to take the bus so, okay, I could do this. I was meant to use the cane, I mean, actually navigate with it, bounce it back and forth, back and forth, to continually check my footing. He failed me as it was obvious I had no confidence about where to put my foot for that next step based on the use of a cane.

"A dog is not a car, but he's a little like a car: he doesn't know where he's going, so you need to 'drive' him. And that's what I wasn't doing: I simply couldn't do it. And if you don't have confidence walking with a cane, there is no way you can walk with a dog. So I failed, but was told to try again.

"I think anything that's worth anything is hard work. And so the same day I failed, I took my cane, went out, and started practicing. I wasn't going to fail again. Tom Sullivan did it, and I could if he could. I took my cane to school, even though I was still a little embarrassed because

people knew me without it, and all of a sudden they were seeing me with it. A lot of my previous actions probably made sense that day, as people realized that I just coldn't see. I practiced a lot, and my tester kept in touch with the mobility instructor at the blind center, telling him how and why I failed the first time. I called my mobility instructor to ask for his help, and we went all sorts of places: to the hospital to learn about halls, and to the avenues to understand how to work curves and streets. I called for help and it was there. Finally, it was time to take the test again, I was ready – and I passed!

"When I went to the Guide Dog school I was valedictorian of my class, and that was because of a big, monstrous, yellow Lab called Libo. Libo was long-legged, about 110lb (50kg), the biggest dog in class. So beautiful, so big he almost didn't make it as a Guide Dog. He did his job so well they were just waiting for someone with the legs and the speed to match, and that was me!

"Libo was my first Guide Dog, my first partner. It was just Libo and I at that time, and our bond became great immediately, with a strong, unique kind of loyalty to one another. He was amazing. Libo was why I was valedictorian; he was a true champion. He was beautiful: everyone would always comment on how beautiful he was, but they didn't need to tell me, I just knew.

"One of my requests was for a dog who would walk fast, and so both of my dogs really moved. That's one of the great things about this school; they ask what your lifestyle is, they watch you walk without a cane, more questions, they watch and analyze everything you do at the school without you even knowing.

"And finally, on that third day, after they have watched you walk around and interact with everyone and all of the dogs, they pick your partner. When they gave me Libo I was so intimidated. I could hear him across the room – heavy panting sounds – and they said 'Okay, we're going to let him go and he'll run over to you, so be ready.' Wow! He ran right over and he was so huge, I was thinking how could this big, monstrous, muscular thing get me to all the places we needed to go? He seemed like such a

Sachmo watches as Clint practices with one of the members of his wrestling team. Sachmo's awareness of Clint's every move demonstrates his protective nature, as he waits, patient and attentive, until it's time to wear his harness and go to work again.

big oaf but he was just a big, happy, fun dog when he was out of harness.

"With his harness on he changed, and that big muscular body easily negotiated any street corner, any hall, and any doorway I could imagine. Libo took me to work, and we traveled on airplanes, trains and automobiles. There were no restrictions because of my blindness – not any more.

"The training class was four weeks in San Raphael, California, but before you get the honor of going home with your new dog, your partner, the last test is a drive downtown, where you are dropped off and told where to go and how much time to take, just you and your partner. My instructors told me that my destination was a bar when really it was a mortuary. They were just joking, trying to make the scary a little funny, though at the time it probably wasn't funny at all. I had to ask where I was, to swallow my pride and ask for help, which has never been easy for me. I had to get back to the meeting place so that day I did ask and we got back on time.

"It's difficult to describe how rewarding this achievement was. Alone – though not really as Libo was with me – I got where I needed to without the help of someone's arm, without stumbling, and without a cane. Holy cow: I (we) can do this by myself (Libo and I)! That's what I mean when I say, he is I, I am he, our purpose is so totally the same, the meeting of minds, the uniting of souls, a synergy like no other.

"When you're at the school training for a month with the instructors, they are watching all you do, checking your commands and correcting your handler efforts. But when they put you on the plane and you go home, well, it's like all those instructions go out the window. I even forgot how to talk to Libo, I was just really, really scared, and lost my confidence without someone to hold my hand. Warned this could happen, it actually did take about two or three months to conquer those feelings of fear. Fortunately, Libo was smarter, and just put up with all my mistakes, giving me the necessary time to grow into our relationship. He was solid in his training and didn't miss a step.

"What makes a dog stand out, why does he get things done ahead of everyone else, how does he see what needs to be done when no one else has a clue?

"The runaway orange juice – an interesting example of this – occurred at the Guide Dog school. Our group was walking down the hall toward class one day when a student began going into diabetic shock, and needed sugar immediately. We knew juice in a can was quickly available from a vending machine, except we dropped the can, and it began rolling down the hall. Everyone in that hall was blind, but we could hear the can rolling, and tried to follow its direction. Libo pulled his harness out of my hand, excitedly retrieved the can, and even punctured it so that we could give the student what she needed. What a dog! No wonder I was valedictorian of that class. The teeth marks were a cute touch, but we could have used the pull-tab, Libo!

"Settling into a job that allowed for my assertive energy whilst not stifling my creative side proved hard. I never finished college; I kept looking for something more fun than classes. I had started in music therapy but I was really more into girls, meeting chicks, but they still don't give a degree for that.

"I struggled with jobs that didn't allow me to be my own boss. My learning curve found me traveling from job to job on the bus with Libo in one hand, a Braille typewriter bumping on his back whilst I juggled my guitar on his other side. Libo never complained; he just took me from one job, one gig, one wrestling practice to another. We made quite a pair as I kept trying to settle down or settle into something that worked for me.

"During most of this time I had been coaching at my old junior high school, a job I actually held for seven years. Since a coaching job is seasonal it allowed development of other interests. Speaking at a health class about my blindness was really the break I had been looking for. That first request led to more requests, and then a school assembly, and I began a new and exciting career that took me all over the US. An Orem booking agent kept Libo and I busy for the next year traveling from school to school in Utah.

It was exciting and fulfilling, as day after day Libo and I traveled by bus to a new and different school to give what I hoped was an inspirational, entertaining speech, or to coach wrestling. Life was really good and our bond grew as the two of us, both in our prime, stepped out to experience new people and unique places.

"Finally, however, I needed another booking location because almost everybody in Utah had heard our speech. Fortunately, I found a nationwide company that gave me a contract to tour seven states in six weeks. It was a hard sell because it was the wrong time of year, and bookings had already been filled for which I had not auditioned. Not even my experience, or persistent calls seemed to help.

"Someone else's misfortune, however, was my good fortune, and resulted in a six-week trial and what was to be one of the scariest, most difficult and yet ultimately rewarding experiences of my life.

"The booking agent asked if I had a driver because so many of the places I had to go were too rural to have a bus service. Did I have a ride? 'Yes!' was my reply, although the reality was that Libo and I set off with a large backpack, his dog food duct-taped to the back, and a list of small towns in Wyoming, Nevada, Idaho and Montana, South and North Dakota, New Mexico, and Colorado.

"The very first gig on the road was in Burley, Idaho, and I still don't know exactly where I was dropped off (from the bus that did run there). I want to tell you that it was on the freeway because I heard a lot of cars and stuff, but I know a bus can't just stop and drop you off on the freeway, so I really don't know where I was. Asking the driver for directions he told me which way to go, pointed (I assume), and was off. It was about three in the morning, and whether or not I went the way he said I will never know, because, of course, I could not see the direction he may have pointed out.

"Libo and I walked for a long time, for at least a mile, with me wondering whether I should turn round, or would that take us further away from someplace – anyplace! So we continued walking, wondering what had made me think I could do this, what was I doing on this road trip! This was my first speaking gig, and I couldn't even get to it because not only did I not know where the hotel was, I didn't know where we were!

"After walking for an hour or more I realized that Libo was walking me up to someone's front door: obviously not the hotel door but Libo knew we were lost, and had decided to ask for help. On the porch steps I felt for the door and just started knocking. I knew I was going to make someone very angry, considering the time, but I needed help. It was late to be knocking on someone's front door, and they were probably a little scared about who it might be, but finally they answered and I explained my situation.

"I told them I was blind – probably obvious, with Libo at my side – and they were absolutely great, and drove us to the motel room. And that's how the whole thing started: our six-week tour began in Burley, Idaho, sometime between three and four o'clock in the morning.

"That night, I learned to listen to my partner, and I also learned to ask for help. It was rewarding, and it was hell, and I'm very proud of myself for that one. It obviously would not have happened without Libo.

"From school to school and state to state I traveled for the next four weeks, working out transportation by asking anyone around me for directions or a ride. Eventually, however, the pressure, the exhaustion, and trying to maintain a schedule in the remote locations of my bookings did get to me. My booking agent was under the impressions that I had my dad with me, because I was never late and everything went great, everyone was happy and there were no complaints. But the challenges were getting greater every day and I was wearing out. I did finish the six-week tour, though, and was given a contract for the next year-and-a-half. My agent said I had proven myself reliable under tough circumstances, and the quality of my talks was exceptional.

"So I found a driver – my new wife – and we went on tour. My agent was very fair; he made it work for us, and we had a great new traveling van with all the bells and whistles. I thought I was going to be the next Elvis: I really thought I was going to go on the road and be discovered. How silly of me; it was a dream, which kept me in debt for a long time. Meanwhile, we hit 38 states in 18 months, going as far as New Orleans, Delaware, Alabama, and Florida – we went everywhere, and there are only nine states that I haven't given a talk in. My wife was a real trooper as we traveled over 86 thousand miles in that time. It was a great experience, our rural towns keep us going; they are really awesome.

"The time came when I settled into a hometown job, coaching wrestling, of course, and raising my son while he recuperated after being hit by a car. It was a special time for the three of us, Tyler, Libo, and me. I started playing my music again, remarried, and helped my new wife raise her young daughter. Home commitments keep me from going on the road like before, but I would still like to check out those nine states I missed, keep coaching wrestling at the junior high school, and book some singing gigs. It's not too late to become the first blind Elvis ...

"Throughout my college experiences, balancing the Braille typewriter, guitar and backpack on the bus, and then when I first started on the road, Libo was in his prime, with me every step of the way. When I settled into my coaching job, and when I changed schools to coach and be with my son, Libo walked a mile twice a day with me traveling to school and back. But it finally came time to retire Libo, a day I thought would never arrive. My life experiences, my career, my dreams, would not have been possible without him, and the thought of another dog was impossible to accept, but Libo couldn't keep working, and I needed another dog to get through my day, to function.

"This is a situation that everyone who works as intimately with his canine partner as I do has to face. Taking care of your old partner while trying to establish a relationship with a new dog, a dog that you need to make your partner because your daily life depends on it, well, it seemed impossible. How did I do that without breaking Libo's heart, or mine, for that matter? Finding Libo

another home for his retirement years didn't bear thinking about, but I was only thinking of myself, as I was to learn. Yes, I kept Libo at my side some of the time, and, yes, I still hugged him and told him 'Good boy!' – when I wasn't hugging and saying the same to Sachmo, my new, big, beautiful, yellow Lab.

"For the first time in our life together, Libo came second. When they approached me Sachmo would knock Libo or push him aside. It was just awful. It was so hard to watch Sachmo bully Libo, pushing him away.

"Libo slept a lot, and whilst sleeping he had started panting in a harsh, deep, raspy voice. Libo had always been such an alpha dog, such a tough man, but now he was a feeble man and he was dying. I made the decision that it was time. Libo died on Sept 27, 2002 aged 13. My veterinarian came to my home, and I asked him not to talk to me because I knew I would cry, just to touch my shoulder and leave.

"The first injection was to make Libo relaxed and sleepy, and he gave a big sigh. Right at that second, I just wanted to say 'never mind, never mind we'll just let him sleep,' but it was time, and I knew that. I was sitting on the floor with Libo nestled in my lap when the second injection was given. A big exhalation of breath, that final sound of life, followed the injection. Sitting and holding Libo, crying and remembering, I was barely aware of the doctor leaving. After all the preparation, after all the turmoil and the getting ready for this moment, it was over. It was really over, and I needed one more moment alone to say goodbye.

"Silently, Tyler, my son, left too. Tyler had shared so much with us throughout Libo's life, but he knew these last few minutes needed to be for just the two of us. It was important I do this alone as it was the last thing I would ever be able to do for Libo.

"Arrangements had been made to have Libo buried in Logan on a plateau overlooking a dairy herd. I remember putting his body in the back of the truck. I didn't want anybody to help me with Libo's body. I was his dad, and so I carried him. I will always remember the difference as I placed his body in the back of the truck: the difference between that hundred pounds just minutes ago, and now.

"My farmer friend had already dug a large hole on his mountain, so everything was ready when we arrived. His family had prepared an initial prayer and then a final prayer while covering Libo's body: it was a real funeral. We planted tulips which I know come up every year. I've only been back to that plateau once because it's so far away, but I know the tulips keep blooming for Libo.

"I buried Libo there because he had started life as a mountain pup. I felt the mountain was the right place for him to rest. Libo dying was an amazing moment, which I will always remember. I know his soul was not in his body, his body was not my Libo, he was not there. I'll never, never forget that moment!

"What will I do next time, when it's time to retire Sachmo? Any answer I give today will only be a guess. With Libo, I could not think of giving my partner to someone else, all the time wondering how he was, did he miss me as much as I missed him, was he happy? After Libo died, I told myself that next time I would wait until this happened before getting anogther dog, but the reality is that if I don't have a canine partner to help get me to work and through the day, I'd be isolated, unable to go anywhere without a cane, and I simply can't go back to that. I can love a dog but I can't love a cane, and I need that love.

"Are my partners tools? If you take away the emotion, and consider only the practicalities of what you can and can't do without them in your life, then, maybe. But anyone who has experienced that type of life-sustaining relationship knows that the love given freely and forever is what makes the partnership so very special. And that is something that no tool, no object can ever provide ..."

Clint

A loving bond is crucial, but without the ability to boldly sense danger; to hear oncoming traffic, to see holes in the street, sense a deadly coma, or apprehend the bad guy, it is simply a loving bond, which, to the blind and law enforcement is not enough. Fortunately, these inborn senses also provide pack protection and nurturing; enabling strength of character and courage that facilitates intelligent disobedience whilst uniting partners in purpose, enabling two to achieve goals that cannot be accomplished by one.

Glimpses of canine heart are seen in all of the stories in this chapter, together with trust and communication between species. Are the dogs tools? Is the relationship symbiotic? Both are terms used by the stories' authors. When used in the appropriate context, these descriptions really do add clarity to the deeper dimension of this unique relationship, which permits basic daily functioning as well as create that special bond; the very essence of life for the blind partners.

Confident, nurturing Guide Dogs and tough, intimidating K9s become family members. And like all of the other canine partners in this book they spontaneously react and use intelligent disobedience when a situation requires immediate action; not waiting for commands or directions, they sense and react instinctively to environmental dangers.

Because the very lives of their human partners can depend on their sense of perception and physical strength, the result is a partnership with a unique unity of purpose that enables basic tasks to be safely accomplished, and is integral to every action, every moment of every day, giving a normalcy that allows living.

Experiencing the deep and intimate depth of my relationship with Katie, and having worked for years with law enforcement and Search and Rescue, I can only attest to the fact that there is a difference. These stories illustrate that difference, which, although subtle, is not understandable in every respect, or even easily described. But the blind and the police know and live that difference, and so do the canine partners walking at their side.

> "By creating powerful Guide Dog partnerships, we empower capable people to fulfill their dreams." – Guide Dogs for the Blind fact sheet[7]

Therapy partners

A gift to those in pain

Our therapy partners possess a unique mystical ability that touches not only the heart, but also the soul of those in pain. Most of what a therapy partner does defies explanation, and all the obedience classes and socialization in the world will only produce a social, obedient partner: the ability to reach into the soul of someone in pain, that's instinct, and extremely rare. A well-behaved therapy partner working in nursing homes, schools, libraries, and hospitals is priceless, prompting smiles and tender moments that benefit emotional and physical wellbeing. But the stories which follow are about that deeper innate ability – canine heart – that soothes and calms a tormented spirit.

Therapy partners instil a sense of tranquility and wellbeing, which, in some cases, allows healing to begin.

Providing a glimpse of therapy dogs in action was not difficult because dozens and dozens of volunteers step forward, train exhaustively, and then give much of their time to let others enjoy the big brown eyes and soft nose of a dog which say: I am here for you – I am here *just* for you. Therapy partners can single out the one person in a room full of strangers who needs help. Their olfactory senses are sensitive to the changes in our bodies; they know when something is not right, and in some cases, they know this before the person does. Animals who sense imminent death, or physical or emotional

"Far from being a luxury, pets are now recognized as a necessity – friends who fortify us daily with their gifts of love, loyalty and laughter." – Dr Allen Schoen

crises are drawn to the individual to provide comfort.

The therapy animals in the stories which follow offered all of themselves without holding back, something rarely experienced, especially between different species and with complete strangers, as the following story about my retired narcotics specialist, Lex, who was also an intuitive therapy partner until her passing in 2012, illustrates.

Nan and Lex

The smell of chemicals in the ward seemed especially strong as I looked around to give some direction to Lex, but she had already climbed onto the couch and into his arms, positioning her muzzle in his long, gray beard, which looked as though it might weigh the same as he did. Small in stature, he gently cradled 75lb (34kg) of German Shepherd as his tears fell into his beard, rolling onto her muzzle. For more than five minutes all of us – patients, nurses, me – sat motionless, not wanting to intrude.

What took place in those five minutes? I've contemplated those moments over and over, and I still don't understand why or how Lex knew this man needed her. How did he communicate his need to her? Why did she respond with such total compassion and submission? Their silent communion went on forever, it seemed: did he have so much pain to ease?

A week later the same man knelt to greet Lex, scratching her ears and speaking softly, but with renewed confidence and strength, and then they both simply moved on. As an afterthought, he turned to me and said "She knows, she knows I don't need her today?" Some seven months after that, a chance meeting in a parking lot placed these two together once again. As the man knelt to scratch her ears, these once-intimate strangers, seemingly remembering 'that time, that pain,' gently touched then went on their way."
Nan

Therapy partners are capable of amazing things: noting the slightest change in the eye's pupil; distinguishing the fingerprints of identical

Nan and Lex.

twins; sensing imminent strokes (a neurological disease) and cancer (a physiological disease). And when these partners are repeatedly exposed to the pain of humankind, their giving and compassion help in ways that can't be equalled.

Pain can throw up a wall of isolation and hostility often impenetrable to family, friends, and medical help, withdrawal for the sake of self-preservation becoming the only answer. Introducing a safe, non-threatening element, breaching those barriers, if only for a few minutes, has proven beneficial in all manner of health issues. And that is exactly what a therapy canine partner can do, offering a temporary buffer against the pain and isolation with safe, uncomplicated love, by way of a simple physical connection which allows the body to experience enhanced relaxation and restored health.

Lisa and Hoop and Dunk
Pain that is shared lessens; love that is enjoyed grows
"There's something about humans and their inner hearts and souls that become moved and enlightened by the presence of an animal. Sometimes it may be just looking at a dog, or wrapping two arms around that furry being which gives back unconditional love. Therapy animals provide just that!

"The benefits of animal therapy, the ability of these creatures to break through barriers and

"Until one has loved an animal, part of their soul remains unawakened." – Anatole France, *For the Love of Saint Thais*

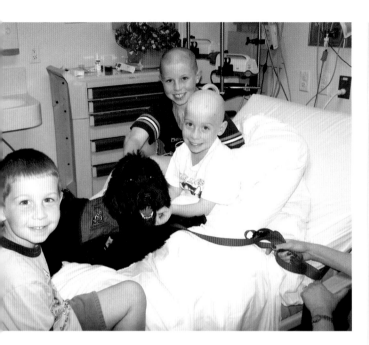

At times of family crisis the comfort provided by the presence of a therapy partner can create priceless memories.

"There has never been a breed of dog designed to enjoy encroachment from strangers. Dogs who actually enjoy interaction in clinical and educational settings are very rare, and the uniqueness of their talent should be appreciated.

"For dogs, the effects of real human emotion, the stress of having large numbers of unfamiliar humans grabbing and hugging them, contact with toxic surfaces, and overcoming sensory stimuli are not simply training issues.

"Nothing else dogs do compares to the kinds of intrinsically stressful social interactions that takes place when they visit clinical, educational, or post-trauma situations. No other canine-related events, no sport nor competition requires a dog to enter the intimate zones of unfamiliar humans and remain there for several minutes of petting and hugging." – Kris Butler, *Therapy Dogs Today – Their Gifts, Our Obligation*

form healing bonds, have been well documented. Hoop was my first therapy dog: a beautiful Golden Retriever. He understood when he needed to jump up on a bed, how to match his pace to that of a patient, or when to reach out with a slobbery kiss, and he did his job better than most.

"The plan from the very first day was, hopefully, to end up with a well-adjusted, trained therapy dog, but it wasn't until Hoop was a year old that we discovered that the limping we thought was 'overdoing it' or 'growing pains' was actually elbow dysplasia. His elbows were simply malformed at birth and untreatable. Since Hoop was already our family's treasured companion as well as a therapy dog, my goal was to preserve his elbows the best way I could: controlling his weight and preventing any jumping down on his front legs.

"Hoop always got high-spirited when I got out his therapy bag and vest: he loved to go to work! In a rehab situation Hoop truly became a very unique therapeutic tool. Standing up more because they weren't afraid of losing their balance, Hoop helped patients work longer and harder. Making their therapy fun while at the same time challenging them to do just a little more brightened their day without causing the usual anxiety or fear.

"One of our favorite volunteer positions was in a hospital Inpatient Adult Rehabilitation Unit. My Retriever's passion was playing fetch with a tennis ball, which may seem like fun and games, but can assist many goals in therapy. These could include standing or sitting balance; weight-bearing, arm control, vocalization – the list is endless. We had received special permission to play unleashed with the ball in a controlled environment, where patient safety would not be compromised, so Hoop freely chased his ball to the delight of the patients.

"Often, even a patient who appears outgoing and cheery is dealing with a traumatic life-altering illness or injury. The genuine smiles and tears of happiness when someone thanks my dog for helping with the therapy warm my heart, and is just plain good for my soul. This positive, happy feeling occurs not only within my patient and myself, but also their family, the nurses, and other therapy people involved.

"One of Hoop's greatest success stories was an eighteen-year-old girl who was semi-comatose after suffering a traumatic brain injury in a car accident. After three months in the hospital with no apparent recovery, Nicole's therapists and parents were extremely worried about her lack of progress. She had not opened her eyes, moved her limbs purposefully, nor spoken in that whole time, and there was the very real possibility that she would be moved to an extended care facility from the rehab unit where she would receive much less therapy.

"Then one day Hoop was introduced to Nicole as she lay on the mat. He snuggled up next to her and she slowly reached out her arms, as if in a trance, and hugged him. Her mother had tears in her eyes as she told us how much Nicole loved animals. Although Nicole didn't open her eyes, she clearly craved the love and feeling of Hoop's warm, hairy body. Everyone begged me to bring him back as soon as possible. Although I usually volunteered at this location weekly, I felt Hoop's presence was paramount to Nicole's recovery, so we went almost every day.

"Nicole continued her spontaneous dog petting, hugging and snuggling, and slowly, over the following days and weeks, she progressed to sitting up with help, still reaching for and grasping Hoop. She still seemed to be in a fog, moving slowly, not talking, and appearing sleepy, but finally opened her eyes and began to follow simple commands, such as pointing to various body parts on Hoop.

"Her mother said, 'Hoop is the one thing Nicole has connected with immediately, the one

"... it [enhanced relaxation] produces health and longevity. This is the powerful lesson that animal companions have taught us ...The Delta Society plays a major role in educating society about the health benefits of animal companions. Whether it is the enhanced relaxation produced by pet animals in the classroom when children read books aloud, or the lowering of blood pressure in the elderly when they pet an animal, or the role animals play in social support and long-term survival of heart patients, the evidence is overwhelming.

"Animals, and nature in general, are a marvelous health tonic. If we include them in our lives, if our physiology is set in a way that includes the rest of the living world, then we live longer and certainly more rewarding lives. The Delta Society has a very real role in helping more members of our society live their lives in an inclusive fashion, to reach out to others, to educate our educators about a new type of biology – one that is living and interactive, and to help end the ever-rising tide of human loneliness and social disconnectedness, which is the great plague of the new millennium." – James J Lynch PhD, Delta Society[8] magazine

thing that makes her feel normal. Usually she is so detached, but with Hoop, she is definitely awake and responsive. He drew things from her effortlessly when no one else could. Her expression has softened from a tense, clenched jaw and tight shoulders to a relaxed mouth and shoulders. It's wonderful. Hoop is a Godsend.'

"Nicole's therapists were pleased with the rapid progress she was now making with Hoop. When she was finally able to stand with assistance, Nicole reached for a ball and dropped it for Hoop, and soon progressed to throwing it. She continued to improve physically and mentally, starting to talk and balancing upright on her own. She could say Hoop's name, and would reach for biscuits to feed him, picking a biscuit's color with 100 percent accuracy. Without doubt, Hoop had a dramatic impact, helping Nicole to come out of her coma, and making a tremendous difference to her recovery.

"Hoop also worked weekly with a twelve-year-old boy in a Pediatric Residential Treatment Center for nine months. Tim was learning how to love and trust after being neglected, abused, and abandoned by his mother. The boy believed he was learning to care for a dog named Hoop, and train him to follow his commands, as well as loving Hoop. In addition, he was also learning important nurturing, social, and play skills for which he'd not previously had role models: skills which would later carry over to his relationships with people, with the help of his psychologists, although this would take much time and therapy. Eventually, Tim was ready to go to a new foster home: Hoop had made a huge impact.

"Hoop himself lived with the chronic pain of his poor, malformed elbows, understood imperfection, and knew about courage. Somehow this dog instinctively knew this universal lesson: pain that is shared is lessened; love that is enjoyed grows, and this made him a worthy friend indeed. He finally crossed the bridge at the ripe old age of twelve-and-a-half years. We were deeply saddened, but his time here with us had been well spent, and shared with many others.

"After we got Hoop, our beautiful Golden Retriever, and my whole family had fallen in love with him, as previously noted, we were disappointed to learn that he had malformed elbows which would deteriorate over time. At this point he was already a therapy dog and working in two different hospitals.

"His breeder offered us a female puppy, sort of as a gesture to compensate for our already limping but beloved dog. We accepted and Hoop's little half-sister, Dunk, arrived when Hoop was two. Although an afterthought, Dunk immediately settled in with her very own built-in 'mom' – Hoop.

"I noticed that Dunk was very loving, but also very timid, so encouraged everyone to pet and interact with her to build her confidence. She needed more than the usual amount of socializing, which included taking her to many different locations and asking people we met there if they would please pet her! We were very successful with this phase of her training because who wouldn't want to pet a fluffy Golden Retriever puppy?

"Obedience training was an absolute breeze for Dunk, some of which may be down to her breed as Goldens are smart and lovable, of course. Dunk's greatest quality was her absolute desire to please; I could teach her some things in just a day. She automatically watched my face closely, not only to receive love and affection, but also to follow any requests. I taught Dunk to give just a single bark to alert me to outside occurrences and objects, and then come to me for an affectionate 'well done!' This allows a dog to forget about what she has alerted you to by the time he or she has received praise. I had forgotten I had taught her this just the once, so when Dunk did it the next time and came running to me, looking into my face, I wondered what it was she wanted. Suddenly, I realized that she was reinforcing the new behavior with me!

"Dunk passed the Delta Society Pet Partner exam with flying colors at just a year old, as had Hoop, so away we went! I worked several programs, using Hoop for some and Dunk for others. Hoop was a hard act to follow, as he had already won numerous awards and been in newspapers, magazines, a movie, and on TV! He was certainly well known. Dunk, however, was the better therapy dog in my opinion: food tray smells or refuse containers didn't distract her! When she was working, she was working 100 percent.

"Dunk was one of those special K9s: a therapy dog who knew just what a patient needed at just the right time. Her biggest asset was her ability to transfer her concentration, love, obedience and inspiration from me to her client/patient, and then be able to switch gears again as she worked with a new patient.

"Her patients loved this attention, the feeling of connection and freedom to play and interact with Dunk. She sensed when patients wanted to be with her and got up close to them, allowing them to pet her and love her. She frequently licked a hand, then looked up expectantly in the hope it would respond with some rubbing and petting. I never had to encourage her to get closer or pay attention to someone.

"When Dunk was about five years old, we encountered a speech and language therapist with a young man in the main open area of the Rehabilitation Center. The therapist, called Sue, was just standing there, seemingly at a complete loss about what to do with her patient. Approaching us, she asked if we could work together in what appeared to be 'last ditch' desperation.

"Bill, her patient, had suffered some kind of brain trauma, although appeared completely normal physically. His problems centered on speech and comprehension, and he was confused, agitated, and didn't seem to know what to do apart from randomly walk about. Sue told me that Bill's rehab team of therapists had not witnessed any appropriate automatic speech, were unable to get Bill to follow any simple commands, or even point to pictures or simple words as a form of communication. He did not repeat words on request, only occasionally voicing what seemed to be gibberish. Although not certain, it was felt that very little comprehension was present (known medically as expressive and receptive aphasia). When no information seems to flow in or out of a patient, this is known as global aphasia, and Sue and the team feared that this was the case with Bill.

"As soon as we approached Bill with Dunk, it became immediately obvious he loved dogs, as he went down on one knee and wrapped his arms around her, speaking gibberish as he hugged, rubbed, and generally loved her all over. I was so pleased to see this very wonderful connection between Dunk and Bill, and, from then on, Sue stepped back and out of the therapy session and Dunk and I took over.

"I decided to try some ball playing with Bill, since sometimes it works as an automatic reaction to toss a ball to a dog. After I got Bill's attention, I asked him if he would like to take off Dunk's leash. I didn't indicate, or reach down to help, but he pointed to the leash and collar, looked at me quizzically, and asked 'Here?' and proceeded to

remove it. Sue and I made eye contact, wearing big smiles: this was one of the first verbal requests Bill had followed since coming to the unit! He understood what the ball was for, and immediately started throwing it for Dunk.

"At this point, I stepped back as well and let Dunk work her magic. She was concentrating one-on-one with Bill, and wasn't even thinking about me any more. Bill started yelling out to Dunk, some of which was gibberish, some clearer, and some a combination. The words and phrases he attempted or was able to voice were: 'get it,' 'come here,' 'sit,' and happy exhilarated cries of 'good dog' and 'yeah!' He was not able to say 'down' or 'stay,' but still got Dunk to understand with his own set of physical cues. He never could say 'ball' or 'Dunk,' but Bill was able to ask her to kiss him on the lips (which she normally would not do) by saying 'smoochie, smoochie.' He also asked her to 'shake,' which she did, and played the game of balancing treats on her nose that I had provided and demonstrated, releasing her to get the treat with a resounding 'okay!'

"People had gradually gathered to watch, amazed and delighted with Bill's communication,

The first time Bill followed a verbal request since arriving at the rehab unit. (Courtesy Laura Seitz, Deseret News)

Only a moment in time, but a lifetime to these children: therapy partners beget joyful smiles in a cold, sterile setting. Whatever, wherever, and whenever it is needed, the dogs give and give, with no regard to an environment full of pain and noxious odors, without animal comforts. Their objective is to provide tender succour to strangers in pain – and from the look on the faces of these children that's precisely what they're doing!

understanding, and joy in creating his own therapy. Dunk had responded to all of his needs and desires with love and enthusiasm; that was the kind of therapy dog she was: always there for the one she was helping.

"At the end of the session I calmly asked Bill if he would like to put her leash back on, with no visual cues or inflection in my voice, and he responded immediately by picking it up from the floor and clicking it onto her collar. Sue looked at me and her one word said it all: 'WOW!'

"The therapists were thrilled with this astonishing demonstration of capabilities they did not know their patient possessed because they had not been able to tap into them. Of course, I occasionally gave some gentle guidance, but Bill really did communicate with my dog using his own version of English and a few physical cues. One fluffy dog was able to do what several therapists with college degrees could not – and Bill sure proved them all wrong!

"This was only one example of how Dunk, during her tragically short life, filled therapists, families, and me with joy and delight. At just six years old, pancreatis took Dunk from us, leaving my family, Hoop and the many others who knew her or were touched by her to mourn her passing. A few short months later, Hoop had to retire, partly because of his poor elbows, but mostly his broken heart.

"My wonderful memories of Hoop and Dunk as my therapy partners and pets live on, and I know they helped the recovery and lives of so many people. They were both special partners, able to make special connections as they gave freely of their loving spirits to patients, families, and staff. Every time I think about Hoop and Dunk, it's their eager-to-please personalities and adoring way that each of them nudged us in pursuit of love and attention are what I think about most. Hoop and Dunk will always be missed!"
Lisa

Kathy and Jerry Lee
Pure happiness, pure love
"Jerry Lee was special from the very beginning: he had something, a special something I had seen

in only one other dog. Jerry Lee had the ability to make people love him, trust him and want to be near him, and I adopted him from the Salt Lake County Animal Shelter when he was nine months old in the fall of 1993. An Akita/Shepherd mix, he looked like a German Shepherd, with the fur and fluffy tail of an Akita. He was beautiful! We bonded quickly; it was as if I had had him all his life.

"The summer of 1994 I noticed the neighborhood children came over whenever Jerry Lee was outside in the front yard. These were kids of all ages, and I'd look over and see Jerry Lee laying under the cherry tree, with them laying down next to him, and even *on* him at times! He didn't seem to mind; he loved the kids and the attention he was getting.

"One night, a few years after I adopted Jerry Lee, I was sitting in the living room reading a story in *Reader's Digest*, and an article about a German Shepherd therapy dog caught my eye. As I read I was thinking to myself that Jerry Lee would be good at that, as he had the same gentle quality that the dog in the story did. At the end of the article there was a phone number to call, so I did. I told the person with ITA (Intermountain Therapy Animals[9]) about Jerry Lee, and he said he thought Jerry Lee would be a good candidate for that kind of therapy.

"A few weeks later Jerry Lee and I went to do our test of general commands, and determine whether medical equipment would bother him. We passed and were certified April 24, 1999.

"Our first session was at Shriner's Children's Hospital. I wasn't sure what to expect, but Jerry Lee wasn't worried: he seemed thrilled to be there. We walked into the recreation room where the staff supervised the children doing arts and crafts, watching TV, playing basketball, or just hanging out. Another therapy team – Pam and her dog, Tigger – was already there, and as Pam was in charge I followed her lead. The children were mostly non-English-speaking but this didn't seem to matter to them or Jerry Lee, as we walked from child to child, or they came to us to take turns petting him. Some knew enough English to ask his name.

"Every other Wednesday we went to the hospital, and after a while some of the nursing staff asked if I could take Jerry Lee to some children who couldn't get out of bed, because they'd just had surgery, or were too weak, or simply didn't feel like going into the recreation room.

"Going from room to room, we asked if they would like us to visit. Most were happy for us to do so, though some did not show interest. From the very first time we did this Jerry Lee seemed to know just what to do, very careful about putting his paws on the bed so he could see and be seen and petted by the child. It's hard to explain but he seemed to know to be especially gentle with these sick children. He would carefully negotiate close enough to the bed to get his front feet up without becoming entangled in the IVs, or any of the medical equipment present.

"The children and their parents would ask questions about Jerry Lee and what we did: how long had we been volunteering, and whether or not Jerry Lee was my dog. Some of the kids had been away from home for some time, and were missing their own dogs or pets, so our visits were a release for them.

"Some parents wanted to get a picture of Jerry Lee with their child, so he's had his picture taken with a lot of kids. Some kids wouldn't say much, just want to pet his fur. There were many children during the three years we went to Shriner's, but one really sticks in my mind.

"A little girl, sweet as can be, about 4 or 5 maybe, was staying there for a few days while her mother was having a baby. I think she had been a patient there before because the staff seemed to know her and her history. I'm not sure what her medical condition was but she couldn't talk, and I think she was, for the most part, blind.

"When Jerry Lee and I walked up to where she was laying in a red wagon and she felt his fur, her whole face lit up. The smile was as big as any I had ever seen since I had been going to Shriner's. Jerry Lee just sat there and let her pet him for as long as she wanted. He didn't try to get up or leave, just sat there. I'm not sure how long we were there with her but the sun had set. I didn't want to leave her; children like her are the reason

"What is man without the beasts? If all the beasts were gone, man would die from great loneliness of spirit, for whatever happens to the beasts also happens to man. All things are connected." – Chief Seattle, 1855

why I wanted to do this type of therapy with Jerry Lee. I wanted people to feel the same thing I felt when I was with him, that pure happiness, pure love which, even if they felt it for only a little while, let them know how special Jerry Lee was.

"After I got married, my husband, Mat, wanted to see what we did, so he came with us to Shriner's a few times, and after he saw the way the children reacted to the dogs, he understood why volunteering was so special to me.

"We also did the READ [Reading Education Assistance Dogs program[10]]. Jerry Lee and I would go to the old Salt Lake City Library, and sit with kids who wanted to read but were shy about reading out loud, though had no problem reading to dogs or animals in general.

"One time, a little boy came up to us and asked if he could 'try and read to him' [Jerry Lee]. He said he wasn't a very good reader but I have never seen anyone try so hard to sound out each word as he did. While he was reading to us he had one hand on Jerry, and used the other to turn the pages. It took him a while to finish a book but he did it. Every few minutes he would have trouble with a word and I would help him out, but when he was finished with that book he went and grabbed another and came right back to where we were sitting and started to read.

"After a few years of volunteering I had to retire Jerry Lee, as it was getting hard for him to get in and out of my truck. For almost 14 years Jerry Lee was my constant companion and my shadow, but on July 14, 2007 I had to say goodbye to my best friend. I knew that this day would come, and I will always have the precious memories of him with my family, my friends, and our time together at Shriner's Children Hospital, which will forever put a smile on my face – and bring a tear to my eye.

"This is for you, Jerry Lee Bear. I will love you forever."

Kathy

Right: Gently encouraging the child by sitting calmly and patiently as he reads.

Our working partners' focus and resultant attention to task is predictable. They warn their blind partner of imminent dangers, chase the bandit, locate drugs, track and find the lost,

accomplishing what they are trained to do when we ask them to do it. And the 'heart' that they bring to their partner and his family becomes as intrinsic to this relationship as their working drives, centered mainly on those in his immediate environment. However, most of the canine partners possess that insight which lets them somehow 'know' things, which would extend beyond their immediate family if the opportunity arose.

The therapy partners in this section possess a different level of trust that does reach out to complete strangers. Unlike 'leading man' and 'tracking for man,' both of which use instinctive skills, these therapy dogs seem to come equipped with a unique compassion for man and his pain. Sensing the anguish and distress of strangers elicits their canine nurturing, and a unique and powerful connection occurs as they give the same

> **"I, who had had my heart full for hours, took advantage of an early moment of solitude, to cry in it very bitterly.**
>
> **"Suddenly, a little hairy head thrust itself from behind my pillow into my face, rubbing its ears and nose against me in a responsive agitation, and drying the tears as they came."**
> **– Frederick Kenyon, *Letters from Elizabeth Barrett Browning***

amazing unconditional love that their partners receive every day.

Especially in the case of children, canines have been giving that extra something since that day 26,000 years ago when a small child and a dog walked together, and the following stories are examples of intense involvement in a classroom setting where children – and particularly those with special needs – receive that 'extra,' that canine heart.

Judy and Barrett, Jim and Truman
Barrett helped students to calm down; Truman lifted spirits that were sad

Barrett
"From the first moment that I felt his soft warmth, I knew Barrett was special. He was beautiful; his appearance invited touch, which brought on an amazing sense of calm and wellbeing, a profound sense of love and acceptance. Looking into his beautiful brown eyes, I understood that Barrett possessed an ancient knowledge that I might only barely grasp.

"Barrett came to us as a small and fluffy Guide Dog puppy, and our job as puppy raisers was to keep this darling yellow Labrador Retriever long enough to give him good, basic obedience skills, along with the skills he needed to be in public and around many types of people and animals. A quiet, calm, sweet-natured, obedient puppy, Barrett naturally tuned into the world, and especially the beings around him. He wasn't hard to train, and accompanied us everywhere – to the store, the movies, to work, to school, on vacation. He settled in with us, nicely complementing our other dogs, cats and birds. Nothing seemed to faze him, and he became a permanent fixture in my special education classroom. He would have made a terrific Guide Dog, but, as it turned out, that wasn't to be his purpose in life.

"When Barrett was young, a Great Dane running off leash attacked him, and, as a result, he became fearful of other dogs – any other dog, small, large, elderly, or young – and would focus on other dogs, rather than his handler. Often, dogs who are attacked become aggressive, but Barrett became more timid, hiding behind my legs when other dogs were around, which was quite amusing if the other dog was a Chihuahua or a Dachshund as Barrett weighed in at 84lb (38kg). If the other dog got close enough to sniff Barrett, he would dance around as if on a bed of nails.

"This behaviour was observed by staff visiting from Guide Dogs for the Blind, and Barrett was placed on a watch. After some attempts at desensitization, and further discussion, we removed his Guide Dog ID and he became my boy.

"When he was six months old I took Barrett to the local Festival of Trees. At the entrance was a line of senior citizens in wheelchairs, waiting to move through the displays, their hands in their laps, some with their heads bowed. Barrett moved to the first in line and laid his head in her lap. Once she was smiling, he moved to the next, and then the next, until he had visited everyone. I knew then that he had a unique gift. Barrett was special: peace emanated from him; just one touch told you that.

"I once took a Breema class [a special type of touch and massage] and took Barrett along. At breaktime, the teacher came over to pet him. Laying a hand on him she exclaimed 'Oh, my gosh! You don't need Breema with this dog. You have only to touch him to feel calm and peacefulness,' which was exactly right. My blood pressure dropped 20 points when I got him, but after he was gone, the 20 points returned.

"Because Barrett had been going to school in my special education classroom, it felt natural to have him continue in that capacity, so we had him assessed by Delta Pet Partner evaluators to see if he was suitable for therapy work, and he passed with flying colors. In my classroom, therapy dogs helped with behavior, physical exercise, motor control, and functional academics. They helped students learn how to care for another creature, gave them a topic to write about, and helped them cope with the ups and downs of Junior High.

"While Barrett worked in my room, we needed no time-out booths, no level system, no discipline plan or reward system. If a child was 'off,' we would simply suggest they sit with Barrett, and they would immediately calm down after only a second or two. On walks through the halls during passing time, every child would reach out a hand to stroke his fur, just a small stroke, and then be on their way.

"As we passed the counseling office one morning, a young lady was sitting on the bench, crying silently. Barrett left my side and laid his head in her lap. She looked at his sweet face and soon began to touch his head. Her tears stopped, her trembling ceased, she began to smile and sat up straighter. When he sensed she was okay, Barrett moved back to my side, and we carried on.

"School staff would often drop by the classroom to have 'Barrett time' when they were having a bad day, and counseling staff began to call and ask for him when they had a student who was particularly upset or despondent. Finally, at the end of the day, the track team would stop to take Barrett on their run: he loved running all-out, and what a wonderful release after being so good all day!

"My students became very attached to Barrett. One student, Laura, was fairly non-verbal, and would become easily upset by noises: her hearing was so sensitive that she could hear the office flip the switch for the intercom.

"One day, as she began to scream and hit the table, I said, 'Laura, you're upsetting Barrett.'

Barrett had placed himself at her feet and was looking up at her. She stopped, mid-scream, and turned to Barrett, saying, 'Sorry, Barrett.' It was the first that she had spoken directly to anyone. We all stared with our mouths hanging open.

"Laura began to talk to the dogs (we also had a beautiful Shepherd called Di). Just a word or two, and then a sentence. Next, she began writing them notes. Then Laura began to talk to us, and other students. The screaming stopped. With Barrett or Di by her side, she was able to handle the stimulation in classes that she could not before. When she began to feel upset, she would move to sit with the dogs. To this day, we credit the dogs in our classroom with opening up her communication.

"Teddy, a new student to my classroom, was brought to visit me before school started. New people, places, and routines are often difficult for students with autism. His mother came into my room, but Teddy stayed at the end of the hall, fearful. I moved to the door and peeked out; Barrett also moved to the door and peeked out. I said to Teddy, 'Barrett would like to meet you,' and moved back into the room. Barrett watched him a bit longer, and then followed me into the room. Teddy followed Barrett and the pair immediately bonded. Whenever he had a difficult day, Teddy would find Barrett and lie with him, head on Barrett's side. Barrett went with Teddy to PE and English, and Teddy would do his laps holding on to one of Barrett's two leashes. Barrett would walk carefully by his side.

"Bobby, a timid seventh grader with a great fear of dogs, arrived at our school. Wheelchair-bound, he had been told ahead of time that our school had dogs. The first day he and I talked about the dogs he told me he was afraid, and began to cry, I told him not to worry; the dogs did not roam free, and were therapy dogs. I explained what they did and said when he felt ready to meet one, to let me know.

"For the first two weeks I slowly walked Barrett to Bobby's classroom door, where we would stop, Barrett would sit, and I would wave. About the second week, Bobby beckoned us closer, so we walked into the class and stopped about five feet away. I introduced Barrett and we left. I did this again for the next two days.

"Then, Bobby asked us to come closer, and we walked slowly to his chair where I put Barrett into a 'down' at his side. The next day, after doing this, Bobby reached out and tentatively touched Barrett's head. Bobby gradually became comfortable with Barrett, taking his leash as we moved his chair from class to class.

"Barrett was in my classroom for five years before the school district banned animals in schools. Teddy would move to the 'sun spot' where Barrett had lain and say, 'I miss my Barrett.' As a matter of fact, we all did.

Truman

"Truman began coming to school at about this time. He, too, had been a Guide Dog puppy, but because of some physical problems was also 'career changed.' Bobby and I talked about Truman and how he was different from Barrett: not as calm and quiet. Truman was a happy-go-lucky Golden, not a responsible Lab, but Bobby quickly came to love Truman.

"Bobby liked to participate in his classes, but one involved an activity on the floor. Bobby couldn't sit without support, so often had to stay in his wheelchair during the fun. One particular day, Bobby wanted to try the floor. We thought we could brace his back on the desk, but before we could get him there, Truman moved behind Bobby and lay on the floor right behind him, where he stayed, supporting his back, allowing Bobby to participate the same as every other student.

"Truman also tuned into seizures. He and another dog, a German Shepherd called Connie, would move to the side of a student just as they began to seize. Truman would lie by their side and not move until they were 'with us' again.

"One day a student began to have cluster seizures: seizing, stopping, seizing, stopping. We called his mother who was unable to come immediately, but asked us to hold off calling the paramedics as she would get there as soon as possible. Truman stayed by the boy's side for an hour-and-a-half, and when his mother arrived she said 'Thank you, Truman, for caring for Paul.'

Straight after that she began to look for a seizure alert dog for her child.

"About the time the dogs were banned from school, my husband, Jim, began to work at Salt Lake Catholic Community Services in a homeless outreach program. Barrett had always been around teenagers and children with disabilities, which he seemed to get on best with. We began to do the READ program in libraries, grief camps, burn camps, and Easter Seals programs, and Barratt did amazing things. He loved kids, and just seemed to know who needed a caring presence in their life.

"Truman, on the other hand – a typical Golden – loved everyone: he didn't care how old or young, if they had a disability, were dirty or under the influence; he greeted everyone on the same terms. 'Hello, (woo, woo woo) I love you, I'm your friend, rub my tummy.' Truman began to go to work with Jim shortly after he began employment with Catholic Community Services of Utah at the St Vincent de Paul's Resource Center. The facility is a homeless outreach program, one of the largest on the Wasatch Front, providing an average of 800 meals per day, and a day room for the homeless to get out of the cold or the heat. Truman was an instant hit, and Jim quickly realized that he would be a valuable member of the mission and our homeless family.

"Jim's job at the center was a combination of daily operations and security. He was

It was obvious why Barrett and Truman were there, touching so many different hearts.

constantly making rounds and responding to fights or medical issues, with Truman as his constant companion.

"Drug and alcohol abuse often results in people having seizures, so if someone was 'down' for any reason, Truman would get as close as possible to them, lying by their side, cuddling in. Jim stopped him doing this at first until he noticed how it comforted the people who were sick, so he let Truman get on with doing his thing as he checked the person medically while waiting for emergency medical services. Truman did this so often that when the paramedics arrived they would say 'We'll take it from here, Truman.'

"Jim once fell down the stairs at home, badly injuring his arm. Truman 'cuddled in' and stayed by his side until he felt he could move, then walked beside him up the stairs so he could get help.

"Jim's and Truman's daily routine involved daily visits to the day room, where Truman would walk past each row of chairs, getting loved and talked to. The next stop was the Head Start Program, filled with kids who lived in the shelter in the neighborhood or in their cars. Truman was their dog, and parents brought in cameras so they could get their photos taken with Truman.

"When Truman first went to St Vincent's, Jim had a client named Kay who, as far as he could tell, had never spoken a word to him or anyone else. Which is not to say she didn't talk – she did – just never directly to anyone, but rather people who weren't there, or to thin air. Kay was sitting in the courtyard talking to herself one day when Truman, as was his custom, sat in front of her and put his head in her lap. Kay looked at Truman, and her chatter slowed, but that was about it. Jim and Truman would see Kay every day in her usual spot, and Truman would put his head in her lap, and Kay's talking would slow, but not much, and she would never acknowledge Jim.

"After about a week or two of this, Kay finally reached down and rubbed Truman's head, and this became the new routine when they stopped by to visit Kay. One morning about three months after first meeting him, Kay looked down at Truman and said 'Hello.' Kay would only talk

to Truman for a while, but finally included Jim in their conversation. Kay told Jim: 'When I touch Truman, the voices stop and I can hear God.' Truman helped Jim reach Kay and, although she stayed on the street, they could communicate through Truman.

"Jim was walking the food line one lunch period, monitoring the queue for problems. Standing near the front was a client new to St Vincent's: pretty ragged-looking, and also intoxicated. Jim was holding Truman on a lead, talking to another client, when the new fellow looked at Truman and stated rather loudly that he wasn't going to eat anyplace that allowed a stinking dog. Before Jim could begin his usual talk about the value of therapy dogs and certification requirements, several other St Vincent clients had surrounded the new guy, and one of Truman's friends had him by the shoulder, explaining that Truman was cleaner and probably smarter than him, and if he didn't like Truman he could get the hell out of town! Jim defused the situation and got everyone settled down, but I was amazed at how protective these people – the castoffs of society – were of a pudgy Golden.

"Truman was everyone's dog, and received Christmas cards and postcards from all over the country, as well as gifts of toys, doggie bones, and stuffed animals. Many of the homeless are transient, and cards would come in from all over addressed to Truman Upton. Some were written in English and some would simply say 'bark, bark, woof, woof.'

"And Truman became a star when he was 'miked-up' and followed on his rounds by Channels 5 and 13, and appeared on Channels 2 and 4 in Utah, as well as featuring on the front page of *The Tribune* and *Desert News*. Jim once Googled 'Truman' and found his photo in a foreign newspaper! He couldn't read the article but the picture showed Truman visiting with a family in the dining room of St Vincent. Before United Way [a coalition of charitable organizations] scheduled St Vincent tours, it always wanted to be sure Truman was around. He was best at soliciting donations, and was voted the Dog of the Year for

Intermountain Therapy Animals, though totally unimpressed by all the fuss.

"Truman loved his work, and found complete joy in coming to work, and, just as he enjoyed St Vincent, he also enjoyed the READ program, children's camps, nursing homes, and hospitals. Once when I borrowed Truman for a READ day at the city library, one of Jim's clients approached and asked me what I thought I was doing with Truman! I had to explain that I was Jim's wife and was just borrowing him for the day at the library. I knew that Truman would handle the huge crowds there like a champ, and so he did.

"When Truman passed away, the homeless clients donated the money for a tree to plant in the courtyard of St Vincent. A memorial service was held and attended by clients, staff, other homeless services providers, and many loved ones. And everyone wept.

"We have had many, many dogs in our lives, but Barrett and Truman were something else. Amazing to watch, they taught us how to love wholly and unreservedly. We miss them sorely, but would not forego a minute of our time with them to avoid the pain of their leaving. They were here for a reason, and many are better because of it."
Jim and Judy

The loss of a partner is felt by everyone in their world. In the context of therapy, the ability to use their special skills in an everyday working environment is unusual, and gives these partners the chance to intimately touch so many lives, reaching more and more hearts. Those places and organizations which allow and encourage visits and the presence of these dogs appreciate and understand their intrinsic value, and the succour they give to sometimes lost souls.

Lyn and Holly
Small but mighty

"Holiday Champagne – Holly – came into my life Thanksgiving 1992, and was to become a blond angel in a fur coat, though I didn't know that then, of course. Small in stature, but mighty in heart, this diminutive Cocker Spaniel skillfully reached

> "... dogs can be wise, compassionate, loyal, courageous, self-sacrificing, and altruistic. Most of all, they can give the purest, most unconditional love." – Allen and Linda Anderson, *Angel Dogs: Divine Messengers of Love*

into the souls of lost children, both the serious, tough, street kids, and the bruised and abused little child.

"Initially, I felt I had been coerced into having Holly, as she was the only dog I had never gone looking for. I had become friends, over a seven-year period, with my mail carrier, Jan, and she loved my little black Cocker, Chewy, who always greeted her with a wagging 'merry-tail' when she brought my mail.

"When I first knew Jan she told me: 'I raise Cockers with longer, smoother hair that doesn't matt easily,' adding: 'I think Chewy needs a friend.' I laughed and told her no, thanks. I'd had several dogs at a time, but since my husband and I were getting near retirement, we wanted to travel more, so one dog was enough. This conversation was one we had many times over the years as each new batch of puppies was born.

"Boys who participated in the therapy dog program were better behaved and did better in their classes." The dogs were a privilege, and many boys worked hard not to lose that privilege.

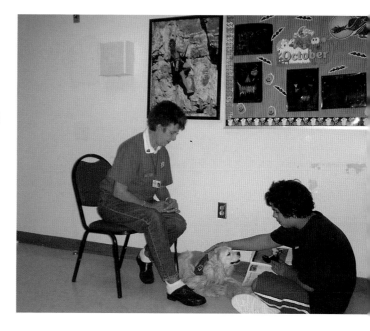

"One day in late fall my doorbell rang. It was Jan, who told me that her mama dog, Champagne, was getting older, so this would be her last pregnancy, and my last chance to have one of her puppies. My answer was still a firm 'no.' A few weeks after the puppies were born I passed Jan in my car as she was walking up my street. I thought she looked like she was crying, so I waited for her. The sad news was that a puppy had died. Jan had never lost a pup before, and was devastated. I consoled her the best I could, but a couple of days later another died: the pups had caught a respiratory infection. I asked Jan each day how the remaining puppies were doing. Oh, oh, getting too involved, I thought ...

"The day before Thanksgiving, Jan rang my doorbell. 'I have only one pup left, and I haven't been able to sell her. She's getting older, more shots are due, and I can no longer afford to keep her.' she told me. 'I know you would give her a good home so you can have her for free.' I replied, 'Jan, I can afford the dog, but we are heading out of the country after Christmas, and the lady who tends Chewy won't tend two dogs,' to which she replied 'I'll tend her for you when you travel.' 'Oh boy, Jan,' I said, 'I don't know if you're making this easy or hard, but let me think about it and talk to my husband.'

"Jan wanted us to stop by on Thanksgiving 'just to look' at the puppy, so, complete with our four-year-old granddaughter who we were babysitting, we headed to Jan's. The other puppies had been sold, but were being held for Christmas. My granddaughter whispered in my ear, 'Please can we have one?' and that was the beginning.

"As are all puppies, Holly was darling, cute, and mischievous. Chewy was less than thrilled with her new housemate, who was getting way too much attention. It was a very hard, cold, snowy winter in our state of Utah, and Holly was proving difficult to train outside. We would stand out in the cold and she would shiver and shiver and do nothing. I would feel sorry for her and bring her in, and in a few minutes she would slip off to a nice warm spot and pee on the floor.

"By the time Holly was a year old, she still wasn't properly house-trained, and pretty much did as she pleased; she didn't even seem to know her name. When she got out of the yard, she would sniff around and wander away, oblivious to my calling, not coming to me but not running away either: I had to go get her.

"Although I had taught many dogs to heel, and always enjoyed taking them for a walk, Holly wouldn't obey this instruction, and trying to walk her and Chewy at the same time was a hassle, as Holly would dash forward and back, around and around, tangling me in the leash. I tried an extending leash so she could walk ahead, but that was even worse as then she *really* tied me up, and I fell over on more than one occasion. I began walking the dogs separately, which was annoying and time-consuming, or left Holly at home, which made me feel guilty.

"By the time she was three, Holly was not a dog I was enjoying, but I keep my pets for life, no matter what. When she was due her annual shots, I lamented to my vet about her, and asked if he knew of a good trainer who would come to my house. Thankfully, he did. Our life was about to change for the better.

"Shawn showed up to give a free assessment of Holly, and asked: 'What is your goal?' 'To be able to walk my two dogs at the same time without Holly tripping me,' I told him. I watched through the living room window as Shawn took Holly out into our cul-de-sac to work with her, and in ten minutes she was walking to heel: I could not believe my eyes. Shawn had good news and bad news. The bad news was that Holly's happy-go-lucky personality meant she did not pay much regard to what was asked of her, but the good news was that she was smart, so with firmness and consistency would be easy to train. And there was me thinking she was a total airhead and the dumbest dog I had ever had. I had a thing or two to learn.

"I signed up for five lessons, and we practiced several times a day for short periods, as Shawn emphasized that this had to be fun for both of us. Praise – over and over – was Holly's reward, but consistent discipline was doled out if she didn't comply: her happy-go-lucky personality meant she couldn't be allowed to get away, even once, with disobedience. There was a lot of discipline at first, and Shawn had to remind me not to raise my voice to her, but to change my tone, telling me 'Standing next to you she can hear your heartbeat, you don't have to shout.'

"Five lessons went by very quickly, and I was amazed at how fast Holly was learning. I was having so much fun with her and we were definitely bonding. I decided to take a further five lessons in off-leash training, which Shawn warned me would be harder. 'With her personality, and off her leash, she will really want to do things her way.' he told me.

"Holly had to learn that I was the pack leader, but when walking her off-leash, Shawn pointed out that she never looked back to see where I was: she just didn't care. To get her to want to know where I was I had to play tricks on her by hiding behind trees and bushes, and she learned very fast.

"On our graduation day from obedience training, Shawn was accompanied by his constant companion and training partner, KC the German Shepherd. He also brought to the park his wife and son, his Bull Mastiff, Rottweiler, and large mixed breed dog to create a lot of confusion to see if it would break Holly's concentration. His wife and son played ball while the dogs ran around, but Holly paid absolutely no attention to them as she stayed totally focused on my commands and me.

"The last test was to put Holly on a 'sit-stay' command a good distance away. Shawn positioned his dogs in a circle between Holly and me, telling me 'Give her the "come" command.' When I did, Holly took off at a run, straight for me, right through the middle of the huge dogs. Shawn was really impressed, expecting her to run around the other dogs to get to me: 'She is fearless,' he said. He couldn't break her concentration and couldn't intimidate her. Shawn told me he had really enjoyed working with us, and thought Holly was a good-natured, brave and smart little dog. We passed! He was proud of us both.

"'That was sure a lot of time and expense to just get my dog to walk nicely on a leash' was the thought that crossed my mind, but I was happy, and so was my obedient little couch potato.

"One morning, when reading the daily newspaper, an article about an organization in Salt Lake City called Intermountain Therapy Animals jumped off the page at me. It was a fairly new organization, which was looking for dogs and cats to attend classes to become visiting therapy animals, after passing obedience and behavioral tests. A phone number was given for more information, so I called and set up an appointment.

"I had no idea what we were getting into, but it sounded like fun. The woman evaluator was very stern-looking and made me feel nervous, but Holly just did her stump-of-a-tail-wagging hula. When I think back to it now, I'm sure we received a perfect score, as I don't think we made any mistakes. The test for Holly was in two parts, first obedience and then behavioral. I learned later that many dogs coming into evaluations passed the obedience test, but would become intimidated and afraid during the behavioral test. Nothing scared Holly, and she loved everyone.

"Soon, we were off to work, all decked out in our red-and-black uniforms. Most of the visits in the early days of Intermountain Therapy Animals were to nursing homes, and Holly loved the attention and petting she received at these, though for me these visits brought back sad memories of my mother, who had passed away in a nursing home after many years suffering from Alzheimer's.

"The organization grew by leaps and bounds as word of our service spread, and new fields and opportunities were opening up. I received a call from ITA to ask if I would be willing to go to a locked-down juvenile rehabilitation facility near me. I had worked in the psychiatric unit of a hospital for many years, so wasn't uncomfortable with the assignment. This facility was for boys of eleven through to young adult, and all of the residents were from out-of-state (the majority from Chicago and Philadelphia); mostly court-ordered into the program for three years.

"The residents were big guys, mostly gang members with drug abuse issues, and crimes

Holly: a little blond angel in a fur coat.

ranging from sexual offences through robbery, and, in some cases, attempted murder. I was always accompanied by a member of staff when I visited, but my concern, that first time, was that these boys would not want anything to do with a little, well groomed, pretty, foo-foo-looking fluff-butt like Holly.

"Well, I was wrong as the guys loved her. She was not intimidating to them so they were comfortable with her. Many of these boys had been chased by police K9s, which meant they were afraid of big dogs. However, whenever I asked a resident if they had a dog, I always received the same answer: 'Yes, a Pit Bull and a Rottweiler,' whether or not this was true! Some of these boys had been involved in dog fighting, and part of their therapy was to treat the therapy dogs with respect. Dogs have no prejudices – if you treat them well they love you unconditionally – and I learned to view these boys through Holly's eyes, trying not to be judgmental.

"Holly and I launched a program that became our special project for eight years. As requested by the boys, Holly learned to do tricks: she would shake with either paw, sit up, high-five with a paw, and roll over for treats. We recruited into the program other pet partner teams that visited on a regular basis.

"ITA introduced the Reading Education Assistance Dogs (READ) program for children with reading difficulties. Our juvenile behavioral system heard about READ, and requested it for some of the boys with reading problems. The ITA director and I met with the staff of the facility, as inclusion of teenagers was a new area for READ. The director insisted that the program would be used as part of the boys' therapy, and not as reward or punishment, with which the staff agreed. There were times when Holly and I conducted reading sessions in a locked-down, solitary confinement room when a boy had broken the rules and was in trouble for his behavior.

"Rehabilitation, whether physical or mental, can be a long, sometimes tedious process. Change doesn't happen overnight, and sometimes you wonder if you really are making a difference, but patience almost always pays

off, and there are memorable moments. We were called to work with a stroke patient at a rehab hospital who was becoming bored with therapy. His therapist wanted to make throwing a ball (to work his afflicted arm) more fun. We were met in the rehab area by the therapist, who warned us that this patient sometimes told tall tales, so 'not to pay them any attention.' Just the previous night, apparently, he had reported that his sister had come and beat him up, which wasn't true, of course.

"I met the elderly gentleman, and introduced myself, saying: 'This is my dog, Holly.' The man replied, 'I have a dog like that, called Molly.' Oh sure, I thought, Holly and Molly, one of his stories.

"The therapist encouraged the patient to try and throw the ball farther for Holly, which, of course, exercised his arm. During our workout, a man came in to watch (I assumed he was staff), but after our session he came over to say 'Hi Dad, I'm going to tell Molly you were playing with another dog who looks just like her, and she's going to be jealous.' The joke was on me for sure.

"More places to visit were added to our now very busy schedule. On a regular basis we called on an adult psych unit at our local hospital, where most of the patients were suffering from depression. One young man said to me: 'I wish I was a fruit fly.' Why? I asked. 'Because, they only have to live for one day,' was his reply. We were able to get a smile out of him when he petted Holly, so we visited often, wanting him to have something to look forward to. When he left the hospital he told me he wanted to get a dog to help him cope with his stress and emotional pain, and bring fun into his life.

"Our therapy program made a profound impression on a social worker trying to help a severely physically and mentally disabled young man. Stopping at his room one day we found the social worker working with him, using colored, plastic alphabet letters. We offered to come back later but, as the patient began to smile and squeal in delight when he saw Holly, the social worker asked us to stay, saying she hadn't been able to get his attention at all. With Holly there, the patient worked on his letters to show Holly what he could do. We made a difference that day.

"Holly loved working with teenage boys and little children as they always played with her and gave her treats, and one little girl was particularly memorable. This darling little four-year-old had been removed from her abusive family, and was to be placed for adoption by a loving family. One problem in being able to place her was she had stopped talking and eating, and was on a child's liquid supplement diet. It was hoped that a therapy dog could help her, and for this assignment we had to commit to six months for there to be consistency for this little girl.

"Holly and I first met Missy, along with her therapist, in a playroom. She had a sad expression on her little face, and made no eye contact, mostly ignoring our presence. Nothing of any note was accomplished during the first of many visits. Missy didn't seem to be afraid of Holly; she just didn't pay attention to her.

"There was a large basket of toys in the playroom, through which Missy would sort without enthusiasm. I would throw a ball for Holly and she would bring it back to Missy, but, again, there was no interest. It was frustrating work, and it felt like we weren't getting anywhere.

"On our next visit Holly seemed to decide to take charge, going over to the basket and digging through its contents. Toys were flying all over the place – and Missy was watching. At the bottom of the basket was a small, rubber elephant that squeaked, which Holly took over to Missy and began playing with, making it squeak and squeal. Suddenly, Missy picked up the toy and threw it for Holly to retrieve over and over. Missy was finally smiling!

"The most memorable visit was when Missy picked up Holly's ear and whispered into it. Fascinated by Holly's long, silky Cocker ears, for many visits this is what she did, whilst continuing to have fun with the squeaky elephant, which she always enjoyed letting Holly find in the basket. Eventually, Missy began to talk out loud to Holly whilst petting and playing with her. Therapy was progressing nicely.

"Missy liked to dress Holly in doll's

Free to move between these special needs students, this therapy partner encourages relaxation and creativity. She is obviously enjoying and responding to this child asking her to speak. He, in turn, is delighted by her attention and keeps trying ...
(Courtesy Jim Dowling)

Her patient, calming, attentive presence can bring momentary peace to an otherwise out-of-balance day.

clothes, so I made some outfits and hats suitable for a dog's anatomy. Holly didn't mind at all; she loved the attention, and Missy was talking more and more.

"I brought baby carrots and pieces of cracker for Missy to feed to Holly while she had her usual snack drink, and Missy began to bring a little cup of popcorn to our therapy sessions, which she liked to feed, piece by piece, to Holly. One day she also had a cup of milk, which she dipped popcorn into and gave to Holly. To our surprise, she then dipped popcorn in the milk and ate it herself, continuing to share, back and forth. Soon, she was sharing the baby carrots and crackers, too! On our next visit her therapist told me that Missy was beginning to eat other types of solid food, and was talking out loud to the children in her pre-school class. Real progress had been made.

"Just before our six months were up, I received a call from the facility with heart-warming news. Missy had been adopted and Holly and I were invited for one last visit. As a going away gift I gave our sweet, (now) talkative little girl a blond Cocker Beanie Baby exactly like Holly, complete with a red scarf. I watched with tears in my eyes when she said her goodbyes, hugging Holly and her own 'Holly dog.' It's nice, and does your heart good to have a happy and successful ending.

"On returning home one day some time later, I found Holly curled up in her chair, sound asleep. She hadn't greeted me at the door, and was startled when I touched her. The senior years were creeping up on her, and I realized she was losing her hearing. In her original training, Shawn had me use voice commands *and* hand signals. I had not bothered with the hand signals since, but wondered if she would remember them. She had not forgotten them at all!

"Holly was such a pro at her work that most people did not realise she was deaf, and the boys still liked to read to her as she sat patiently by their sides. Every two years, therapy dogs have to be re-evaluated, and, using only hand signals for the test, Holly passed with an almost perfect score.

"A further two years on I knew it was time to hang up Holly's ITA leash and scarf. She was beginning to lose her sight, now, and arthritis was slowing her down. It was time to let her enjoy the life of leisure she had earned and well deserved. All of our clients and facilities were sad to see us retire, and at surprise going away parties there were tears all around. We were very proud of the work we had accomplished.

"A year later, I held Holly in my arms as, with dignity and peace, she crossed over Rainbow Bridge to go play with her old pal, Chewy. In her honor and memory, I placed her ashes in her favorite place where she was happiest – under the trees on the beautifully landscaped facility where 'her boys' reside.

"I knew in my heart that this little blond angel in a fur coat found me, as I had certainly not gone looking for her. The extraordinary bond that we had allowed us to do something very special. My pet partner will be forever missed."
Lyn

As if lifesaving hospital visits weren't enough, Holly also stepped into a new endeavor without hesitation, giving children with reading difficulties a safe, comfortable environment in which to learn. The READ program she helped initiate is still going strong, worldwide (the picture on page 140 was taken 12 years after Holly's initial visit to the same facility where she shared her heart). The success of the program serves to illustrate the need for that unique connection forged when our therapy partners provide our children with unconditional love and support.

Therapy partners offer all of themselves to complete strangers – strangers in need, strangers in pain and distress – with an emotional strength of character that is astounding. The fortitude needed as they absorb the pain is palpable: not physical endurance, speed or agility, but emotional strength and personality, an almost mystical level of trust, and a rare spiritual degree of self-confidence.

Driven by the same innate instincts that give all of our working dogs their edge, therapy partners ignore the emotional obstacles and barriers that the people they help sometimes erect, and simply move in gently to present themselves in a moment of total uncomplicated tenderness. Head in lap, wet tongue on cold hands, soft, brown eyes filled with trusting love, or silky ears into which to whisper secrets, all momentarily relieve the pain and soothe the spirit.

Therapy canines achieve a very special connection, which words cannot ever adequately describe, although pictures can sometimes capture those moments: that joy, that connection, the simple warmth and tenderness. The very essence of this book is written on the faces of the children pictured within its pages, that tell the tale of *Partners* like no words ever could ...

"... he will be our friend for always and always and always." – Rudyard Kipling, *Just So Stories for Little Children*

Initiating a touch, in a moment of complete assurance that everything is okay, this child responds with poignant tenderness.

With children – as with dogs – truth and honesty shines out as acceptance, and complete, uncomplicated love.

... being heroes every day

Epilogue

Highlighting the canine senses that drive all dog behaviors, the stories in *Partners* shed light on the instincts behind the behavior: the very same instincts present in every domestic dog born and living today.

From the seemingly simple task to the most heroic event, canine senses get the job done: dogs don't know they are our heroes in so many ways, they only know they're doing what we want them to – what they were born to do.

Her gentle, loving attentiveness as she observes the area surrounding this child is intense and protective. Completely undirected, her every survival instinct is totally engaged.

In this place, for this single moment, these two embody total togetherness. Honest and uncomplicated, this unique connection and bond spans centuries of interspecies symbiosis: a relationship simply like no other.

"You shall not find, in nature's immense crucible, a single living being that has shown a like suppleness, a similar abundance of forms, the same prodigious faculty of accommodation to our wishes.

"This is because, in the world which we know, among the different and primitive geniuses of life that preside over the evolution of the several species, there exists not one, excepting that of the dog, that ever gave a thought to the presence of man." – Maurice Materlinck, *My Dog*

Impossible to pinpoint the exact day the relationship began, sometime during our past mankind became a family member of the species canidae, and a bond born of necessity was forged, enabling our species to thrive by making use of a dog's basic survival skills.

The unique ability of our dogs to know our hearts and needs does have a plausible explanation, which is based on the physiological make-up of their senses, and not mysticism or fairytales. Working in unison with their emotional essence – their canine heart – these senses allow ability and action beyond basic animal instinct, and are responsible for the intrinsic value our working partners bring to our lives every day: present not only in Tommy guiding Brad around holes in the street, or Enzo pulling the bad guy from under the dark bridge, but there, also, in the small lap dog and the big hunting Lab lying at our feet.

Walking at our sides throughout history, the need for these inherent survival senses has become much reduced in a world that, in most cases, has no call for what dogs were born to give. So, dogs have adapted to meet what needs we *do* have – and will undoubtedly continue to do so – and we must protect and provide for them the way they have for us: as one family member to another.

Except for the working dogs around the world who find themselves serving in capacities sometimes beyond imagination, most dogs have nothing to do. Thankfully, because of our age-old connection, man and dog – two entirely different and separate species – cling together out of mutual need and desire. As many of our canine companions find themselves without a purpose, without a job, so they chew shoes, bark at cars, are made homeless, and create problems for themselves and society.

Dogs need a purpose, so give your faithful friend a job and meaning to his day; a reason to use the skills he was born with. Then stand back and watch his life expand as he excitedly explores the full potential of his inborn instincts.

Bibliography

My Dog; Materlinck, Maurice; George Allen, 1906; pages 5, 10 & 153

Men of the Old Stone Age: Their Environment, Life and Art; Osborn, Henry Fairfield; Charles Scribner's Sons, 1915; page 10

The New Work of Dogs: Tending to Life, Love, and Family; Katz, Jon; Random House Trade Paperbacks, 2004; page 10

Scent and the Scenting Dog; Syrotuck, William G; Barkleigh Productions Inc, 1972; pages 12, 18 & 80

The Language of Smell; Burton, Robert; Routledge & Kegan Paul Books, 1976; page 13.

Jacobson's Organ – And the Remarkable Nature of Smell (1st edition); Watson, Lyal; W W Norton & Company, 2000; pages 13, 19 & 89

Dog Behavior: Why Dogs Do What They Do; Dunbar, Ian; Tfh Publications, Inc,1979; pages 13 & 86

The Dog's Mind: Understanding Your Dog's Behavior; Fogle, Bruce; Howell Book House, 1990; pages 14, 16 & 17

Scent: Training to Track, Search and Rescue; Pearsall, Milo D and Verbruggen, Hugo MD; Alpine Publications Inc, 1982; pages 14, 29 & 30

'Making Sense of Your dog's World;' Wells, Virginia; courtesy PetPlace.com (www.petplace.com); the definitive online source for pet news, health, and wellness information; page 17

'The use of scent-detection dogs;' Browne, Clare, Kevin Stafford and Robin Fordham; *Irish Veterinary Journal* (Volume 59 (2): February, 2006); page 18

'Canine Scenting Ability Makes Teaching Tracking a Treat;' Priest, Julia (www.working dogs.com/doc0181htm); page 19

'Developing a Physiology of Inclusion: recognizing the Health Benefits of Animal companions' Lynch, James J PhD; Life Health Care – *Delta Society Magazine*, 2003; page 35

I & Dog; The Monks of New Skete; courtesy Yorkville Press, Inc; page 46

'Get to know your Working Dog;' Mancuso, Theresa; *Dog World Magazine;* November 1995; page 57

'Prey Train the Young Prospect;' Bradshaw, Jerry (www.schutzhund-training.net/puppy/prey-training-young.html); page 58

'Drive Channeling in the Working Dog;' Bradshaw, Jerry (www.docstoc.com/docs); page 70

'Search and Rescue Dog;' Mitchell, Michael W; *Dog Sports Magazine*, April, July, December 1998; August 1999; pages 80, 81 & 90

'Wilderness Strategy for Dog Handlers;' Koenig, Marcia; *Response* (March/April 1987); pages 81 & 96

'Working for Wildlife;' Mackay, Paula; *Bark Magazine*; 2005; page 87

Ready! Training the Search and Rescue Dog (Kennel Club Pro); Bulanda, Susan & Larry; Kennel Club Books, 2010;

reprinted with permission of the publisher. Available at www.shopanimalnetwork.com; pages 88 & 93

Search Dog Training; Bryson, Sandra; The Boxwood Press, 1984; page 92

'Nevada TNT Explosion;' Hammond, Shirley; *Dog Sports Magazine*, August 1998; page 99

More Than Courage. Real Life Stories of Horses and Dogs and People Who Have Loved Them (1st edition); Lawson, Patrick; Whitman Publising Co, 1960; page 102

'Through Buddy's Eyes;' Frank, Morris; Morris Frank's visionary efforts revolutionized life for Americans with visual impairments. *Vanderbilt Magazine* James Summerville, 1983; pages 108 &109

Schoen, Allen Dr; The Land of Pure Gold Foundation is the world's largest Golden-inspired website, which strives to help others strenthen and lengthen the bond, as well as provide cancer treatment grants for working dogs, and fund research in comparative oncology; http://landofpuregold.com/about.htm; page 132

For the Love of Saint Thais; France, Anatole; ThaiSunset Publications, 1890; english translation by Robert B Douglas from original; CreateSpace Independent Publishing Platform, 2010; page 133

Therapy Dogs Today: Their Gifts, Our Obligation; Butler, Kris; Funpuddle Publishing Associates, 2004; page 134

Seattle, Chief, 1855; page 140

Letters from Elizabeth Barrett Browning; Frederick Kenyon; page 141

Angel Dogs – Divine Messengers of Love; Anderson, Allen and Linda; New World Library, 2002; page 145

'The Cat that Walked by Himself' *Just So Stories for Little Children;* Kipling, Rudyard; George S. Morang & Co, Limited 1902; page 151

Turnbull, Agnes Sligh; page 154

Notes

[1] 'The Wolf at the Door – Dogs may have been man's best friend for thousands of years longer than we realized' by Pat Shipman *(American Scientist Magazine)* explores the scientific evidence leading to this date

[2] *The Rainbow Bridge* poem: author unknown

"Just this side of heaven is a place called Rainbow Bridge.

"When an animal dies that has been especially close to someone here, that pet goes to Rainbow Bridge. There are meadows and hills for all of our special friends so they can run and play together.There is plenty of food, water and sunshine, and our friends are warm and comfortable.

"All the animals who had been ill and old are restored to health and vigor; those who were hurt or maimed are made whole and strong again, just as we remember them in our dreams of days and times gone by. The animals are happy and content, except for one small thing; they each miss someone very special to them, who had to be left behind.

"They all run and play together, but the day comes when one suddenly stops and looks into the distance. His bright eyes are intent; his eager body quivers. Suddenly he begins to run from the group, flying over the green grass, his legs carrying him faster and faster.

"You have been spotted, and when you and your special friend finally meet, you cling together in joyous reunion, never to be parted again. The happy kisses rain upon your face; your hands again caress the beloved head, and you look once more into the trusting eyes of your pet, so long gone from your life but never absent from your heart.

"Then you cross Rainbow Bridge together ...."

[3] During JJ's fight with cancer Mike's financial situation and the limitations of his department responsibilities were somewhat eased by a network of fellow officers and their financial support. Providing that same kind of support to other handlers is the goal of 'JJ's Police Dog Fund' (www.jjpolicedogfund.org.

[4] OC spray is commonly referred to as pepper spray, and causes pain, tearing and irritation to the eyes. It is used in riot control and personal self-defense

[5] Rocky Mountain Rescue Dogs Inc of Utah was established in 1980, and is an all-volunteer, non-profit service organization that provides qualified dog teams to assist governmental agencies locate missing persons, and provide first aid if necessary in areas such as urban, wilderness, avalanche, water, and disaster. All of the SAR stories in *Partners* are about certified Rocky Mountain Rescue Dogs teams (www.rockymountainrescuedogs)

[6] NASAR (National Association for Search and Rescue: www.nasar.org) has dedicated itself to preparing all those involved in search and rescue. Search and rescue is a life-saving vocation, and the ability to save a life is often dependent on how quickly the person can be found and accessed. If the missing person is one of your loved ones, you will expect well-equipped, well-trained search and rescue professionals to bring your loved one home safely to you

[7] Guide Dogs for the Blind provides enhanced mobility to qualified individuals through partnership with dogs whose unique skills are developed and nurtured by dedicated volunteers and professional staff.

Established in 1942, Guide Dogs for the Blind ('use our Power of Partnering to improve quality of life') continues its dedication to providing quality student training services and extensive follow-up support for graduates. Programs are made possible through the teamwork of staff, volunteers and generous donors. Services are provided to students from the United States and Canada at no cost to them (www.guidedogs.com)

[8] The Delta Society mission is 'to improve human health and well-being by promoting mutually beneficial contact with animals and nature,' helping people throughout the world become healthier and happier by incorporating therapy, service and companion animals into their lives (www.deltasociety.org/)

[9] Intermountain Therapy Animals' mission is 'enhancing quality of life through the human-animal bond:' its motto 'Pets Helping People.' The stories in the therapy chapter of *Partners* were all provided by certified ITA teams (www.therapyanimals.org/)

[10] The mission of Reading Education Assistance Dogs (READ is to improve the literacy skills of children through the assistance of registered therapy teams as literacy mentors. READ dogs are registered therapy animals who, with their owner/handlers, volunteer as reading companions for children in schools, libraries, and many other settings.

Intermountain Therapy Animals – a non-profit organization – launched READ in 1999 as the first comprehensive literacy program built around the appealing idea of reading to dogs, and the program has been spreading rapidly and happily ever since! (www.therapyanimals.org)

Visit Hubble and Hattie on the web: www.hubbleandhattie.com and www.hubbleandhattie.blogspot.com

 twitter

Details of all books • Special offers • Newsletter • New book news

... being heroes every day

Adapt 5, 8, 9, 12, 17, 18, 37, 46, 74, 154
Aggression 48, 57
Air-scenting 18, 29, 80, 92, 101
Apprehension 48, 57, 70
Avalanche 6, 14, 43, 75, 84

Behavior 5, 9, 12-14, 17, 20, 25, 27, 37, 46, 65, 70, 72, 86, 89, 90, 118, 121, 147, 152, 154
Body language 14, 20, 23, 27, 65, 69, 72, 92, 93, 112, 113
Bond 5-9, 11, 12, 14, 16, 17, 27, 31, 37, 41, 47-49, 52, 57, 63, 70-72, 77, 89, 96, 100, 101-103, 106-108, 110, 112, 116, 118, 121, 126, 129, 131, 134, 139, 142, 147, 150, 153, 154
Bond born of necessity 11, 108, 154

Cane 103, 104, 114, 110-112, 115, 116, 124-126, 128, 131
Canidae 5, 154
Canine heart 12, 17, 46, 48, 50, 82, 87, 96, 103, 108, 112, 116, 130-132, 140, 141, 154
Canine humor 77
Canine language 93
Canine species 4, 6, 10, 11, 13, 16, 18, 20, 27, 43, 45, 118, 133, 153, 154
Canis lupus familiaris 5
Cognitive senses 17, 70
Communication 5, 6, 8, 9, 11-14, 16, 27, 47, 48, 50, 63, 80, 82, 86-88, 92, 93, 96, 99-102, 106, 108, 118, 121, 133
Connection 6-8, 10, 14, 16, 37, 80, 96, 99, 103, 108, 110, 121, 133, 136-138, 140, 150, 151, 154

Defense training 70
Detain 48, 51, 52, 54, 62, 70, 71, 74, 79
DNA 13, 18
Drives 14, 21, 27, 48-51, 57, 70, 74, 81, 86, 96, 140, 150, 152
Dual-purpose 18, 31, 48, 60, 74, 76

Eyes 12, 13, 16, 133

Fight drive 49, 70, 74
Find 14, 19, 18, 27, 29, 31, 46, 80, 83, 85-88, 90-102

Finish 23, 33, 35, 41, 44, 87
Focus/refocus 12, 14, 19, 21, 27, 36, 43, 45, 46, 48, 50, 51, 61, 68, 80, 92, 96, 102, 105-109, 113, 114, 140

Goal 11, 41, 47, 81, 102, 109, 131

Hasty search 81, 96
Hearing 12, 16, 93, 112, 117
Herding instinct 80, 86
Hunt instinct 14, 16, 21, 27, 29, 41, 48, 49, 70, 74, 80, 96, 102, 103

Inherent instinct 5, 9, 14, 37, 50, 70, 93, 154
Innate senses 5, 11, 12, 14, 27, 37, 39, 46, 57, 92, 96, 107, 112, 118, 122, 131, 132, 150, 154
Instinct 5, 7-9, 11-14, 46, 57, 70, 89, 96, 107, 112, 117, 118, 124, 131, 132, 136, 140, 150, 152, 154
Intelligence 12, 46, 52, 57, 96, 102, 112, 118
Intelligent disobedience 46, 74, 80, 92, 96, 103, 106, 112, 121, 124, 131
Interspecies relationship 10, 103, 118, 131, 133, 153

Job 6, 9, 12, 14, 18, 20, 22, 31, 37, 41, 44-46, 48, 60, 74, 81, 84, 87-90, 92, 95, 109, 111, 116, 119, 124, 126, 134, 152, 154

Living tool 20, 22, 41, 48, 57, 59, 70, 79, 82, 103, 131, 134

Motivation 19, 20, 48, 57, 99
Mysticism 8, 12, 132, 150, 154

Obedience 49, 50, 63, 70, 122, 124, 136, 141
Odor 12, 13, 18, 21, 27, 29, 32, 66, 80, 89, 132, 138
Olfactory 8, 12-14, 17, 18, 27, 35, 37, 41, 43, 47, 63, 74, 80, 85, 92, 132

Pack instinct 8, 9, 12, 13, 16, 18, 45, 47, 49, 70, 103, 108-110, 124, 131, 154
Partnerships 5, 6, 41, 48, 70, 96, 99, 103, 104, 108, 109, 116, 118, 121, 123, 131
Patrol work 32, 35, 36, 48, 57, 60-64, 69, 70, 71, 74, 76

Pee-mail 13
Play drive 63, 99
Prey drive 10, 13,14, 17, 29, 48, 49, 57, 58, 70, 74
Protection instinct 58, 70, 74, 76, 131, 154

Quartering 27

Recall 83, 85, 86, 94
Relationship 7, 8, 10, 12, 14, 17, 48, 63, 95, 99, 103, 110, 115, 116, 118, 124, 128, 130, 131, 136, 140, 153, 154
Reward 16, 17, 20, 27-29, 49, 50, 51, 53, 55, 57, 84, 87, 99, 106, 128, 129, 146
Runaways 20, 75

Scent 12-14, 18, 19, 21, 26, 27, 29-31, 45, 46, 51, 79, 80, 87, 89, 96, 101
Scent article 21, 45, 80, 83, 86, 88, 90, 92
Scent discrimination 12, 75, 80, 87, 88
Scent-specific molecules 18, 29, 80
Search 18, 26, 27, 29, 30, 46, 59, 80-102
Senses 5, 8-17, 46, 47, 57, 70, 109, 117, 136, 152, 154

Skill-sets 11, 12-14, 16, 18, 19, 21, 27
Sniff 12, 13, 21, 30, 31, 41-44
Spontaneous engagement 55, 74, 131
Survival instincts 8, 9, 11-17, 27, 47, 49, 50, 70, 74, 102, 109, 110, 152, 154
Symbiosis/synergy 12, 103, 128, 131, 153, 154

Tool 48, 70, 82, 103, 131, 134
Touch 12, 14, 16, 17, 63, 87, 133, 141-144
Tracking 18-21, 26, 27, 29, 37, 48, 67, 68, 87, 92, 101
Training 9, 12-14, 17, 27-30, 41, 46-48, 51, 63, 69, 74, 80, 84, 86, 88-92, 96, 101, 105, 106, 109, 110, 112, 113, 117, 118, 120-124, 132, 134
Trust 5-8, 11, 12, 14, 27, 41, 46, 47, 48, 50, 56, 63, 80, 102, 106-108, 110, 112, 115, 116, 118, 120, 121, 131, 140, 150

Unity of purpose 111, 128, 131, 154

Working dogs 5, 6, 8, 9, 12, 14, 37, 57, 103, 104, 106-109, 113, 114, 116, 118, 119, 124, 130, 132, 134-136, 147, 140, 150, 154